NARRATIVES From the
CLASSROOM
An Introduction to Teaching

For Hiro

愛している。

Paul Chamness Miller, Editor

Division of Teacher Education, University of Cincinnati

Foreword by William Ayers

NARRATIVES From the CLASSROOM

An Introduction to Teaching

SAGE Publications
Thousand Oaks ■ London ■ New Delhi

For information:

Sage Publications, Inc.
2455 Teller Road
Thousand Oaks, California 91320
E-mail: order@sagepub.com

Sage Publications Ltd.
1 Oliver's Yard
55 City Road
London EC1Y 1SP
United Kingdom

Sage Publications India Pvt. Ltd.
B-42, Panchsheel Enclave
Post Box 4109
New Delhi 110017   India

Printed in the United States of America

Library of Congress Cataloging-in-Publication Data

Narratives from the classroom: An introduction to teaching / edited by Paul Chamness Miller.
      p. cm.
Includes bibliographical references and index.
ISBN 1-4129-0407-2 (cloth) — ISBN 1-4129-0408-0 (pbk.)
    1. Education—Biographical methods. 2. Teaching—Psychological aspects. 3. Teachers—Training of. I. Miller, Paul Chamness.
LB1029.B55N37 2005
371.102—dc22

                                                    2004016439

04   05   06   07   10   9   8   7   6   5   4   3   2   1

Acquiring Editor:	Diane McDaniel
Editorial Assistant:	Margo Crouppen
Production Editor:	Diana E. Axelsen
Copy Editor:	Frances Andersen/Mattson Publishing
Typesetter:	C&M Digitals (P) Ltd.
Indexer:	David Luljak
Cover Designer:	Edward Abarca

Contents

Foreword

What Future Teachers Need to Know

William Ayers

C harles Dickens published *Hard Times* in London in 1854—I'll do the
math for you, that's exactly 150 years ago. In the opening paragraphs,
Dickens describes with fierce precision the first thing future teachers need
to know. This is the fraught world of 19th-century English schooling,
remarkably like the one new teachers will face in modern America:

> "Now, what I want is, Facts. Teach these boys and girls nothing but Facts.
> Facts alone are wanted in life. Plant nothing else, and root out everything
> else. You can only form the minds of reasoning animals upon Facts: nothing
> else will ever be of any service to them. This is the principle on which I bring
> up my own children, and this is the principle on which I bring up these
> children. Stick to Facts, Sir!" . . .
>
> The speaker, and the schoolmaster . . . swept with their eyes the inclined
> plane of little vessels then and there arranged in order, ready to have imperial
> gallons of facts poured into them until they were full to the brim.

Most people picking up this text are just now entering or are perhaps
in the beginning stages of a teacher education or credentialing program,
while others may be completing their student teaching. There is good
news and bad news to keep in mind regardless of where you are in your
program. The bad news first: You can't be a wise teacher before you've
been an innocent and naïve one, smart before foolish, experienced before
inexperienced. This is obvious, but so many *new* teachers berate themselves
simply for being new, that it bears noting at the start. Learning to teach
takes more time. You are a work in progress. Keep going.

The good news? You can hold onto your humanistic ideals as a teacher, negotiate the troubled waters of teaching, continue to grow, and learn for your entire life in classrooms. Committing to the task of continuous experimentation, investigation, inquiry, and study is essential. One way to proceed is to engage in an intergenerational dialogue with other teachers, a space for problem posing and problem solving, historical and theoretical considerations, storytelling and critical reflection. This text is one site where you can begin that dialogue.

There's so much more to learn. Too often future teachers have experienced little more than a few courses in educational philosophy and psychology, the history of education, then the methods of teaching, and finally a synthesizing moment when everything is theoretically brought together in student teaching. This approach structures the separation of thought from action, rips one from another, and walls the mind off from the body, weakening both. It's lazy at best, miseducative always. But worse, it ignores the humanizing mission of teaching.

The humanizing mission focuses on the humanity of students, multidimensional creatures with bodies, minds, hearts, spirits, and also hopes, dreams, aspirations, and desires. These are some courses we might have wanted to take in college: Turning Toward the Student as Fellow Creature (Not Dirt Bag of Deficits); Building a Republic of Many Voices Where Each Can Be Heard, Each Seen; Creating Community with and for Students and Families; Finding Critical Allies in Parents and Community; Developing Courage and Confidence; Becoming a Student of Our Students; Practicing Creative Insubordination; Transgression 101; Lifting the Weight of the World; Resisting Orthodoxy; Teaching Toward Freedom, How To.

There's a message here, of course, about what is to be valued and why, just as the message in the existing standard curriculum tells us what is to be valued and why. I want teachers to resist the mindless and the soulless in teaching in favor of attention to the ethical and intellectual dimensions of their efforts. I want teachers to be aware of the stakes, aware as well that there is no simple technique or linear path that will take them to where they need to go, and then allow them to live out settled teaching lives, untroubled and finished. There is no promised land in teaching, just that aching persistent tension between reality and possibility. This book might help.

I want teachers to figure out what they're teaching for, and what they're teaching against. I know I want to teach against oppression and subjugation, exploitation, unfairness, and unkindness. I want to teach toward freedom, for enlightenment and awareness, wide-awakeness, protection of the weak, cooperation, generosity, compassion, and love.

I want my teaching to mean something worthwhile in the lives of my students and in the larger worlds they will inhabit and create. I want it to mean something in mine. The teachers presented in these pages have lived meaningful teaching lives—listen and learn; think, reflect, and talk back to them.

I want future teachers to commit to a path with a certain direction and rhythm: Love life, embrace your students, breathe in and breathe out, love your neighbors, open up, listen, love yourself, be generous, act and doubt, learn from your students, question everything, talk with everyone you meet, defend the outcast and the despised, challenge and nourish yourself and others, become a student of your students and allow them to become a teacher to their teacher, seek balance. I want future teachers to develop a wild and eclectic and dynamic list they can refer to when the night is dark and they feel themselves to be far from home. Here is Walt Whitman, in one of his many prefaces to *Leaves of Grass*, offering advice to his fellow poets:

This is what you shall do:

Love the earth and sun and the animals, despise riches, give alms to everyone that asks, stand up for the stupid and crazy, devote your income and labor to others, hate tyrants, argue not concerning God, have patience and indulgence toward the people, take off your hat to nothing known or unknown or to any man or number of men, go freely with powerful uneducated persons and with the young and with the mothers of families, re-examine all you have been told at school or church or in any book, dismiss whatever insults your own soul, and your very flesh shall be a great poem and have the richest fluency not only in its words but in the silent lines of its lips and face and between the lashes of your eyes and in every motion and joint of your body . . .

Wow! That's a list to laminate and carry along in your backpack, a list to tape to your wall. It's written to poets, but it stands as advice to free and future teachers, too, a nice start to our own lists. There are wonderful elements in the following pages to begin constructing your own list, your own rules to live by. The important thing is this: Don't let your teaching life make a mockery of your teaching values.

Preface

Paul Chamness Miller

In the several years that I have been an instructor in teacher education, I have come to the realization that preservice teachers enter the program with rose-colored glasses and preconceived notions of what teaching really is; many students in teacher education programs across the country are not aware of the various issues that concern the profession of teaching. This concern is often coupled with insufficient exposure to real classrooms, schools, and teachers because of constraints of time, available teachers, and course loads. However, in order for the preservice teacher to fully understand what it means to choose teaching as a career, it is important to make connections with teachers to see what occurs within the walls of schools. One possible supplement to experiencing the classroom firsthand is to provide the preservice teacher with narrative accounts of teachers' experiences with students, parents, administrators, and colleagues, in order to obtain a clearer picture of what teaching involves. JoAnn Phillion, in the first chapter of this book, provides a description of what narrative is, why it is important, and how a preservice teacher might use the narratives of experienced teachers to affirm his or her decision to become a teacher and to gain a deeper understanding of the host of issues that make up this important career.

This book is a collection of narratives and opinions from experienced teachers and teacher educators who want to share their lives as teachers with those who are considering joining them in the profession. While no book could ever replace the invaluable experience of being in a classroom and working closely with a seasoned teacher, this book does afford the reader a few moments with several carefully selected educators who understand the importance of sharing their teaching experiences. It is also important to note that the topics selected for this book are not exhaustive, nor do they represent all points of view of the issues addressed. The authors selected for this book have presented their personal experiences, making each chapter unique. In the traditional form of contact with teachers, one is often limited to the expertise of one teacher at a time. This book provides the opportunity for the preservice teacher to have a glimpse into the classrooms and minds of 15 individual teachers. Each of these teachers comes from a different walk of life and a different location. The authors are also of varying ethnic backgrounds, a combination that provides a rich variation of experiences and opinions. Knowing this, the reader should not take what is presented as the "gospel" on the topic; instead, it would be preferable to ponder what is discussed, perhaps look into the topic further, gather contrasting arguments on the topic, debate the issue with classmates and other teachers, and attempt to sort out where one stands on each issue. It is often beneficial to organize one's thoughts in a journal or narrative of one's own. Knowing where one stands will prepare the future teacher for situations that will arise in the classroom, future courses, and job interviews.

Because the issues that involve teaching are so varied, I have organized the book into sections, with each section focusing on a particular theme. These sections will help the reader understand how particular topics are related to each other rather than giving the impression that each topic is an isolated issue. What is more, the reader will find that the topics are often intertwined. For example, the role of the teacher is defined in current curricular issues, instructional methodologies, dealing with students and parents, and so forth. It is, therefore, not surprising to find the same issues resurface in several of the chapters included in this book.

Part I presents two chapters that deal with understanding the purpose of schools and teachers. In order to fully understand what the purpose of teachers is, it is important to understand their roles as Kin Chee describes in Chapter 2. He shares his thoughts on how his role as a teacher is continually redefined with each new student. Teaching is more than the instructional part of the job and this chapter encourages the reader to begin considering what this profession truly entails. To help the reader understand the role of schools, Christopher Blake and Connie Monroe present, in Chapter 3, a difficult topic related to the purpose of schools, one that is often overlooked in teacher education: moral education. Teaching morals is inevitable; whether we teach them overtly or not, students experience character education every day that is spent in the classroom. This chapter, however, proposes a new approach to this type of education considering the diversification of our society and schools.

The reader is challenged to think about how one determines what is "moral" in a diverse society where there is perhaps minimal consensus.

Part II focuses on the policies that are commonly established in schools and perhaps mandated by the government. Jill Underly, in Chapter 4, addresses the role that politics plays in the profession of teaching. Politics is involved in education at all levels—from federal, state, and local governments to school boards and individual schools. This chapter depicts one teacher's experiences with these various facets of politics and how they have affected what she understands to be the "inner workings of the school." Chapter 5 presents Wayne Au's views on tracking and the effect it has on students' success or failure in school. While some tracking occurs beyond the control of the individual teacher, there is also another form of tracking that is often employed within the classroom, and this chapter challenges the reader to consider the potential results of a tracking system and how it may affect the learner in the end.

Part III has as its theme the topic of school programs, an issue that is of major concern in recent years. Betty Eng provides a detailed account of her personal teaching experiences with curriculum programs in Chapter 6. Her focus is on how educational reform in Hong Kong has resulted in a shift in the curricula used in classrooms around the world, and she challenges the reader to consider what education truly is and how to help students achieve this notion of education. Many schools have programs to work with nonnative speakers of English, but these programs are not enough to help meet these students' needs. Chris Carger, in Chapter 7, addresses, through many of her own personal experiences, how diverse classrooms have demanded that she take a different approach to teaching and learning. She emphasizes the importance of getting to know the students, their backgrounds, and their needs.

Part IV centers on the instructional practices that might be addressed in greater detail in the preservice teacher's methods courses. In Chapter 8, Teresa Rishel and Paul Chamness Miller address the importance of establishing relationships with students, parents, administrators, and the community, in order to achieve greater success in teaching. Crystal Reimer addresses, in Chapter 9, preventative measures that teachers could take to avoid potential behavioral problems by once again reinforcing the idea that the teacher must get to know the students as individuals. Teresa Rishel, in Chapter 10, discusses the issue of safety, another part of classroom management, focusing primarily on the mental well-being of students in order to understand better what goes on in the minds of young people who engage in acts of violence such as suicide or school shootings. This is a topic that is often unpleasant to consider, but one that cannot be ignored in today's world. In Chapter 11, Magdalena Mok discusses how in the 21st century assessment is changing, especially concerning standardized testing and its effect on curriculum. Along with this shift in emphasis on standardized testing comes the idea of comparing the assessment *of* learning and the assessment *for* learning. Chapter 12 is an account of Pamela Miller's experiences in learning to use technology in the classroom as a teacher who did not grow up with computers as current preservice teachers typically experience. In today's teacher job market, it is imperative that future teachers have significant skills in using technology to its fullest potential in the delivery of instruction, and this chapter discusses some of the technologies that may be available to the new teacher.

The last section, Part V, addresses issues that are important for preparing the preservice teacher for entering the workforce as a teacher. Joseph McSparran's Chapter 13 is an account of his experiences as principal and superintendent in hiring new teachers. In order to make the most of this important time in the preservice teacher's career, it is imperative to begin thinking about the job search at the beginning of one's education, rather than waiting until it is time to interview. Chapter 14 is an account of Erin Mikulec's experiences during her first year of teaching in the public schools. Regardless of the quantity of courses a preservice teacher takes, there will always be unanswered questions. This is due to the fact that teaching is not prescriptive; each teacher, student, administrator, school, and parent is unique. While the experiences presented in this chapter may never be shared by anyone else, the goal of the chapter is to let the reader know that, despite the challenges that arise in the first year, teaching does become easier with time.

I have included within each chapter a brief note explaining why the particular topic was included in the book and to help contextualize the topic. At the end of the chapter is a list of suggested further reading that a preservice teacher may choose to read outside of class if he or she finds the topic of particular interest. Most of the suggested readings were also written by experienced classroom teachers. This is particularly important because, as previously mentioned, the chapters presented in this book are of one individual's opinions. By reading other books on similar topics, the future teacher will gain additional perspectives on the issue, affording him or her a greater opportunity to develop an informed opinion on the matter. In addition to these suggested readings is a list of suggested questions that may be used to write one's own narratives and personal journal responses to the readings. Writing responses to the chapters will allow the reader the opportunity to organize thoughts and develop an opinion. This may aid the reader in realizing where he or she might have questions that remain unanswered on the topic or perhaps it will enable the reader to simply express in words those thoughts that might be in his or her mind but not yet formally formulated. By having these thoughts organized on paper, one is better prepared for an interview where questions about these issues may arise. It is also suggested that these questions be used to facilitate discussions in the classroom or with a cooperating teacher in a field experience. Through discussion, one is able to gain a better grasp of the situation. What is more, hearing opposing perspectives may not change one's opinion but will engage a group of students in a healthy debate to perhaps appreciate another point of view. These methods are not only important to the learning process, but to the development of one's individual beliefs and philosophies on teaching and learning.

As a former high school teacher and now teacher educator, I have intended to provide preservice teachers with a solid understanding of the issues included in this book in order to prepare them for what lies ahead. My colleagues and I firmly believe that teaching is more than delivering instruction; as the following chapters will indicate, there is a plethora of issues that every preservice teacher must consider prior to entering the profession. My goal for the reader of this book is to develop an informed opinion about various topics that will ultimately prepare him or her for what is waiting down the road.

1

Narrative in Teacher Education

JoAnn Phillion

This book presents experiences and ideas about teaching in a different form from that to which the reader may be accustomed. Narratives provide a rich, detailed experience that is often ignored in teacher education courses. Narrative also offers information that other forms of writing do not. Dr. Phillion describes what narrative is, explains why it is important for future teachers to read narratives, and offers suggestions for getting the most out of the narratives that are read in this book or in others.

♦ ♦ ♦

As a classroom teacher, first in Japan, then later in Canada, I found that my fellow teachers often told me stories. These stories were full of the richness of experience and practice, full of the struggles and triumphs of teaching, full of the life of classrooms. Some stories teachers shared were humorous, some tragic, some a mixture of both. They were always about real-life situations, about the nitty-gritty details of teaching. As I listened to the stories, and reflected on them, I learned about the meaning of being a teacher. I learned that teaching is an art, one that develops over time. I learned that teaching is a relationship between teachers, administrators, students, and parents. I learned that teaching students in a new country (Japan) and teaching immigrant students in my own country (Canada) was going to be a challenge. I also learned that teaching was something I cared about passionately.

Now, years later, as a teacher educator living and working in the United States, I find that I appreciate sharing my own classroom stories with my students and having them share their stories. I also have my students read stories of teachers, or teacher narratives, such as the ones in the following chapters of *Narratives From the Classroom: An Introduction to Teaching*. Over the years, I have come to realize that I value narratives because they allow access to the heart and soul of teaching. As students read and reflect on these detailed accounts of teachers' experiences, they can begin to imagine who they will be as teachers, how they will relate to students and parents, and how they will live their classroom life. I find this aspect of reading teacher narratives important for all students, but particularly so for the beginning preservice teachers in the program I teach.

I also value narratives because through reading them we have access to different forms of knowledge than that of the more formal knowledge of research literature and textbooks. This narrative knowledge, derived from personal and professional experience, from face-to-face encounters with students, from years spent in schools and classrooms, is multifaceted and multidimensional. It is not easily "transmitted" to someone else; it seems best communicated through stories and narratives. This experiential knowledge is termed "personal, practical knowledge" in teacher education (Connelly & Clandinin, 1988).

Personal practical knowledge is

> a term designed to capture the idea of experience in a way that allows us to talk about teachers as knowledgeable and knowing persons. Personal practical knowledge is in the teacher's past experience, in the teacher's present mind and body, and in the future plans and actions. Personal practical knowledge is found in the teacher's practice. It is, for any one teacher, a particular way of reconstructing the past and the intentions of the future to deal with the exigencies of a present situation. (p. 25)

In *Narratives From the Classroom*, you will read teacher narratives that depict the complexity of what it means to be a teacher. These narratives—first-person accounts, close to life, and often deeply moving—reveal the hidden dimensions of teachers' personal practical knowledge. As narratives, they are like stories; they have settings, characters, timelines, and plots. They have moral struggles embedded in them. The power of the teacher narratives in this book lies in the ability to capture the complexity of teaching, to express the emotions of teaching, and to reveal what goes on behind the closed doors of practice. These narratives reveal that teaching is posing questions, and often being unsure of the answers. They reveal that teaching is ongoing experimentation, and often being unsure of the direction in which to go. They also reveal that the lives of teachers in today's classrooms are challenging and rewarding. In this way, the narratives in the book illuminate many of the issues teachers, preservice students, and teacher educators grapple with on a daily basis.

Narratives also shed light on research being done in teacher education; narrative, however, humanizes and personalizes the issues. With narratives, unlike abstract theoretical literature, we can delve deeply into the emotional aspects of teaching. Emotions are often neglected in writing about teaching, but why should that be so when we clearly realize that teaching is a relationship? In *Narratives from the Classroom*, the authors, many of them classroom teachers, some of them from countries other than the United States, discuss the broad landscape of teaching and how much of it involves work outside the doors of the classroom and outside the traditional notions of subject area teaching. We also learn how teaching is an act of heart, not just of mind. These aspects of teaching are not often dealt with in teacher education programs, which through the traditional system of teaching "courses" are somewhat reductionist in what it means to be a teacher. For me, there is no better way to communicate the complexity of teaching, and its joys and sorrows, than through teacher narratives.

Why Narrative?

In the social sciences: Narrative has a long history of use in the social sciences. I will briefly sketch the background in this section and then discuss the uses of narrative in teacher education in detail (see also Phillion & He, 2001). Donald Polkinghorne (1988), a psychologist, examined narrative in social science disciplines and found that narrative has a long history of use by practitioners (e.g., psychotherapists, historians). Why would narrative be used by practitioners? He claimed that the power of narrative lies in its ability to bridge theory and practice and to make research more relevant to practitioners. For Polkinghorne, narrative is a way to organize complex events and human actions and to focus attention on existence as it is lived, experienced, and interpreted by the individual. Jerome Bruner (1986), also in psychology, stated that narrative is the primary way that human beings think, make meaning of experience, and communicate understanding of experience.

Clifford Geertz (1995), an anthropologist, claimed that narrative is the way we make meaning as we reflect on the past, form accounts of change over time and place, and weave fact and interpretation to craft coherent accounts of complex experiences. For anthropologist Mary Catherine Bateson (1994), narrative is a means of capturing the complexity of changing life experience, of recognizing patterns within changing experience, of sharing learning from reflection on experience, and of improvising new ways of living (and teaching) that savor the ambiguity of life experience. For Geertz and Bateson, and others in the social sciences, narrative is an essential way humans make meaning of experience and communicate that meaning.

In teacher education: Narrative has a developing history in teacher education, one that is growing every day in both research and practice (e.g., Carter, 1993; Connelly & Clandinin, 1988; Florio-Ruane, 2001). Teacher educators use narrative in many different ways and for many different reasons; those using *Narratives from the Classroom* will find that each chapter lends itself to a different form of exploration and for different reasons. Many teacher educators use narrative to bring life to topics that otherwise might seem distant to students and unrelated to their lives. Many use narrative to build understanding that our personal experiences impact what we believe about teaching and how we engage in practice. Many use narratives to inspire their students to believe that teachers can and do make a difference in the lives of their students. An example of such a narrative is *To Teach: The Journey of a Teacher* (2001), by William Ayers, author of the foreword to this book. With much of the media rhetoric giving the opposite impression, narratives such as this are essential reading.

One of the primary reasons teacher educators such as myself, and others interested in diversity, are turning to narrative is its potential use as a way to connect students' experiences to those of children they will teach and as a way to develop empathy with "other people's children" (Delpit, 1995). Chris Carger's work (author of Chapter 7 in this book) is an excellent example of what I mean by developing empathy through reading narratives. In *Of Borders and Dreams: A Mexican-American Experience of Urban Education* (1996), Carger has written a narrative of the teaching and learning of Alejandro Juarez, a Mexican American child in inner-city Chicago. I use this book in my teacher education classes because it can bring my students directly into Alejandro's life in school, into his classes, into interactions with his peers and with his parents. Many of my students have backgrounds very different from Alejandro's and have had little, if any, contact with second-language learners. Through reading this rich, contextualized story, my students can begin to imagine what it might be like to be (mis)educated as an English-as-a-second-language student, to be marginalized, and to be a parent of a student having these experiences. I feel that this narrative can help them develop empathy, not only for Alejandro, but also for the children like him whom they will encounter over the years in their own ever-diversifying classrooms. Also, and importantly, I find that reading this narrative affords my students the opportunity to examine their assumptions about immigrant children and those learning English as a second language. Through the detailed accounts of Alejandro's teacher, students can see how a teacher's assumptions about students impact classroom practice and, in Alejandro's case, how the teacher's assumptions about his abilities curtailed his potential.

In addition to developing empathy and allowing for examination of assumptions, another reason I have for using narratives is that they can foster cross-cultural understanding. In the world today, this kind of understanding cannot be overemphasized. We need to get along with people different from ourselves and with people in different parts of the world. We need to be able to teach students different from ourselves in terms of language, culture, ethnicity, class, and experience. We need to begin to think of ourselves as "world citizens" (Nussbaum, 1997), not just as citizens of our local communities and countries. I can think of no more important task in teacher education than preparing teachers to think of themselves in this way.

Ming Fang He's (2003) narrative, *A River Forever Flowing: Cross-cultural Lives and Identities in the Multicultural Landscape,* is a powerful example of the potential of narrative to foster this kind of growth. In her book, we meet three women from Mainland China and follow their journeys from their birth during political upheavals in China, through the Cultural Revolution (1966–1976) and their lives on the reforming farms, to immersion in the beginnings of a Western education in university in China, then to graduate work in Canada. Beautifully and emotionally written, the narrative enables us to picture the women's lives unfolding before our eyes and understand their dilemmas of who they are and how they will live their lives. A narrative such as He's allows students to see "others" as individuals, with experiences, with pasts, and with futures. In coming into contact with "others" through narratives, some of the barriers between cultures can begin to dissolve. This glimpse into these lives reaches across continents and cultures and cultivates a sense of how interconnected we all are.

The ability of narrative to foster empathy and cross-cultural understanding relates to the ability of narrative to foster multicultural understanding. My own work in a Canadian inner-city school is an example of the potential of narrative to raise awareness of multicultural understanding. In *Narrative Inquiry in a Multicultural Landscape: Multicultural Teaching and Learning* (Phillion, 2002), we meet Pam, a teacher in a low-income school, and follow her through two years of teaching children from all over the world. We get an up-close look at multicultural life in schools and of multicultural practice in action. We see how Pam uses her "personal practical knowledge" (Connelly & Clandinin, 1988), knowledge derived from her life experiences, her years of teaching, and her work with children, to develop a practice that works for her children in her school.

Teacher educators with other foci and other goals will also find the narratives in this book useful. Authors in this book discuss teaching diverse students, student-teacher and parent-teacher relationships, the moral components of teaching, classroom discipline, technology use by experienced teachers, and important concerns in school and student safety. Practical advice on preparing for the job market, relating to administrators, and stories of surviving the first year are shared. Topics related to standardized testing, tracking, and diversity in the classroom are also discussed, and through the focus on personal experience, somewhat demystified. Discussion questions at the end of each chapter provide the opportunity for students and teachers to engage in lively debate over the issues. A list of additional recommended readings further develops the ideas in each chapter.

What are some other ways we can use narrative in teacher education? Narrative is more than telling and reading stories. Narrative is also an approach to teacher education, one that centers on understanding personal experience. Narrative focuses on experience as it is lived by the person (the teacher, student, or other character telling the story) and also focuses on the way a person makes meaning of the experience. Narrative is also a way of communicating the meaning of lived experience. Narrative arises out of practice and as such opens up understanding of personal practical knowledge, not only the knowledge of the author of the narrative, but also our own knowledge as we reflect on the story and our own experiences.

The idea of using narrative in teacher education was pioneered by Jean Clandinin and Michael Connelly. For them, narrative is not only the texts we read, such as the narratives in this book, but also a way to think about teaching and learning as well as research into teaching and learning (see Clandinin & Connelly, 2000). A narrative approach to teacher education is based on the idea that we make meaning through reflection. Reflection leads to understanding, which can lead to action; in the case of teachers, reflection and understanding can be transformed into renewed and revitalized practice.

In conjunction with reading the teacher narratives in this book, students may find it useful to engage in some of the following reflective activities. These activities are adapted from *Teachers as Curriculum Planners: Narratives of Experience* (Connelly & Clandinin, 1988). I use this approach in my undergraduate and graduate work with preservice and in-service teachers. (See my Web site at http://www.edci.purdue.edu/phillion/ for additional details.) These activities focus on understanding experience, and reflecting on experience, to create in-depth understanding of self and others. These activities can illuminate personal practical knowledge. Many of these activities can be done collaboratively.

Autobiographies: Autobiographies can be written with general goals of exploration of who we are. In the case of beginning teachers, it is useful to do these explorations as they are directly related to education. Students in my classes begin with a brief overview of their education by responding to questions such as: Where did you go to school? What sort of schools were they? What were the teachers like? What were the students like? If students changed schools and communities a number of times, they might include a chart showing each grade, teacher, year, and school location as an aid to the narrative. Students can ask their parents and teachers what they remember about their (the students') educational experiences. Next, students write about special events connected to their education that influenced their attitudes about school, teaching, or learning. Students describe these events in detail, telling what happened, how the event made them feel, and the attitude it engendered. Finally, they discuss how these prior experiences and attitudes influenced them to consider becoming teachers. Some students enjoy including photographs with their autobiographies; some enjoy creating CD-ROMs with music and photographs.

Reflective journals: My students keep reflective journals to explore developing understandings of self in relation to their students. Such journals are places to explore what students are seeing in field experiences and what they are reading in texts and narratives in their classes. Initially, students can focus on physical descriptions of schools and classrooms; later, they can reflect on student-teacher interactions and their developing understanding of pedagogical practices. It is important that journals be kept over a period of time so that students can return to earlier entries and reflect on them. Journal entries are based primarily on students' participant observations in local schools. In an additional program I oversee, students engage in technology-mediated observations of a distant, highly diverse school, through video-conferencing and the Internet. They also write journal entries.

Stories: Stories written about past educational experiences can shed light on our implicit beliefs about teaching and learning. Stories about experiences as a teacher or a student that include detailed information on the following questions are useful: Who were the characters? What was the setting? When did the story take place? These stories do not need to be long; some brief stories can capture experiences. Sharing the stories and having fellow students or the instructor respond to them is also useful. In fact, sharing stories and engaging in dialogue around stories, is a powerful way for students to connect to each other and to their teachers.

Interviews: Preservice teachers can benefit from interviewing practicing teachers or administrators. These conversations, focused on practice, can shed light on the experienced teacher's personal practical knowledge and show glimpses of the complexity of teaching. I have students reflect with cooperating teachers they work with in their field experiences. Some guiding questions I suggest students ask are: Why did you decide to become a teacher? What was school (elementary/middle/high) like for you? Why did you decide to teach at this level and/or this subject? What age level do you prefer to teach? How do you plan your daily lessons? Do you think first of the children, or the curriculum content, or the standards you have to meet? What do you do when students' attention shifts? Who decides on classroom rules? These interviews are particularly helpful after students have been in the classroom for several weeks and have a context for the conversation.

E-mail exchanges: E-mail exchanges from as close by as between students in the same class, or as far apart as students in different parts of the world, are wonderful ways to explore experiences. Betty Eng (a teacher educator friend in Hong Kong who wrote Chapter 6 in this book) and I had our students read stories of teaching and learning we both had written. All students' responses were shared through e-mail. We believed that our students learned about the role of place and context in education through this type of cross-cultural exploration.

Educational philosophies: Any of the narrative activities described previously are useful to include in educational philosophies. By engaging in the narrative explorations, students have a better understanding of themselves and their beliefs about teaching and learning. These systematic explorations enable students to articulate their thinking. In writing an educational philosophy, students pull their developing ideas and beliefs together with evidence from activities in which they have engaged. This can be the culminating piece for a narrative program of teacher education. In my program, we also have an additional layer of reflection when students prepare an electronic portfolio that includes material from many of the preceding activities.

Teacher Narratives: The Beginning of a Journey in Self-Understanding and the Understanding of Others

Narrative and story are essential aspects of being human and are the ways we understand experience and relate meaning of our experiences to others. The use of narrative crosses cultures, countries, languages, and disciplines. Why is that? I think it is because there is something intrinsically appealing about a narrative. I think it is because narrative allows for the possibility of understanding the experiences of others, those different from ourselves, those with different kinds of personal practical knowledge. Narrative also allows access to the heart and soul of experience; in the case of *Narratives from the Classroom,* we have access to emotional aspects of teaching in ways that other forms of writing do not offer. Narrative fosters growth in understanding others, developing empathy and a sense of connection.

Narrative also works hand in hand with imagination. As you read the chapters in this book, and as you reflect on the narratives through class discussion, conversations with friends, or some of the suggested activities, think about what matters to you as a teacher, or your future as a teacher. Imagine possibilities for your classroom. As you read and reflect on the detailed accounts of teachers' experiences in *Narratives from the Classroom,* imagine who you will be as a teacher, how you will relate to students and parents, and how you will live your classroom life. Imagine yourself as a teacher.

What Do You Think?

1. What are narratives? Why would we use them in teacher education?

2. What is personal practical knowledge? Do you feel this is a valuable form of knowledge? Explain your answer.

3. Share a story of your own educational experience with a student in the class. You can do this either in writing or orally. Remember the key elements of a story: characters, plot, timeline, setting, etc. After sharing the story, discuss it with your partner.

4. Share a story of a teacher who has impacted your life. Discuss it with a partner.

Suggestions for Further Reading

TEACHER NARRATIVES

Ayers, W. (2001). *To teach: The journey of a teacher.* New York: Teachers College Press.

Ayers' narrative is an honest, thoughtful account of his own personal experiences as a teacher and the lessons he has learned. This book will challenge many to stretch their ways of thinking about teaching.

Baldacci, L. (2004). *Inside Mrs. B's classroom: Courage, hope and learning on Chicago's South Side*. New York: McGraw-Hill.

This book describes the personal account of a woman who worked as a reporter for many years before becoming a teacher. This narrative is almost a glimpse into Baldacci's personal diary, as she recounts her experiences in transitioning from her previous career to teaching.

Carger, C. (1996). *Of borders and dreams: A Mexican-American experience of urban education*. New York: Teachers College Press.

This is a narrative account of Carger's experience working with a Latino student and getting to know his family in Chicago. Her message is that an effective teacher is one who gets to know students as individuals who are dealing with real life situations.

Johnson, L. (1992). *Dangerous minds*. New York: St. Martin's Press.

Dangerous Minds is a narrative describing Johnson's experience working in urban schools with students that many other teachers had deemed "unteachable." Johnson demonstrates the importance of teaching students based on their needs and their life experiences rather than on our own preconceived ideas of what teaching is.

Solnicki, J. (1992). *The real me is gonna be a shock*. Toronto: Lester.

This is another example of a teacher's narrative. Solnicki describes her coming to terms with being a privileged white woman teaching students who are in poverty and have low self-esteem. She tells of her experiences in getting to know these students and addresses important questions that pertain to students who don't believe in themselves.

TEXTS ON USING NARRATIVE IN TEACHER EDUCATION

Connelly, F. M., & Clandinin, D. J. (1988). *Teachers as curriculum planners: Narratives of experience*. New York: Teachers College Press.

Connelly and Clandinin focus on how teachers' personal experiences play a role in planning and developing the curriculum at all levels. Their arguments are supported with many examples of narratives, case studies, and other real classroom experiences. Narrative is described as a tool that both teachers and students use to make meaning of their lives.

Florio-Ruane, S. (2001). *Teacher education and the cultural imagination: Autobiography, conversation, and narrative*. Mahwah, NJ: Erlbaum.

This book is unique in that it blends research and narrative together in a form of participatory research. The author claims that teachers can learn about themselves and others through ethnic autobiography. To that end, she describes her experience as a member of a book club—where she collected personal stories of the other members—and provides analysis of the data.

References

Ayers, W. (2001). *To teach: The journey of a teacher.* New York: Teachers College Press.

Bateson, M. C. (1994). *Peripheral visions.* New York: HarperCollins.

Bruner, J. (1986). *Acts of meaning.* Cambridge, MA: Harvard University Press.

Carger, C. (1996). *Of borders and dreams: A Mexican-American experience of urban education.* New York: Teachers College Press.

Carter, K. (1993). The place of story in the study of teaching and teacher education. *Educational Researcher, 22*(1), 5–12, 18.

Clandinin, D. J., & Connelly, F. M. (2000). *Narrative inquiry: Experience and story in qualitative research.* San Francisco: Jossey-Bass.

Connelly, F. M., & Clandinin, D. J. (1988). *Teachers as curriculum planners: Narratives of experience.* New York: Teachers College Press.

Delpit, L. (1995). *Other people's children: Cultural conflicts in the classroom.* New York: New Press.

Florio-Ruane, S. (2001). *Teacher education and the cultural imagination: Autobiography, conversation, and narrative.* Mahwah, NJ: Erlbaum.

Geertz, C. (1995). *After the fact: Two countries, four decades, one anthropologist.* Cambridge, MA: Harvard University Press.

He, M. F. (2003). *A river forever flowing: Cross-cultural lives and identities in the multicultural landscape.* Greenwich, CT: Information Age.

Nussbaum, M. (1997). *Cultivating humanity: A classical defense of reform in liberal education.* Cambridge, MA: Harvard University Press.

Phillion, J. (2002). *Narrative inquiry in a multicultural landscape: Multicultural teaching and learning.* Westport, CT: Ablex.

Phillion, J., & He, M. F. (2001). Narrative inquiry in educational research. *Journal of Critical Inquiry into Curriculum and Instruction, 3*(2), 14–20.

Polkinghorne, D. (1988). *Narrative knowing and the human sciences.* Albany: State University of New York Press.

Part I

Purposes

2

My Thoughts on the Role of the Teacher After 12 Years in the Field

Kin T. Chee

Understanding what students, parents, and administrators expect of teachers is a difficult task at times. Often, one chooses teaching as a career because of one's passion for a subject or for the general sake of learning, but teaching involves more than simply delivering instruction, a concept that may not be entirely clear to the preservice teacher. Mr. Chee discusses the various roles he has been obligated to assume on a daily basis to afford the reader a glimpse at what might be expected of him or her in the future. He maintains that the role the teacher must assume is determined at least partly by the needs of the students. This chapter is not intended to define all of the roles of the teacher; rather, the author attempts to describe some of the roles he has assumed in his tenure as a teacher in order to give the preservice teacher an idea of what is expected; being a teacher is more than disseminating knowledge.

♦ ♦ ♦

Introduction

This is a true story. Some time ago, three teachers sat down together for dinner at a Korean restaurant. The discussion somehow led to a spirited exchange of views on the role of the teacher in the classroom. One participant was a visiting instructor from Japan, who was in the United States on a yearlong assignment, teaching Japanese at a middle school. The second was a senior lecturer of Japanese at a major state university in the northeast; and the third individual was a high school teacher of Japanese. The combined years of teaching experience of this trio of teachers spanned some 20 years across grades 1 to 16. The first teacher vehemently argued that she had knowledge to impart to students and that the teacher's primary role is to "teach" (i.e., transmission of knowledge). The second teacher suggested that her task was to "coach" students through the materials and to "facilitate" the transmission of that knowledge with activities based on students' needs and learning styles. The third teacher, while agreeing with the others, suggested that most students armed with the right motivation, discipline, interests, and materials can acquire knowledge and skills just as well on their own, with or without direct academic intervention (i.e., instruction) by the teacher. To him, the mere transmission and subsequent internalization of that knowledge by students is only a small fraction of what a teacher does in the classroom on a daily basis. What happens in the learning community, particularly the development of relationships, is far more important in firing the engine of learning among students.

What, then, is the preservice teacher or someone who is thinking about entering the field to make of the role of the teacher in today's class-room? Has the role of the teacher changed that much over the years beyond simply "teaching"? What does it mean to "teach"? Indeed, if the role of the teacher is not just to "teach," what function(s) does the teacher perform in the school? Is the understanding of the role of the teacher so disparate and varied among students, parents, administrators, and even practitioners in the field?

This chapter contains snapshots of one teacher's experience in six public schools and one college in the United States, Japan, and Singapore over the course of 12 years. The hope is to shed some light on the role of the teacher in today's classroom, which this writer strongly believes is shaped by one's implicit and explicit teaching goal(s) and what he or she has to do in order to attain them. In short, the part you play as a teacher, whether as a coach, an advocate, or a counselor, is dictated by what you hope to accomplish, both in the short and long run, and by what you do in the classroom on a daily basis.

The Reason I Became a Teacher

Like most teachers, the reason I became one was borne of conviction, per-haps naively so. I was in my third year of study at the university, majoring in English with teaching minors in Chinese and Japanese. This was in the early 1990s, and the Japanese economy, although waning, still had the strength of a bull. The Japanese yen was relatively strong. American auto companies seemed unable to stem the tide of better and cheaper vehicles coming into the country from Japanese competitors, which added to the trade deficit between the United States and Japan. Critics also regularly spoke of the Japanese "buying up America," which ostensibly damaged our national pride. Inevitably, the anger aimed at Japan hit all Asian Americans, reaching its peak with the wrongful murder in 1982 of Vincent Chin, a Chinese American engineer, by two disillusioned white autoworkers who thought he was of Japanese descent. As an Asian person and a student of the Japanese language and culture, I was acutely aware of the political rhetoric as well as sentiments toward Japan bashing in the country. I felt compelled to act, to change minds and hearts, and the way to do it was to become a teacher. Beyond mere vocabulary and grammar, I wanted to share with students my passion for languages, and through language, to see and understand the "other" as human and by extension a real person. I wanted students to see the beauty in languages and to realize the power of words. I wanted students to know that with knowledge comes understanding. More important, I wanted them to know that they can effect changes in the world, through words and deeds. With these teaching goals in mind, I became an English teacher and later taught Japanese as well.

At the time, there was indeed a critical shortage of teachers, especially in low-income rural and urban school districts. There were many programs in place—including the now-disbanded Center for Urban Teacher Education (CUTE), in which I was a participant; Teach for America; and so on—whose mission was to assign well-educated and well-meaning young people fresh out of college to teach at troubled school districts. The expressed goal of these organizations was to help academically challenged students attain a level playing field with more affluent students. The participants of these programs were certainly imbued with this almost zealot-like fervor to eliminate educational inequity in this country and to help students succeed in all aspects of their lives. I was one of them. I wanted to help. I wanted them to succeed. Little did I know that my expectations were to come up against the most trying realities that tested my strength and will to continue in the teaching profession.

The First Act: Reality Check

What I discovered during the months of my student teaching is that good intentions alone are insufficient for teaching, particularly in an environment where a multitude of needs are in constant play that demands your every attention. It is not that the students were unusually defiant or uncooperative. They wanted to learn and succeed, and they really wanted to please the teacher. However, it came as a profound realization to me that for these students who were poorly schooled in academics and classroom routines, learning just did not come easy! One reason is that many students came to school distrusting adults in general. Their contempt may well have been an immature attempt to exert their independence. However, my experience pointed to the fact that their mistrust invariably came from adult figures who (may have) failed them in the past. It is certainly not news to learn that teachers do at times give up on their students despite their better inclination or judgment.

In addition, most students came to class lacking skills in reading and writing. They also lacked basic knowledge in core disciplines such as math, science, and social studies. Somehow, they had reached their present grade levels having retained very little from previous grades. Why? Indeed, why do American students consistently fail to perform on par with students from other countries on international tests? I can only surmise that either they were not taught the materials or that the instruction they received was less than sufficient for the information to stick. The end result is that they were often confronted with newer materials that exceeded their understanding. In response, they became frustrated and withdrawn at its most benign or they exhibited episodes of acting out to signal their state of discomfort or insecurity. The students I encountered could not or were unwilling to tackle content materials that were a little beyond what they were capable of at the time. Their academic preparation for school was, in essence, checkered, unstable, and/or nonexistent! What should a teacher do, then, other than abandon the curriculum at hand to return to the basics? This, together with often impoverished economic resources at home as well as less than ideal family conditions, has the effect of pushing the students even farther behind academically compared to other students in more affluent environments.

In such circumstances, the traditional teaching model of simply teaching facts and figures did not work. The students did not know how to learn; their study habits were not well developed. They needed preparatory work to repair the gaps in their knowledge before embarking on more advanced materials. More important, the students had to know that the teacher truly cared about them, had faith in them, and would be there to help them should they falter. In addition, they had to realize that they had the strength, will, and courage within themselves to negotiate and continue in this academic maze. Above all, the necessary motivation and drive to succeed had to come from them.

How does one even begin to teach these life skills? The lessons I learned through the teacher preparatory program offered few concrete solutions, least of all consolation in the face of such crushing and immediate needs. So, what did I do? Yes, I knew that there are different ways of knowing, different ways of learning, and certainly different ways of demonstrating knowledge. However, what really counted at that particular school was scores on standardized tests. Because of this, I struggled daily to come up with activities to mediate between content demands and students' needs. It was truly a process of trial and error. I did not have a script to fall back on. However, the clarity of my objectives made the process more manageable. The end goal was to help students learn and be successful!

Perhaps what I did can best be described by the following messages that were given to me by two students, both 12th graders, at the end of my student teaching experience. The first was written by Felicia, an African American who was tall, beautiful, smart, articulate, but unfortunately lacking in self-esteem and confidence in her own abilities. The other was written by Tim, who was athletic (quarterback on the football team), tall, handsome, well liked by others, and always ready to compensate for his academic inadequacy with a big, disarming smile, and sweet words.

Personally, you have showed me the other side of education. I will miss your enthusiasm and dedication. Thank you for believing in my capability. You made me feel smart, when I felt like an average student. Thanks for your kindness and your positive attitude . . . I hope I am as academically sound as you.

Love, Felicia

Most teachers don't get through to me because I am very stubborn, and sometimes I just refuse to learn. But with you I never had a chance to refuse, because you always took it past the textbook level. And you did it effectively . . . promise me that no matter how tough it is, never let teaching get the best of you. And never give up. I'll end with this one word, *CONSISTANCEY* (his spelling and emphasis).

Tim

What made these responses so heartening was the fact that they were unsolicited. They came from the students themselves, who really saw through my schemes (with numerous missteps along the way) to help them learn and responded in kind. Indeed, they really wanted to learn. Aside from subject competence, what is also clear from these statements is that students want their teachers to have conviction in their voices and "consistency" in their deeds. Never give the students the opportunity to refuse, as Tim puts it, is one mantra I still carry with me as I continue teaching today.

Teaching is also part salesmanship, demanding "enthusiasm," "dedication," and "a positive attitude" on the part of the teacher. The students can see through you if your heart is not in it. Additionally, the teacher is also part counselor and part preacher—able to see the good in everyone, which is not always easy. He or she has to muster every ounce of faith in the student's ability to succeed, even " . . . when [the student] felt like an average student" like Felicia. The students need you to cheer them on when they are down. In terms of content, the teacher has the responsibility of bridging dry and often isolated materials with the larger world beyond the classroom walls. This taking it "past the textbook level" (Tim), in effect, creates relevancy and students can thus see the value in what they are learning.

These students and their needs essentially set the tone of the classroom and determined the various parts I played in it. My original game plan to teach tolerance and reverence for language had to be put aside somewhat to accommodate the more pressing and immediate needs of the students. It struck me then, even as it does now, just how fluid and changeable a teacher's role can be in the act we called "teaching" and its intended effect of "learning."

The Next Chapter in Teaching

My first teaching position brought me to a large urban high school in a midwestern town. There were some 2,500 students in all at the school, administered by one principal, one vice-principal, and three associate principals. Like most large urban centers, the school district was experiencing a growing loss of students to the outlying schools in the suburbs. In spite of its relative affluence with its military installation as well as several blue-chip companies, the community had pockets of extreme poverty, which, in turn, affected the learning/teaching climate at the school. The building itself was an august fixture in the community, dating back to the early years of the city's founding. In order to stop the hemorrhaging of the students to the suburbs, the school instituted the highly rigorous and prestigious preuniversity course of study called the International Baccalaureate (IB) Diploma Program. This is a European-based college preparatory program that incorporates the best aspects of national education systems without being based on any one. At the same time, it allows students to fulfill their state education requirements. To gain entry into the program, prospective students had to have excellent grades and references, undergo a rigorous interview, provide several writing samples, and sit for an aptitude test. The idea here was to create a school-within-a-school that caters to highly motivated, college-bound students. Armed with the lessons I had learned from students such as Felicia and Tim during my student teaching, I readily took on the new challenges presented to me by the students in the IB program. Admittedly, the disciplinary problems here were limited to students not turning in their assignments on time. One phone call to their parents quickly resolved that issue. I felt so fortunate to have students such as these. The students in the IB program were without doubt amazing young people. They were articulate, intellectually curious, intrinsically motivated, goal oriented, self-assured, and hard working. Of course, they were not immune from problems in day-to-day living, such as their parents' divorces and loss of jobs and the pains from lost loves. Nonetheless, these sporadic setbacks did not hold them back from achieving high scores on their IB examinations and attending Yale University, Dartmouth College, Carlton College, Duke University, and the like upon graduation from high school. I would like to think I had a hand, albeit a small one, in their successes. What did I do? Were the lessons I learned from Felicia and Tim adequate to the task at hand, that is, to serve the needs of these students and help them achieve their goals?

Is Teaching a Science or an Art?

The IB students were ravenous where content was concerned. It did not matter how I presented the materials in class. Whether it was a lecture, hands-on activity, paired interview, game, watching a video, or group research, the students readily took in whatever materials I offered and they were still asking for more, peppering the lesson with their comments, asking questions, and seeking clarifications. Again, the needs of the students dictated my role in the teaching-learning continuum—here I am simply a conduit, facilitating the transfer of knowledge in meaningful contexts.

The question as to whether teaching is a science or an art is not new. What I like to propose, however, is that they are not mutually exclusive. Depending on your "destination" (i.e., teaching goals) and the "vehicle of choice" (i.e., classroom activities) you employ to arrive at your objective, the role that a teacher plays will, of course, differ accordingly. Like an architect, the science of teaching rests in the groundwork that a teacher lays prior to the lesson itself. Careful attention to developing a curriculum as well as connecting to or reinforcing other content areas all add to the calculus of effective instruction. This is where the notion of recycling materials in different contexts is crucial for information to stick.

In addition, I realized just how important test scores were to these IB students, which invariably generated tremendous stress among them. In fact, I have seen students literally shaking at the end of major examinations. Thus, at the beginning of each school year, all of us would take a short detour from our regular studies to research the efficacy and end goals of testing. We found that these numbers represent only a snapshot of students' efforts at any given time and can be affected by a host of factors, some of which were beyond their control. In short, these numbers do not represent the sum total of their learning. The students were, by and large, unconvinced. They had been indoctrinated from the start of their academic careers that test scores are the signifiers of success. For my part, I scaled back on the number of tests I gave in class. Formal assessments were only strategically given at points in the lessons for us to measure progress as opposed to achievement. When deficiencies were identified, remedial lessons were given to correct any gaps in knowledge. This certainly had the effect of lessening the pressure on students to excel on tests alone and instead focused their attention on the task of learning.

The art of teaching, I would contend, lies in one's knowledge of the students; one must know when to push and when to pull back; when to probe or test and when to pull back; and when to exert control and when to allow them to explore on their own. Teaching and its corollary, learning, are not linear processes, traversing between two discrete points of the teacher and the students. It struck me at the time, though, how difficult it was for me to give up control of the act of instruction. What good was I if I were not there to teach? Looking at these students, however, made me realize that teaching and learning are collaborative acts of giving and taking, a dance of sort. It was conceivable that with the right music the students could dance very well on their own, in pairs, or in a group, without me! However, this would definitely require a reconfiguration of the teacher-teach and student-learn model to a more student-centered and collaborative model of instruction on my part.

One Song, Different Dances

The years I spent in the IB program were fruitful and contributed immensely to my understanding and growth as a teacher. By the end of this time, the classroom was no longer foreign territory to me and I found myself becoming more comfortable in the multiple roles that I played in a single school day. Still, surprises remained aplenty that continue to challenge my worldview as a teacher today.

An African American student came to me one day with a drop slip and told me that she was dropping my advanced course even though she had been in it for two years. She claimed that the class was too difficult. I did not believe her reasoning and prodded her for clarification. She finally confessed that she resented being labeled as "acting white" by her non-IB friends and she did not want to be picked on and ostracized anymore. "Acting white?" When did doing well in school refer to "acting white"? No amount of pleading, cajoling, and explaining on my part could convince her to change her mind. The conversation I had with the student's mother came to no avail, either. Sadly, that was the last I saw of her, not only in my class but in the IB program as well. This episode was one of many occasions in the years following when I found myself humbled by my own inability to rectify all wrongs. In spite of my best intentions and willingness to help, there was nothing I could do to deflect or lessen the pressures exerted by peers as experienced by this student. It was a painful experience, and I took it personally since I had vowed to help everyone to learn and succeed. In my eyes, I failed both my student and myself in the process. It took years before I came to accept that I could not "save" everyone. This episode, among many, demonstrated my fallibility as a teacher.

In another instance, I found myself in a confrontation with a parent who claimed that I had embarrassed and humiliated his child in front of the entire class with negative comments on a writing assignment. What I did, with the child's stated consent, was to use her assignment as a basis to talk about how a given rubric was used to evaluate the assignment at hand. I thought we had developed enough trust over the course of the program in each other to engage in such a task. Unfortunately, several students came up with rather critical statements in the course of the conversation that could be construed as a personal attack on the author herself. What it boiled down to at the end were my words and intent versus the student's interpretation of the event. In hindsight, of course, I should have used a made-up assignment for this purpose. But the real lesson for me from this event was the importance of initiating and maintaining contacts with the parents of my students in the course of the year. It is not enough to call them when a problem arises; it is far better to establish a working relationship with them at the beginning of the year to solicit the assistance and support a teacher needs to better serve the students in their learning. An incident such as this could, therefore, have been avoided if the parents had known the teacher and could have spoken to his or her intentions. Teaching is not the sole responsibility of the teacher. Successful teaching requires all parties—student, parent, administrator, and teacher alike—to understand the end goal(s) and the responsibilities involved and to participate in the teaching-learning process together.

It is clear, looking at the two incidents discussed previously, that the teacher's role in the classroom is multifaceted, requiring different skills and orientations of mind. One could reasonably argue that I was at once a counselor, a social worker, a peacemaker, a public relations specialist, and more, in addition to being a teacher. However, it must be noted that these various roles do not necessarily contradict each other if one is sure about the end result. In other words, these roles all lead to the same road toward success for students.

Learning New Tricks

After leaving the IB program, I spent the next two years pursuing a master's degree to further hone my craft as a teacher. It was a rigorous program, combining theory and practice. It was there that I learned about action research, which I think all teachers should learn to do. Action research is a pedagogical practice that allows teachers to test and evaluate, among other things, their teaching techniques and assessment strategies. The fact is, most teachers already do this intuitively in their own class-rooms. What action research does is to formalize a series of research pro-tocols that could impact the reliability and validity of the outcomes of one's research. This would surely strengthen the classroom practices of the teacher, which would, in turn, engender greater academic success among students. In recent years, I have explored the use of story-based approaches, including total physical response (TPR), Gouin series, and total physical response-storytelling (TPR-S), to teaching Japanese pragmatics. The goal here was to increase and enhance students' oral production in the target language through the use of pragmatics devices via innovative teaching strategies. In another project, I looked at how Think-Aloud Protocols can be used to reinforce various reading strategies that were introduced in the classroom.

Participation + Discussion + Reflection = Teach, Teaching, and Teacher

Following a six-month stint teaching a sixth-grade class at an elementary school in Singapore and another six months teaching English at a high school in Japan, I accepted a year-long position teaching English at a midwestern high school. Returning to my original goal of teaching toler-ance and acceptance through language, I left the following year for a rural school district in upstate New York where I began teaching Japanese (again). This was indeed a fortuitous move professionally because I soon found myself heavily involved with the regional organization for teachers of Japanese. With the encouragement and support of members of the organization, I have found the voice and confidence to share with my peers at conferences and workshops what I have been doing in the classroom. Their feedback has been invaluable in challenging me to be more deliberate and creative in my teaching. Additionally, I was invited to participate in a panel of teachers who had developed a language proficiency test for 10th-grade students. Many schools across the state have since adopted this assessment tool to evaluate their students. In the process, my participation has made me more aware of what I teach and how I go about testing my students in the classroom.

Teaching is often a solitary act. Teaching is also a private act. Often, it is difficult to discuss your teaching strengths and weaknesses with anyone, least of all your peers in the field. Therefore, it is up to the teacher to find ways to improve himself or herself professionally. Aside from conferences and workshops, reading up on research literature and journals, and consultation with colleagues, it is important to set aside time for personal reflection and rejuvenation. This is a time to look back on lesson(s) taught and to strategize as to how to proceed. This is also a time to center oneself and to become reacquainted with the teacher inside the person and the goals this teacher has set for himself or herself in the classroom. Finally, it is personal time to spend with friends and family. A teacher should never forget that beyond the four walls of the classroom, there are other people who matter in his or her life. It must be remembered that a teacher is also a spouse or significant other, a father or mother, a son or daughter, and a friend. These, too, are critical roles in a teacher's life!

Finally, a note about a teacher's role with regards to school administration: In principle, the administrators are there to support teachers in their teaching endeavors. However, it does not always work out that way, depending on the personalities involved as well as the politics of the school district. It might come as a surprise to novices in the teaching field that a teacher is also an advocate of his or her program of study. During times when money is short, there is every incentive for the central school administration to trim costs by cutting programs deemed to be "frills." It is not unusual for music programs, art programs, technology programs, physical education programs, and foreign language programs to disappear from course catalogues should the need arise for budgets to be slashed. It is, therefore, up to the teacher concerned to speak out, to publicize, and to promote the program. This might involve community-wide activities, fundraising, presentations at board meetings, and so on. It may sound crass, but you may have to "sell" yourself and your program to increase its visibility. Without support from students, the school administration, and the community at large, your program may disappear and the school district is not required to retain you in the school year, with or without tenure. Good teaching alone, and I can certainly attest to that, is insufficient to assure the continuance of your program.

Some Final Thoughts

Perhaps there was a time when a teacher's role was simply to pass on knowledge and skills, but that time is now long gone. Instead, teachers are now faced with students with greater needs, coupled with increasing demands for accountability; teaching has become more difficult than ever before. Still, the game plan that I have had since my student teaching days, modified and tempered by years of experience, remains my playbook in the classroom today. The role of the teacher is not static; it is ever changing based on the exigencies of the day. However, enthusiasm, dedication, and a positive attitude that one carries into the classroom, together with a faith in students and their abilities to succeed, will continue to be essential tenets for teaching. Furthermore, teaching cannot be effective without the support and trust of the students' parents, the school administration, and the community at large. With an eye toward helping students succeed, the role of the teacher changes accordingly, based on needs and audience!

What Do You Think?

1. How has your idea of the roles of the teacher changed from the time that you were in school to the present day? What roles did you see your teachers assume when you were in school?

2. In your field experience, interview your cooperating teacher about the various roles he or she must assume throughout any given school day. What roles must a teacher assume that are more "behind the scenes" that a student may not necessarily observe?

3. Which roles of the teacher do you believe are the most important? Which do you believe are the least important? Explain your answers.

4. Are there any roles that you do not like? How will you deal with taking on those roles if you are required to do so despite your feelings?

5. Are there roles that you believe a teacher should not assume? Why not? Are there roles that you believe are imperative that a teacher assume? Why?

Suggestions for Further Reading

Lambert, L., et al. (1996). *Who will save our schools? Teachers as constructivist leaders.* Thousand Oaks, CA: Corwin Press.
   The authors encourage teachers to take a part in redefining the role of the teacher as the "constructivist leader." It is suggested that creating learning communities is an essential role that teachers should assume. The requirements for becoming a leader and teacher are discussed.

Mills, G. (2002). *Action research: A guide for the teacher researcher* (2nd ed.). Upper Saddle River, NJ: Prentice Hall.
   Mills maintains that the role of the teacher should include action research. He provides a step-by-step description on how to conduct this form of research, how to write it up for publication, and how to analyze the data appropriately. Many examples and resources are also provided.

Palmer, P. J. (1997). *The courage to teach: Exploring the inner landscape of a teacher's life.* Hoboken, NJ: Jossey-Bass.
   This is more of a self-help or psychological book in nature, a book to remind the reader of what teaching is all about. While the primary audience for this book might be the teacher who is "burned out," a preservice or new teacher might also find this book useful for gaining a clear understanding of this profession.

Parkay, F. W., & Stanford, B. H. (2003). *Becoming a teacher* (6th ed.). Upper Saddle River, NJ: Pearson Allyn & Bacon.
   This is an excellent resource for the preservice teacher in order to gain insight into what teaching really entails. The authors address a variety of topics by including discussions on current trends in teaching, social issues, meeting standards, curricular issues, and much more.

3

Moral Education in American Schools

Christopher Blake

Connie Monroe

The issue of teaching values, morals, and ethics receives much debate in education circles. People question whether such topics should be included in the curriculum, and even when there is some consensus about teaching morals, the question of which morals to teach is raised. This chapter addresses the complexities that go along with the idea of teaching morals, from both a historical and a modern perspective. All teachers teach morals and character through their own actions. It is, therefore, imperative that a preservice teacher begin to consider where he or she stands on certain issues before they arise in the classroom.

♦ ♦ ♦

Introduction

The epithet *e pluribus unum* ("out of many, one"), minted on the nation's currency, is a signpost to the American Dream of unity from diversity. The same hope also underpins much talk in the United States currently surrounding moral education. A groundswell of public desire is discernible for post-9/11 American society to cohere around common, core values that will bring consensus of ideas and actions, rather than the cultural fragmentation and diversification that is perceived as prevalent. One main stage on which this play is now being enacted is that of the public school system, despite the historic constitutional separation of church and state. Currently, we see a united call for school action in the moral domain, and a strident claim that education should be leading the way in reforming the hearts, minds, and lifestyles of today's youth (Bennett, 1995; Bloom, 1987; Wynne & Ryan, 1997). The response of the education system to this "hot" issue has, however, been varied. Thomas Lickona (1992), the modern father of the "character education" movement, noted that the summons to education has been initiated from outside the school walls and has resulted from broad public perception of societal and individual decline. Instead of leading the debate on societal values and their relationship to education, the teaching profession has found itself frequently listening and reacting to the rhetoric and ideas of others (Coles, 1997).

This exemplifies the problematic nature of moral education in the United States, where even the term itself is sometimes called character education, values clarification, values education, citizenship education, among other terms (Lawton, 1995). Coupled with this is an increased sense of accelerating changes in cultural life, a rush toward what Kincheloe (1993) called "postmodern hyper-reality," which has thrown into doubt many of education's "sacred cows" and challenged American certainties about educational priorities. Most powerfully, the post-Columbine and post-9/11 perception is that America's core moral values are under attack and need reinforcing among our youth as a defense against both our external enemies and our internal denigrators.

In this chapter, we will present varied aspects of moral education as it exists in America. We will examine the issue from the inside and outside by combining a teacher's narrative that describes her experiences and reflections in varied settings with the contextual commentary of a British educator who has studied various aspects of American education. We will examine two extremes of moral education before presenting several of the more common practices that reflect moral education in mainstream America.

Moral Education: An Exposed Curriculum

When I taught in an independent school for several years, the moral nature of education was clearly revealed. Private schools often have an advantage in the realm of moral education both in their free-dom to openly address moral issues and in their ability to project a cohesive sense of values through their choices of faculty and curriculum. They need not remain unbiased to reflect the public's debate over morality. Although the school where I worked was not religious, the "hidden" curriculum was clearly presented and built into the academic experiences. While the inclusion of certain aspects of the hidden curriculum can be clearly identified at many schools, this school presents it directly as a central theme.

During the regular terms of the school year, classes took place in groups of no more than 15 to create an interactive setting with lively discussions. Problem-solving approaches focused around current issues were used as often as possible creating interdisciplinary applications and requiring discussions of implications. A certain level of participation in extracurricular activities was required of all students with the stated purpose of teaching them to be active, face challenges, and work in teams.

The school culture clearly incorporated a sense of common values and attitudes. Students were held responsible for their work and contribution to class, but teachers were equally responsible to the students. Weekly faculty meetings allowed thorough communication to create interdisciplinary connections and to address concerns about students so that no child would fall between the cracks. On occasions such as Earth Day, community service was also connected to academic activities to make it clear that beyond the responsibility to each other, faculty and students had a responsibility to the greater community.

More unique facets of the curriculum provided experiential teaching experiences that unashamedly included moral education. Trips away from school such as mountain climbing or ropes courses presented challenges requiring students to learn interdependence and to face their fears. In the high school, experience-centered seminars focused small groups of students and teachers around a topic for a period of a month. While some groups studied language, literature, or culture in settings such as Belize or London, others studied ecological issues in settings such as the rain forest or the Baja Peninsula. Students studied homelessness, the handicapped in our society, or Native American art forms in ways that required problem solving, close socialization, and discussions of ethical implications.

Most disciplinary incidents at the school were handled by an elected student advisory group in a setting similar to a trial. One faculty member would present information on the incident and its negative impact; the student and his or her advisor would present any defense or clarifications that were appropriate. The students would then deliberate with a faculty advisor and determine an appropriate consequence. The system worked surprisingly well as both an educational tool and a deterrent. Students who had served on the disciplinary group or encountered its process spoke of the difficulty of deliberations and what they learned of how incidents impact whole communities.

Students also learned to behave responsibly through their interactions with each other in other ways. In one program, students from the secondary grades were assigned buddies from the elementary grades for the year. In addition to helping with the organization at schoolwide activities, it was clear that the older children were to behave as role models. They soon learned how much the younger children looked up to them and emulated them. On several occasions, I noticed how some of the less traditional students would straighten up and modify their behavior in the presence of their little buddies. They might appear to be wild, rebellious teens yet they had accepted a sense of values and responsibility that showed more clearly in their actions than in their outward appearances. The common threads of values built through the curriculum and culture of this school had a significant impact on the moral education of the students.

There are unique features of this school setting, yet many of the values supported by the curriculum of this school reflect traditional aspects of American moral education such as a strong work ethic, creative problem solving, responsibility to others, individual achievement, and teamwork. Traditionally in American education, the moral basis of schooling was fundamental. Although devoid of religious influence, the inculcation of character and virtue was axiomatic to the work of the Common School. Egalitarianism and civic duty could only be attained if certain values were popularly accepted, a fact fully recognized by the school leaders of the 19th century. The central focus of morality in this respect was clear. The publication series known as the McGuffey Readers, named after clergyman and educationalist William Holmes McGuffey (1800–1873), testifies to the importance of moral education in the emerging school experiment. Over 120 million editions of the McGuffey Reader were published across the United States between 1836 and 1920, the largest circulation of any book in the world other than the Bible, thus ensuring the nurturing of certain values across several generations.

When this vision of cultural and moral conformity was at its zenith, American education was able to solidify its values basis around a specific nationalistic vision, secular in form but rooted in Protestant, Anglo-Saxon traditions, and egalitarian in its privileging of conformity and disregard for difference. For commentators since, the argument has been whether the *unum* or the *pluribus* won out in this historic narrative. These contrasting perspectives reflect a broad division and generalization about cultural pluralism in the United States that have far-reaching implications for moral education in today's school. Broadly speaking, egalitarian and pragmatic values in socioeconomic and public life empowered the trend in the 19th and early 20th centuries toward enhanced access and greater participation in the educational sphere. But with these values also came an increasingly partisan view of what counted as desirable culture and a perception of identifiable character and morality traits that might serve the emerging cultural hegemony. The result was that American education came to reflect a broad bias toward white European heritage, and reinforced this bias by inculcating particular notions of the virtuous character and moral life.

Understanding Acceptance or Moral Miseducation?

My year in a poor urban school inspired me to consider the daily aspects of moral education more carefully. I had been a successful teacher prior to that year and enjoyed the respect of both my colleagues and my students in other states and varied settings. New to the area, I accepted a position at a middle school operating on a year-round schedule with classes beginning two weeks after my arrival in the area. While I had taught in urban settings before, I did not realize that this school was one of the poorest in the nation and had very few white students. I was entering a different culture without preparation. As often happens, the experience of another culture led to both dissonance and reflection.

Perhaps the heart of moral education relates to how people treat each other. At that school, I saw extremes in terms of consideration, caring, disrespect, and ill will. In this school, I was physically struck and threatened by both students and parents. I learned that patience and cheerfulness would be interpreted as weakness by some. My colleagues advised me to use discipline methods that I considered demeaning although they were an accepted part of the school culture. I was even reprimanded once for assigning an alternate punishment rather than the standard writing assignment of 50 rules to be copied 10 times for dress code infractions. This may sound antiquated, yet it took place less than a decade ago. It presented one of the dilemmas

I faced that year. While morality is judged by cultural norms, I had to choose between my own conscience and the accepted behaviors that would be respected and effective in that school.

That school also challenged my sense of how people are given a voice and valued as persons. I remember feeling quite comfortable ending a conversation a student tried to pursue in class related to current generations' inherited responsibility for slavery. After all, it was unrelated to the day's learning goals and I knew better than to enter an argument with an adolescent. Unfortunately, the student resented my suggestion that we should save that discussion for another time and refused to participate meaningfully in class from that time forth. It was only a month later that I was told by another student that he didn't have to listen to me as his parents had told him that he didn't have to be bossed around by any white folk. I assumed that he was overinterpreting a remark that had been intended to build confidence. A phone call to parents intended to clarify the situation and seek their assistance taught me that my assumptions were wrong. The parents communicated clearly that their child should take no directions from any white people, including teachers. I felt frustrated, indignant, and devalued by this interaction, but I recognized the same lingering reactions on the part of the student I had cut off. I still feel justified in my classroom decision, but I fear that the other child's parents may also feel justified. I now wonder how those lessons impacted students' views of both justice and equality.

Moral education is interactive in nature; often the moral lessons are being learned by the teacher as well as by the student. I was in my early 30s at that point. My son was enrolled in kindergarten, and I kept his picture behind my desk with other personal objects. When one of my students asked me if that was a picture of my "grandbaby," I alternated between feeling amused and insulted. Later, I listened to this 13-year-old boy mention his 28-year-old mother and his five younger siblings and realized that the student had been serious. Clearly, my traditional approach of using family trees to teach vocabulary would need to be modified. In fact, I became much more careful to consider how such discussions could be descriptive rather than prescriptive. At the same time, the importance and value of family is a concept that was still worth reinforcing. My efforts to remain nonjudgmental were challenged by the fact that morality itself requires decisions based on values, priorities, and ideas of right and wrong.

As the first school I discussed demonstrated a culture unified in shared values, this school demonstrated a culture of disagreement and divisiveness. I should have known it would be a difficult year when, after my original acceptance of the position, I was told that I couldn't enter my classroom until the day before class. I couldn't examine the text being used, as they weren't sure there was one or if there were enough for students—the previous three French teachers had not completed their yearlong contracts and left no information related to resources. The lack of support and concern for the teachers was both a symptom and a cause of the pervasive lack of caring among the student body. Teachers were heard to comment to students that they should ignore other teachers as their subject was irrelevant or that the teacher didn't belong. I heard teachers comment within students' hearing that various aspects of the curriculum didn't matter as they predicted which students would never finish school and which were destined for a life of crime.

It can be argued that these teachers' attitudes were understandable reactions to their experiences; nevertheless, I question the morality of their behavior. If teachers have a moral obligation to teach, lead, and aid their students—then what was being taught? In spite of the pervasive culture of disrespect, there were successful teachers in that school who communicated a sense of possibilities, caring, and responsibility to their students. They chose to remain in that setting where they acted as counterinfluence to the difficulties in the children's lives. They taught morality as they listened to the children, valued their experiences, challenged them to achieve, and demanded that they reason. Explaining that their students wouldn't "care how much their teachers knew until they knew how much their teachers cared," they taught children instead of subjects. Through the years, they maintained a sense of direction by using their own sense of morality as a compass through the chaos.

A friend who continued teaching in that urban school, Maureen, described recently feeling troubled and ambivalent regarding teachers' right to have private lives versus their responsibility to act as role models. Her feelings were brought to a head when she realized that two of the young teachers in her school were pregnant and unmarried. Both teachers had expressed to their colleagues and students that they had no intention of marrying and intended to raise the children themselves. While this has become more socially accepted, Maureen was concerned about the message that the students would take from this. In a setting where teen pregnancy is all too common, do teachers bear a responsibility to live a personal life modeling marriage as the only setting for procreation? Recent trends toward an increase in children born outside marriage raises the question of whether we have a responsibility to support marriage or if that is a proscriptive attitude that is becoming less a part of our social contract.

Although several years have passed since I left that school, various aspects of what I experienced there still trouble me. I have a great deal of respect for the strong teachers who choose to remain in that difficult school setting. They have taken on not only the challenge of teaching in a setting of poverty where little support is given to teachers, but also of maintaining their own sense of values in a setting where moral relativity rules. Students from traditional moral backgrounds with strong religious convictions sit next to the teen mothers and students who wear parole monitors around their ankles. The students receive mixed messages from their teachers related to what is acceptable behavior and what expectations they may have of life. While it is easy to blame the school, in many ways it simply reflects the moral confusion of America and the neighborhood it incorporates.

Twentieth-century history has largely seen the hegemony that used to dominate moral education maintained, but weakened. The practice of cultural domination has remained, but increasingly the exclusion of minority cultures and dysfunctionality of traditional values has impinged uncomfortably on societal consciousness. The initial response was ambivalent. On the one hand, the drive to assimilate more fairly and comprehensively became a priority (Berry & Blassingame, 1982). But while this comprehensive and consensual voice was strengthened, so also was that of a new trend, that of pluralism. For advocates of the latter, the lesson of two centuries was a cultural power play in which America had tried "to have its cake and eat it, too."

The power behind this alternative pluralist perspective lay in the historical reality that the values that had sustained cultural hegemony were, for the first time, now in doubt. Here lies the crux for any theory of moral education in today's democratic societies. In the same way that a relationship existed in the 18th and 19th centuries between the ascendancy of cultural homogeneity and the values of egalitarianism, utility, and secularism, so an inverse relationship can be discerned increasingly in the 20th century between personal values and cultural discourses of heterogeneity and diversity. This fundamental relationship, the contingency or interdependency between values education and cultural discourse, is underscored by the history of school-based character education programs in recent decades.

By the 1960s, this lack of confidence in the epistemological basis to morality had infused popular culture. The priority of individual worth and fulfillment reached a new level of societal consciousness, bringing in its wake the call for freedoms and struggles against various injustices. Here morality was not absent, but sociopolitically oriented toward individual self-expression and legitimacy, over forms of authority and governance, whether just or not. The values clarification approach (Raths, Harmin, & Simon, 1966) relied on proximity between espoused values and personal actions and encouraged students to reflect on how their actions might reflect their values. Critics were quick, however, to pounce on the limitations of this approach, in particular, its replacement of moral content with value-oriented volitions and feelings, needing simply to be "clarified" in the learner.

Diplomatic Efforts in Moral Education: Glimpses from the Middle Ground

My experiences in the two schools I mentioned earlier had profound effects on my own thoughts and attitudes toward moral education, but I don't consider them representative of mainstream American education. Instead, I judge the more common approach toward moral education to be a careful effort to include morality in diplomatic ways that will be inoffensive to most. The experiences of my teaching interns and friends in the classroom have confirmed my own experiences in public schools.

The formal inclusion of moral education ranges from the level of statewide mandates to local school projects. Service learning is now a graduation requirement in the state of Maryland where it takes several forms. College freshmen tell me that their service learning was supposedly incorporated into the regular school day. Theoretically, students planned, enacted, and reflected within classroom activities such as organizing for food drives or assisting in local elementary schools. In reality, many of these students cynically voice that they actually carried out no service and don't know how they earned the credit for service that they received. In other locations, students actually were provided with opportunities to carry out their service learning within the greater community by volunteering in hospitals, child care centers, or retirement homes. Students from these settings express both an appreciation for a meaningful experience and reservations that this should be optional as not all students participated willingly or found the programs convenient to their personal obligations.

Teacher reactions to these programs vary. Irene tells me that she supports it in theory, but she expresses concerns over mandating service and the documentation requirements that necessarily follow. It has become one more curricular mandate that she must fit in and track. Sara, a former Peace Corps volunteer, is more enthusiastic and puts a great deal of time into creating interesting service learning opportunities in her classroom that can tie to the curriculum through various units she teaches.

Moral education can be seen more clearly in the curriculum as districts use their influence to transmit mainstream cultural values to continue the enculturation facet of our educational institutions. An example of this can be seen in a large Maryland district's first-grade curriculum, which includes "recognize the family as a basic unit of society that perpetuates life and promotes healthy growth and development." A teaching intern, Ellen, described this to me as touchy-feely indoctrination, but her mentor teacher supports it fully as she relates how she has seen families change and feels that strengthening family ties ultimately helps her students. She comments, however, on the need to interpret the term *family* broadly as she sees more nontraditional families and does not want any children to feel excluded in her classroom.

A popular program chosen by many districts as a vehicle for moral education is the Character Counts program. It focuses on six "pillars of character," including trustworthiness, respect, responsibility, fairness, caring, and citizenship. While one nearby elementary school applies this through a program that recognizes students who best model these virtues, a neighboring school creates student skits to explain the concepts. The middle school closest to them uses these concepts as a discussion point when analyzing literature to create yet another application of this program. In a district where I taught in Ohio, I remember a similar approach created by a principal to focus on a word of the week as a vehicle to discuss and model virtues and character. That program was credited with improving both test scores and student behavior. These programs usually focus on encouraging virtue by promoting good habits; they avoid controversy and moral relativity by focusing on those character virtues that are fully consensual.

I was always curious about the various ways that morality is addressed more directly in relation to local culture. I remember attending two concerts one week. One middle school in Ohio had a "holiday concert" including cute songs related to snow, while the other middle school 30 miles away had a "Christmas concert" including traditional Christian carols and a religious theme. When I taught in Texas, pep rallies at my rural high schools always included a prayer to conquer the opposing team, which was led by the captain of the appropriate team as a feature between the dance team and the band. In spite of continued controversy over prayer in school, my nieces assure me that this practice continues there. In the same small town, the middle school principal, Ann, took a more diplomatic approach. I remember when she counseled students that their theft of class field trip fees was "inappropriate and antisocial" rather than condemning it as morally wrong. She chose to demonstrate that she was nonjudgmental and sensitive to alternate perspectives. Ann admitted to a background in values clarification approaches and praised its cognitive benefits while mourning its lack of moral certainty.

Individual teachers include moral education in their classrooms in a variety of ways, based on their personal stance. My friend Caroline in Colorado explains that she consciously thinks aloud when making decisions in the classroom as she wants her high school students to understand how adults consider various aspects and moral implications to their choices. In the same neighborhood, Heather uses class meetings with her fourth-grade students to discuss issues in their learning community and explains to observers that she wants the students to consider just solutions and the consequences of choices. They demonstrate the "grappling" approach encouraged by Sizer and Sizer (1999) as Hank does when he encourages lively discussions of right and wrong related to current events study in his social studies class.

Teachers across America make conscious decisions to bring moral education into their classroom by choosing books, movies, and topics that are likely to provoke discussions related to morality and ethics. Many are willing to take on the uncomfortable position of moral educator because of their acceptance of role model status and their desire to provide students with a framework for the moral issues they will face throughout life.

It is important to note the relationship between moral growth and the reproduction of democratic society. This Deweyan (1916) principle recalls that in such matters, both students and teachers are seekers, and once this is acknowledged, a radically different view of pedagogy follows, firmly rooted in traditions of critical and reconstructionist thought. Aristotle once defined teaching as an activity that is done "as to a friend." This means that a teacher is more than a good role model, or curriculum developer, or representative of a moral institution. It is rather a vision of a personal inquirer, seeking to find with others the potential for growth and healing in the face of individual uncertainty and societal ambiguity. Students long for this, but because of its risk and demand in personal terms most teachers are not equipped to be that "friend."

From this it follows that moral education should be perceived as a resource rather than a directive or a goal for education. This point is in real danger of being lost at present. The trend within moral education, clearly visible in numerous character education programs, is to objectify a consensual level of consciousness. The danger of consensus in moral education is that it elevates an ethereal moral core to educational privilege, while failing to engage learners in the critical act of thinking for themselves. Put simply, it gives us a moral fantasy, a calm hallucination, to help shut out the experience of our present disjointed society, which increasingly requires a penetrating moral analysis.

Here, then, lies the diversionary danger of current thinking on moral education. By celebrating only the consensual, it runs the risk of indulging the vacuous. All rational individuals and cultures acknowledge the legitimacy of such principal values as honesty, knowledge, and justice. The role of education, however, lies in its capacity to help us maneuver from the quiet backwaters of consensus into the unsettling undercurrents of real life, where our interpretation of principal values in the human situation confronts us with dilemma, turmoil, and disagreement.

Conclusion: Toward a New Rationale for Moral Education

We are concerned that the historic themes that have long endured and provided the context for moral education are no longer fit for purpose. The traditional themes—egalitarianism, utilitarianism, participative democracy, and secular morality—have prevailed in different forms through most periods of American educational history. But we contend that no longer can moral conformity be legitimized, given the cultural ramifications that such a goal implies and requires. Instead, a new capacity for moral dialogue, a sense of shared, participative moral inquiry, is the essential need of education in the postmodern condition. Education in this picture offers clues for moral growth and participation in society. What scope, then, might moral education offer?

We need to ensure that moral education gives free rein for teachers and students to participate in what Kincheloe (1993) called a "pedagogy of consciousness." Such consciousness starts from a recognition of both the failure of "totalizing" perspectives to provide meaning to our human condition and the ambiguities of our own cultural and personal experiences. But it also goes on to take as axiomatic those experiences as we make moral sense of the dilemmas of daily living. This "relativism" of sorts is not meant to negate the possibility of moral growth, but just the opposite. As Kincheloe (1993) put it: "Educational visions that simply attempt to reveal fixed eternal truths or the great ideas of America . . . fail to engage students with living arguments and with practical forms of understanding that move us to acts of democratic courage" (p. 229).

Such participation is, critically, resistant to totalizing views or consensual pictures. Instead, it takes seriously the arbitrariness of the postmodern condition, but goes on to equip each individual to seek a vision and meaning in its face. This is a grander task than identifying core themes in morality of educational interest. It is about utilizing all our capacities—mental, emotional, personal, and social—in the quest for becoming moral change agents. Such a quest goes beyond even the worthy processes of critical thinking, because it needs to recognize that moral inquiry is about affective and personal investment, as well as cognitive awareness. This is the reality of human experience that led Lenin (1960) to assert that "truth is concrete." By this, he meant that morality does not abide in metaphysical ideals, but in the hopes, struggles, and achievements of our personal and collective lives.

The school and its culture provide such a concreteness. In such a community, we come across what Benhabib (1992) called an "interactive universalism," or the coming together of conflicts among experiences, traditions, ideas, and practices in our diversified culture. The reality is that public education has always been the arena for cultural contestation and regeneration, rather than the homogeneous system that modernism has sought through ideologies such as egalitarianism and utilitarianism. This is the crux for any education in morality. The real strength of such education lies in its potential to awaken and empower us in the face of the arbitrariness of our cultural condition.

This is why advocates of the Religious Right have been so successful recently in the public sphere, in "the guts of American politics," as Shapiro (1995) put it. They alone have provided a moral vision that encompasses the breadth and depth of human experience: Put simply, they treat all our life experiences very seriously. But with their vision also comes a totalizing dogma that is willing to trade in intolerance and closed-mindedness in order to achieve a communal life secure from daily insecurities. This presents a challenge for the moral educator today. On the one hand, education urgently needs to find a moral imperative geared to a participatory, compassionate, and communal society. On the other hand, it must do so without proposing a monolithic, straitjacketing vision that appeases consensus at the expense of meaning and challenge. The task of finding such a moral vision is also made more difficult by the frameworks we commonly adopt in America by trying to standardize everything into a program or a curriculum requirement.

Education in our present social condition instead needs to act like a prism, enabling us to see ourselves, our limitations, our potential, our lifestyles, our communities, our cultures, and our society, and empowering us to struggle together for justice and meaning in our lives. This lesson is not new. It recalls the origins of public education in America, when education and morality were synonymous and absolutely bound with societal survival. In such a context, morality is not a separate part of life, capable of discrete identity, but totally bound to our human consciousness and thus to every act deemed educational. Such a priority needs rediscovering. In America's historical passage from modernity to postmodernity, we need to revisit and reformulate that insight, without accepting the inevitability of cultural hegemony that followed in its wake.

In this sense, despite being an artificial construct of curriculum and school, values education, moral education, and character education, whatever we may term it, can harness morality to the experiences and hopes of our individual and cultural autobiographies and thus point to the reality that we are not educated persons unless we are moral persons. In so doing, it may help us forge a reconstituted society and remind us that all educational quests are ultimately about being human and how we should live as free individuals in the broad human community. This paradoxical hope for shared living in a diverse world—"one out of many"—is ultimately the same ideal on which democracy in general, and American society in particular, rests its legitimacy and aspirations.

What Do You Think?

1. How do you personally define moral/character education?

2. Reflecting on your previous educational experiences, how was moral education incorporated into the curriculum? How did this type of education make you feel? What did you learn from this education?

3. In thinking about a current or past field experience, how has the cooperating teacher with whom you work(ed) incorporated moral education into the curriculum? How do (did) the students respond to this education?

4. In thinking about the issue of moral/character education, do you believe that it should be a part of what is taught in schools? How should a teacher, school, school district, or other entity determine what to include in the content of such education?

Suggestions for Further Reading

Devries, R., & Zan, B. (1994). *Moral classrooms, moral children: Creating a constructivist atmosphere in early education.* New York: Teachers College Press.

The authors argue for a revised constructivist model of teaching that includes opportunities for students to develop socially and morally. They argue that development in these areas occurs as children have opportunities for daily interaction. Devries and Zan provide suggestions for teachers establish interactions to foster this development. Their arguments are grounded with a theoretical approach to the issue.

Noddings, N. (2002). *Educating moral people: A caring alternative to character education.* New York: Teachers College Press.

Noddings proposes that moral education should focus on teaching students to care for others. Part of this caring is truly giving our attention to someone in an open discussion. She maintains that it is also important that educators teach students how to care for themselves and allow others to care for them.

Ryan, K., and Bohlin, K. E. (2003). *Building character in schools: Practical ways to bring moral instruction to life.* Hoboken, NJ: Jossey-Bass.

This book offers the reader a guide for implementing a plan for character education into the classroom or the school at large. It includes a guide for developing a curriculum to lead students to becoming responsible adults as well as establishing ties with parents to achieve this goal.

References

Benhabib, S. (1992). *Situating the self: Gender, community and postmodernism in contemporary ethics.* London: Routledge.

Bennett, W. (1995). *The children's book of virtues.* New York: Simon & Schuster.

Berry, M. F., & Blassingame, J. W. (1982). *Long memory: The black experience in America.* Oxford: Oxford University Press.

Bloom, A. (1987). *The closing of the American mind.* New York: Simon & Schuster.

Coles, R. (1997). *The moral intelligence of children: How to raise a moral child.* New York: Bantam Books.

Dewey, J. (1916). *Democracy and education.* New York: Free Press.

Kincheloe, J. L. (1993). *Toward a critical thinking of teacher thinking: Mapping the postmodern.* Westport, CT: Bergin & Garvey.

Lawton, M. (1995, May 17). Values education: A moral obligation or dilemma? *Education Week,* 1–11.

Lenin, V. I. (1960). *Selected works: Notes to Hegel* (Vol. 2). London: Lawrence & Wishart.

Lickona, T. (1992). *Educating for character: How our schools can teach respect and responsibility.* New York: Bantam Books.

Raths, L., Harmin, M., & Simon, S. (1966). *Values and teaching.* Columbus, OH: Merrill.

Shapiro, S. (1995). Educational change and the crisis of the left: Toward a postmodern educational discourse. In B. Kanpol & P. McLaren (Eds.), *Critical multiculturalism: Uncommon voices in a common struggle* (pp.19–38). Westport, CT: Greenwood.

Sizer, T. R., & Sizer, N. F. (1999). *The students are watching: Schools and the moral contract.* Boston: Beacon Press.

Wynne, E. A., & Ryan, K. (1997). *Reclaiming our schools: Teaching character, academics and discipline* (2nd ed.). Englewood Cliffs, NJ: Merrill/Prentice Hall.

Part II

Policies

4

The Inner Workings of the School

Jill Underly

Regardless of one's stance on politics, whether at the federal, state, or local level, a teacher cannot avoid becoming a part of them. The federal government is taking more of an interest in education, which at one time was left more or less in the hands of each state. State and local governments and elected school boards also have a stake in the education of their children. This chapter discusses the various indirect roles of politics in the life of the teacher based on the personal experiences of Ms. Underly. She addresses many controversial issues from her own perspective. As you read the chapter, think about how you might agree or disagree and think about your own experiences when you were in public school.

♦ ♦ ♦

Introduction

I wanted to become a social studies teacher for as long as I can remember, quite possibly from the moment I conceptualized what a social studies teacher actually was, and what impact I could have on a young person's life. I was fortunate to have good social studies teachers in my educational experience, which molded my view of what a good teacher was supposed to encompass. Throughout my career, I have tried to imitate those professionals and strive to be the best teacher that I possibly could be.

When I first began teaching four years ago, a veteran teacher explained to me that the first year or two would be the most difficult.

I never was as tired before in my life! I would come home from teaching and immediately collapse in exhaustion. There is a lot to learn those first few years. I think in addition to adjusting to lesson plans and grading projects, figuring out how a school works can be quite overwhelming at first.

I know plenty of people who get through their student teaching and then decide that the profession is not for them, and there are plenty of teachers I know as well that finished their first year and did not come back for a second. To survive as a teacher, especially if one is certain that this is the career for him or her, it is important to establish a good support network in order to survive those first years. Teaching is not a profession in which one instantly becomes a professional; it is one that requires extensive preparation for each day, and one that requires that those who teach also remain students for life. What I mean here is that, as teachers, we are required to continually include professional development in our career plans. It is necessary to remain current on new methods and current within the subject area to be a true professional.

There is much more to the organization of a school than the individual teacher and his or her classroom. As I was clueless those first years to the art of teaching, I was also clueless to the concept of teachers' unions and teacher politics. Granted, I knew that the school, as any institution does, has its own internal politics. It took time for me to feel things out and become accustomed to various situations in which I found myself from time to time. There are external politics in the form of teachers' unions, the community, the school board, and state and federal laws that affect the school and the teacher. I have found that in order to be the most effective teacher, I must remain current with the news in both my community and my state because public education continues to be one of the hottest topics in the news as laws continue to change.

Federal Laws and Public Schools

Teachers can learn a lot about politics and government by taking a closer look at the workings of the school district in which they are employed. For example, in 2001, an amendment to the Elementary and Secondary Education Act of 1965, called the No Child Left Behind (NCLB) Act, was signed into law by President George W. Bush. This law is, in essence, an accountability law to make sure that all students, regardless of race, socioeconomic status, and gender, succeed in the classroom and meet the same standards at the national level. In order to "prove" that schools are upholding their commitment to educate everyone who comes through their doors, students will be tested at regular intervals with standardized exams. The scores from these exams will be compared to previous years' scores, and, essentially, each school district must show consecutive improvement. This law came into effect my second year of teaching. At the time, I did not realize the bearing this law would have on me and others in my profession. For those in professions outside of teaching, NCLB possibly means very little or nothing at all to them. However, because I work in a public school, my actions and those of the students I teach are evaluated by the accountability standards set forth by NCLB. There is nothing quite like an accountability law to make you notice what is taking place at the federal government level and notice how it impacts your profession on a daily basis.

Under the act's accountability provisions, states must describe how they will close the achievement gap and make sure all students, including those who are disadvantaged, achieve academic proficiency. One of the troubles that many administrators and educators see with this law is the requirement that all students are tested on achievement. This includes students who are in special education programs who might not do well on exams because of learning disabilities or other circumstances and students whose first language is not English. When the results are revealed, schools must produce annual state and local school district report cards that inform parents and communities about school progress in their district. This, according to critics of the law, is where the problems appear. Because school districts' records are public, those records—especially the test scores from the accountability tests—are compared with neighboring school districts. Included in the report are the numbers of students who do and do not pass the math and verbal sections of the standardized tests. As a result, the media rank the school districts by the number of students who pass, and they label those with higher passing rates as the better school districts. There are many variables that are not disclosed when these reports reach the media: the percentage of students learning English as a new language, the number of special education students whose capabilities are below the test level, the attendance rates, and the number of students who are economically disadvantaged or those whose parents perhaps send them to school without meeting their basic needs. All of these variables impact how well a school district will score collectively on these exams. It is not a surprise that test scores seem to correlate with the socioeconomic level of the population within the school district; as a result, it is a challenge for poorer school districts to go beyond the stigma that ensues, especially when they are compared to neighboring school districts that might be more economically advantaged. There are many studies that indicate that wealthier school districts have students who outperform their counterparts in poorer school districts. Higher teacher and parent expectations of the more affluent students, more opportunities for field trips, and the basics of parental involvement all impact student achievement.

What the No Child Left Behind Act intended was for that gap in learning to be narrowed—that students in poorer or economically disadvantaged school districts (which usually have larger minority student populations) would succeed at the same rate as students in more affluent schools. Is it any wonder teachers protest about this and unions oppose this law? At the heart of it, I believe there are good intentions. But what the federal government has failed to do is accept the responsibility to fund this program. The states are responsible for implementing the No Child Left Behind Act, which has depleted millions of dollars from their already tight budgets. The federal government ideally should fund the program as mandated by law.

Schools that do not make progress must provide supplemental services, such as free tutoring or after-school assistance, take corrective actions, and, if still not making adequate yearly progress after five years, make dramatic changes to the way the school is operated.[1] Still, there are differences in how schools are held accountable, and this varies from state to state.

As a high school student, my most common complaint was that we never made it through all the social studies lessons. The year always started out with quite a bit of promise. Most American history classes began with the American Revolution. Revised curriculum and state and national standards commonly dictate that a secondary-level United States history course must finish with the most current history. However, in my day, the Vietnam War was barely covered, at a time when we should also have been discussing the first Gulf War. I have learned that because of increased testing regulations, there is even less time to spend on the content of the class. Students are tested more frequently under new accountability laws, and teachers and schools are held liable for students' performance on these exams. School districts will do everything possible to guarantee that their students will perform well on these exams, and teachers do their best to make sure that all the curriculum standards are addressed in the allotted amount of time, because they are held accountable if the requirements are not met. Are there concrete answers on how to complete all these tasks in nine months of instruction? Absolutely not. What school administrators look for is efficiency. Plainly spoken, teachers do their best to make sure no time is wasted during the course of the school year. In adjusting to all that is required of me, I have relied on fellow seasoned teachers and the principal at my school for advice. Fortunately, they are always willing to dispense advice on how to be efficient and organized in the classroom.

During my teaching career, I have also seen schools completely revamp their curriculum in favor of enhancing their reading or math scores on accountability exams. Teachers in low-performing school districts are repeatedly finding themselves teaching outside of their content area and reinforcing content in areas stressed on the exams. It is a sad fact of life that as a teacher today part of the school year must be devoted to testing students and retesting those students who failed or missed the exam, along with reviewing and preparing students for the next scheduled exam. The time that remains to actually instruct students is now all the more precious.

Another lesson I have learned through personal experience is that I cannot take personal offense if instructions from the district office appear to be aimed directly at my school or me. Decisions that school district superintendents and school boards make are in the best interest of the students and student achievement, both of which are at the forefront of their agendas.

Networking in the Community and With the School Board

While looking for a teaching position, and before any interviews, it is important to research the community in which one hopes to teach. For some teachers, the ideal position would be in a community that collectively values education, is concerned about its schools, and takes an active interest in the school's academic success. Schools that have high community and parental involvement are generally very good schools. Students who are usually academically minded and motivated to do well, regardless of the educational attainment level of their parents, are found in areas where the community values education. If a candidate is lucky enough to stumble upon one of these idyllic communities, she has found an extraordinary school district. For many teachers, their dream is to teach in a school district that values their talents; low-income, urban school districts thirst for talented teachers.

Talents are valued in a variety of ways, depending on the school district, and where one's talents fit best. I feel that I am a very challenging teacher. I demand a lot of my students and expect from them high performance. These expectations work both in my favor and against me. In my first school district, I was continually frustrated by my students' achievement because I grew up in a culture that was entirely different from theirs. I grew up in an upper-middle-class environment, while my students struggled with poverty in their homes (where meeting basic needs such as meals and warm clothing was a challenge). I did not share any common ground with my students.

This worked against me until I was able to adapt to their situations and be empathetic to their fears. Once I understood what my students were experiencing at home, I was able to teach them in the best ways that I could, contributing to the success we experienced in our studies.

In my current teaching situation, my students come from affluent families. Their goals are overwhelmingly to go on to college and get good jobs and acquire material items, such as nice cars and beautiful homes. I have had to shift my teaching style and methods now to accommodate these students who bring with them an entirely different set of experiences. Both school settings have been challenging to me as a teacher, not only because I was required to constantly challenge my students, but also because my students have different experiences and needs in these two schools; I have had to learn to individualize my teaching to meet their different needs.

Several studies have found a strong correlation between parental involvement in school and student success (Bempechat, 1992). Student success generates high exam scores, which satisfy the accountability requirements set by high-stakes testing, and, for many, a more enjoyable teaching experience in the district. Teachers in these districts are more facilitator than teacher, which has redefined the role of the teacher in the classroom. Schools with higher parental involvement also find themselves without the problems that other school districts face—lack of volunteers for different theater or athletic programs, gang-related problems, and shortages of substitute teachers. These districts are not entirely devoid of problems; they just exist at a different level.

Community involvement and community pride in the local school is a major challenge that communities need to confront directly, for schools are usually at the center of communities. In many communities, property values are determined on the success of the local school district. In my opinion, however, the secret to a successful school is parental involvement. Without parents, a school still may have the best students and the best teachers, but there will be a void where parents are needed—as volunteers, as liaisons, and as a resource for the classroom. Open communication between administrators and parents, as well as teachers and parents, is instrumental in a successful school district. Without an active parental volunteer base, a school district's success is limited. As I previously mentioned, I have taught in two school districts. One district did not have a parent-teacher organization and the other had one that was extremely active within the schools districtwide. This cooperation made a vast difference on school climate. When students, teachers, administrators, and parents all work together to make a school a wonderful learning environment, there are inherently fewer problems within the building and much more community support for the school.

Networking is at the heart of the teaching profession. I make every effort to acquaint myself with the parents who volunteer in my school as well as my own students' parents. I believe it's important to keep the lines of communication open with the parents, whether or not their child is in my class. I have many opportunities to interact with parents with the sports that I coach and the activities that I sponsor. This is important because I often rely on the generosity of parents to help with sporting events or to help chaperone on special occasions. I also rely on parents as guest speakers in my classes as appropriate. I have found that parents are usually more than willing to volunteer their time; the problem is that many of them have never been asked to become involved.

Another important part of networking is getting to know the school board. School board membership and requirements vary from district to district, but commonly the school board is a body of elected members who serve the community through making decisions regarding the public schools. In communities where there is high parental involvement, one will usually find very effective school boards (and competitive elections). It is important to take notice of local school board elections through awareness of the main issues, especially those at the forefront of newspaper articles, because school boards shape school policy. School boards set the budgets for the school year and they determine the details of teachers' contracts, such as salary and health insurance benefits. As all of these issues are important, it is vital for teachers to pay close attention to school board races. It is also imperative for teachers to establish good relationships with school board members. When I have opportunities to meet the members, I always make it a point to introduce myself because it is important to establish these relationships. School board members enjoy talking with and getting to know teachers in the school district despite the fact that it is a thankless job—one that goes unnoticed when things are going well, but one that never fails to draw criticism in bad times.

Through the establishment of these relationships with parents and school board members early on in one's career, another lesson in how schools work—networking—is learned. When a job-related need arises that the principal or superintendent may not be able to fulfill, or if there is an issue that is of pressing importance, one has the option of taking the need to the school board, and having established relationships with several of the members will make this process easier. This type of networking is used by politicians and administrators in all professions; it is essential that teachers know those who make the decisions that affect their employment and the working environment.

When I decided to leave my first teaching position, I was thankful that I was on a first-name basis and on very good terms with my school board members and my school superintendent. I became acquainted with the administration while I was a young teacher on several committees at school. Many people were reluctant to serve on these committees, but I did not hesitate. School policy and law has always interested me, and I think that the school board and superintendent were impressed that I took such an active interest at such an early stage in my career. I became acquainted with them over the course of my years at the school, and I always felt comfortable being honest about my thoughts on different subjects and issues. When I decided to leave the district, I was very honest and upfront with my superintendent as to why I was leaving and where I was hoping to be hired. He fully understood and supported my decision, and when my potential new employer called for a recommendation and evaluation, my superintendent was not caught off guard. This fact alone, according to my new employer, sealed his decision to hire me. He respected my sincere communication with my employer at the time.

Extracurricular Academics and Athletics

Many coaching and sponsoring activities are put on the shoulders of young teachers. This is often because as teachers mature and reach tenure (a point in teachers' careers where their years of experience have reached the level of permanent status) many drop the coaching or sponsoring responsibilities they once had as newer teachers.

I have really enjoyed my extracurricular positions in school communities. It gives me an opportunity to get to know the students in a different setting. I have coached a sport since I started teaching, and while it does occupy a lot of time, it has been incredibly rewarding. It can be a huge responsibility to manage both teaching and coaching tasks, but good teachers can do both. In the beginning, I pledged never to have coaching interfere with my teaching, and I have strived to maintain this goal. In addition to coaching, I am also an academic club sponsor. I find this involvement satisfying because I get to know a completely different set of students whom I do not have in my classes of freshmen and sophomore students. Sponsoring the academic club has been extraordinarily fulfilling as well, and these students participate in a variety of activities that I also enjoy. I enjoy letting the students involved in these activities take responsibility; this allows me as their sponsor to take pride in their accomplishments. My involvement in these activities has helped students feel more comfortable around me, and I feel that they are able to open up to me more and participate more in class because they have established that relationship with me outside of the classroom. When the time arrives, it will be difficult for me to give up my responsibilities as sponsor and coach.

Teachers: Union or Non-Union?

There are two major education employee unions in the United States: the American Federation of Teachers (AFT) and the National Education Association (NEA). All school districts in the United States have employees who are members of either the AFT or the NEA (Cochren, 1998). In either case, both unions offer their members benefits through their respective organizations. Any one can join either union. Both embrace education workers in the public schools, including paraprofessionals and school administrators; the difference is that the AFT is more encompassing, meaning it accepts membership from health workers in the schools and other noneducational workers and aides. Both the NEA and the AFT have lobbyists in Washington, D.C., working for the interests of public education, and if they were ever to merge into one large educational workers' union, it would be a powerful force in Washington, D.C.

Union membership is a personal decision, and it is something that every teacher should consider carefully. Some schools may require all teachers to pay union dues, called "fair share." Through fair share, teachers are still given the option to officially join the union, but if a teacher chooses not to join, she will pay a fee to have the union act as her representative during the negotiation of contracts. It is important to research the benefits of membership, because they do differ; the state union organizations also have benefits that vary from state to state. The local-level benefits are what may be of particular interest to a teacher. Personally, I am an advocate of teachers becoming union members. The membership dues might seem financially steep for a first-year teacher; however, I always look at membership as "job insurance" because of the protective measures unions can take to ensure that I am not wrongfully dismissed from my position as a schoolteacher because of false allegations.

To illustrate some of the activities of teachers' unions, the following are real examples from school districts in which I have worked in the past. In my short tenure as a school employee, I have worked for two school districts. School District A had about 95 percent union membership, while School District B had about 60 percent union membership. In both districts, union representatives negotiated the teachers' contracts for the school year.

They negotiate such items as pay increases, work day and sick day allotments, insurance premiums, and annual teacher evaluations, all of which find their way into the language of the contract. In my personal opinion, School District A had a better contract, one that was more beneficial to the interests of the teachers. The teachers in School District A had high union membership and therefore took a greater interest in their contract and discussed these interests with their school board members and negotiation teams. I found that in School District A the teachers had a more satisfying relationship with their superintendent and their school board, and they were generally more content with their working conditions. School District B employees, where the union membership was lower, were required to perform odd noninstructional jobs at school. For example, many certified teachers found themselves involuntarily serving as club sponsors, working as unpaid crossing guards after school, and serving on committees over the summer without compensation; there were a variety of situations over which teachers had no control but felt obligated to perform.

Critics of my point of view might argue that those of us who go into teaching *must* know what is expected of us ahead of time; otherwise, why would we voluntarily accept positions that pay very little for the hours we put in and the criticism we receive from parents, the community, and lawmakers? Surely teachers know what they are getting into ahead of time, so they must silently accept these responsibilities. While most people entering the field of education do know what is expected when entering the field of education, this does not mean that teachers should be taken advantage of at every opportunity.

Because of increases in litigation against teachers based on allegations of sexual misconduct and physical abuse, even cases that are unfounded and irrational, teachers need to have the protection of unions. Allegations like those described above are damaging to careers and financially burdensome, so much so that it is impossible to handle them alone without the support that unions provide.

As I compare both working environments, they were each great places to work and, depending on one's outlook regarding unions, one might be more comfortable in one setting or the other. Admittedly, there was a certain peer pressure to join the teachers' union in School District A. Personally, I was fine with this pressure because I am a strong believer in the benefits that unions offer. However, some might be more comfortable in School District B, where there is less union involvement and less pressure to become a member. In either case, it is important to be fully aware of the trade-offs involved in a district with low membership as well as one with high membership. It would be a good idea to research union membership and look over the details of the teachers' contract before agreeing to work in a certain school district.

Through teachers' unions, one has the opportunity to become more active in the community at large. Teachers' unions pay close attention to school law at both the state and the federal level, and they are actively involved in issues that affect teachers' contracts. As a member of the contract bargaining team, the insurance committee, and the sick-leave committee, I was heavily involved with the teachers' union while employed at School District B. Because of this involvement, I felt that I had a better command of the issues that affected me directly. I also felt that I had more influence and control and, necessarily, the power to change things within my district just through being actively involved in the decision-making processes.

Role-Model Behavior

When I was going through public school, the teachers' lounge was a very scary place. I remember once in sixth grade, my reading teacher asked me to deliver a message to a fellow teacher in the teachers' lounge. I remember being terrified as I walked up to the frosted glass door adjacent to the cafeteria. I knocked softly the first time and waited for a response. Then I knocked softly again. I waited. No response. Gathering up enough nerve, I knocked slightly harder, all the while shaking in my shoes, fearing the person who would answer the door.

When the door was finally answered (and as cigarette smoke poured out through the open door), I remember trying to peer around the teacher and get a glimpse of the interior of the teachers' lounge. It was never enough of a glimpse to provide me with enough particulars to share with my friends, but it was always very intriguing to look inside that room.

One couldn't help but marvel at what went on or what was discussed inside those walls. From the time we were little, we were taught to revere the teachers' lounge. We were not, as students, to ever enter that room or to even look in if we happened to pass by when the door was slightly ajar. We were taught to respect the privacy of the teachers' lounge. It was a room veiled in this sheath of secrecy, and with very good reason.

Every institution has a teachers' lounge. It could be the break room, the place where teachers unwind, let their hair down, share ideas, share personal information, discuss things "off the record," gripe and complain, fight with each other, or cry tears of joy, sadness, and frustration when they confide in their colleagues and friends. Personal phone calls are made from the teachers' lounge, events talked about in secret with the overall understanding that whatever is said in the lounge stays in the lounge. It is no wonder that this forbidden area is a source of intrigue for the student! (Just in case you were wondering, smoking is no longer allowed inside schools, even in the teachers' lounge.)

As a student, I wondered if teachers talked about students in the lounge. As a full-time teacher, I can answer that—of course they do. There is no way around it. Teachers have students in common first and foremost. Most of the time, conversations are benign: "How is John doing in your class?" or "Why hasn't Jackie been in school these past few days?" Discussion about students is usually out of general concern for that student. But there are occasions when teachers discuss students in an unfavorable light, and there are times when teachers talk about administrators and other staff in a hostile manner. Gossip really has no place in a school, even in the teachers' lounge, but sadly, it is unavoidable. We are all guilty of it at one time or another. As professionals, however, we must be mindful of gossip and be ready to change the subject if conversation turns to this type of chat. Gossiping will usually lead to bad situations and could land a teacher into quite a bit of trouble. Staff members inevitably learn if someone has been gossiping about them, which can put the person responsible for gossip or rumors in awkward situations with other faculty. Gossiping about students and staff is unprofessional, and if one wishes to have the respect of her peers and students, she must strive to remain professional.

I know of some teachers who stay clear of the teachers' lounge because of gossip or negative banter. Ron, a former mentor of mine, was the type of teacher who never set foot in the lounge. He would eat his lunch in his room, mainly because he felt the teachers' lounge was unwelcoming and negative. Ideally, the lounge should be a place where all teachers feel comfortable congregating, eating their lunch, and generally taking a break from students and interacting with other adults. It is not my intent to give the impression that the lounge is bad place; simply a teacher should be able to be herself, become acquainted with colleagues, and read a book or relax while taking a break.

Learn the Rules Concerning Work

When I first started teaching, I realized that there were many things I had to learn that my college professors could not teach me. There are a myriad of duties that make up a routine analysis of work, such as lesson planning and faculty meetings. However, there are also situations that occur on an annual basis such as textbook selection, planning curriculum guides, and special meetings and conferences on student placement. Some regulations, such as dress code and appearance, evaluation procedures, and schedules for faculty meetings are included in my school's teacher handbook. Other concerns such as lesson plans, how to plan effectively, and how to follow the curriculum guide are not included.

Textbook adoption occurs in every state on a regular schedule in a cycle from five to seven years. In Indiana, for example, books are rotated every seven years based on the subject, which means a department will adopt new books for a particular subject one year in the cycle. There is quite a bit of planning involved in textbook adoption. Textbook publishing companies come to the school, make appointments with entire departments, and do everything in their power to convince the school district to choose their textbook. Textbook publishing is a multibillion-dollar business each year, and the textbook companies will attempt to cater to the more politically conservative in content material. Textbooks are aimed at the markets in states that require statewide textbook adoption (the entire state adopts the same text for all the public schools in the state). Texas is the largest adoption state, requiring statewide adoption in all disciplines and at all levels. Cornering the market in Texas or other large adoption states, such as California, results in even greater profits for the textbook publishers. However, in other states, once teachers have selected publishers for their texts, it is common to have a parent committee look over the textbooks and secure their opinion. Finally, once a choice has been made or narrowed down, the department chair or other subject representative will go to the school board and propose that selection for the textbook.

The conservative nature of the books adds to the frustration of many teachers, social studies teachers in particular. The textbooks appear as glossed-over, unexciting versions of American history, or they deliberately include the least offensive and least controversial subjects covered in literature texts. Many textbooks format the material in a way that makes it difficult for the student, or the teacher who does not know much about the subject matter, to discern which information is actually the most important. This stems from the fact that there was a push in the latter part of the 20th century to make textbooks fair and balanced to all events of history and to make them more attractive from a multicultural perspective. A recent book published by education historian Diane Ravitch, *The Language Police* (2003), addresses these issues. Ravitch's argument is that the information presented in social studies textbooks in particular covers everything that has happened in history, but because everything is weighted equally, nothing stands out as truly important. Stemming from the fact that our educational system has shifted toward schoolwide and statewide testing and rankings for accountability, the tests have come to rely heavily on the content of these ordinary, dull textbooks. Evidently, all of this is done at the expense of truth and of historical and literary quality and accuracy. Ravitch's book provides insightful suggestions on how to improve this situation in the textbook industry. In the meantime, however, until these conditions are changed it is up to educators to take control of the content of their courses and enrich the curriculum to the best of their ability. As an educator, I have seen that many topics that I feel are valuable lessons in literature or American history are left out because textbook companies feel this type of subject matter is controversial and perhaps they fear that the larger areas where they hope their book would be purchased might not pledge their support. Since this is often the case in my teaching, it is up to me to select supplemental material to include in my lesson plans. Because I teach in a community that is rather conservative, I always make sure that any supplemental material I choose to include outside of the approved curriculum has at least the approval of my department chair or principal as a precaution.

I love to use community members as guest speakers in my classroom. I once caused controversy within my school because I invited a young man into the classroom to talk about "stigmas" to my sociology class. This young man was HIV positive, and he was to communicate to my students his experiences with others since he had uncovered his stigma—how people have treated him since they found out about his condition, and how this stigma has affected his life. His talk was not to be about AIDS or alternative lifestyles, and he adhered strictly to the topic of stigmas. Unknown to me and the other teacher who arranged for this guest speaker to come to our class, one student was extremely uncomfortable with the fact that the speaker was gay. She called her mother between classes, and the mother then called a school board member. The school board member subsequently called the principal. Even though I had gone through the proper procedure in obtaining prior approval for this guest speaker, this issue arose. According to the principal, there could have *potentially* been some questionable material presented in the talk, which made him uncomfortable. I explained that the class visit was entirely pleasant and informed him that I followed all the correct channels to have this man come speak to my class and that the topic remained on the issue of stigmas. All in all, the issue was resolved calmly and reasonably. The lesson I learned is that even following proper channels will not prevent political issues from surfacing when a teacher chooses a controversial issue to address in class.

In addition to guest speakers and community involvement, I take advantage of the many journal articles, magazine articles, and videos that are produced specifically for education, as they offer a wealth of additional knowledge and are often very interesting. What is more, the students enjoy having them included within their lessons. My students are appreciative of my creativity in choosing appropriate supplements; for example, I included an article on the practice of *Kindertransport,* which was used to relocate several million Jewish children from Germany, Austria, and Czechoslovakia to Denmark and Great Britain during World War II.

Ultimately, I have learned that my actions as a teacher dictate how well my career progresses. I always remember that how I conduct myself is continually being evaluated by the administration and other faculty members, not to mention students; I am on my guard at all times, in the classroom, at faculty meetings, in the teachers' lounge, etc. I have witnessed new teachers fall asleep at meetings, speak out in criticism without any basis or support for their statements, work on other activities during the meeting, whisper, and, worse, talk, while other teachers and administrators might be sharing their views or goals for the meeting. While I don't know if any repercussions resulted from these actions, I feel that I must strive to conduct myself professionally, both for my own reputation and for that of the profession of teaching, which seems to be continually under great scrutiny.

I also try to remember that complaints might lead to actions and consequences that not only affect me but also those with whom I work. One school principal, Edward, was the master on the subject of politics in schools. A veteran teacher went to his office to complain about her class sizes, arguing that these classes were just "too big" for her to be an effective teacher; she insisted on reducing the classes to less than 20 students in each class. Edward declined her wish repeatedly, but with her daily persistence Edward finally gave in to her wish and moved some students from her classes into others within her department—increasing the size of her colleagues' classes in order to make her classes smaller. This exemplifies Edward's expertise in internal politics, as it forced Mary to realize that by making her life "easier," she had ultimately increased the demands and workloads of her colleagues in the department.

It is easy to become overwhelmed with all the expectations and responsibilities that are put on the shoulders of a new or fledgling teacher. It is important to remember, however, that teaching does not automatically become easier with more experience. Instead, coworkers and administrators will look to you more for guidance and leadership, increasing the pressure to always do and say the right thing. Perhaps one of the greatest lessons to learn as a new teacher is to honestly think through your actions before you actually do or say anything. Teachers are role models, not only to their students, but also to the community and even to each other in the buildings in which they teach every day.

Remember, as a teacher, one is not powerless to the proceedings that occur in government or within the community or school; a teacher can become an activist for the teaching profession. At times, it might seem better to succumb to pressures to perform at lower standards because of general expectations of the students or other teachers in the building. However, consider the power that teachers have within their classroom and in their community at large, and the power, then, to change expectations and to make a marked difference on the attitudes of those around them.

Nothing prepares new teachers entirely for their first teaching assignment. Most of what you learn about teaching will come from having a classroom of your own. Similarly, most of what you learn about school and "office" politics comes from being there in the building and interacting with your coworkers, students, and their parents. The lessons in this chapter have as a purpose to encourage the reader to think about how issues in the classroom and the school will affect the life of the teacher and how they are constantly at work within the classroom, the school, and the community. Every teacher must be aware of and educated about all of these influences. Politics is more than what many of us perceive as "government proceedings." Politics are internal and external forces in the form of relationships with students, parents, coworkers, and the community at large. Politics are smaller subject areas we need to master as teachers in addition to our content material in order to be knowledgeable, effective leaders in our schools and our communities.

What Do You Think?

1. Consider how familiar you are with the No Child Left Behind legislation. What is your opinion on school accountability? Will making schools accountable for the success of their students increase student achievement? What are the positive intentions of NCLB as well as the negative effects that it might have on public education?

2. Reflect on the type of school district at which you might like to be a teacher (rural, urban, suburban; large, small; private, public). Why did you choose this type of district? Why not the other settings? Explain your choices.

3. Research the social problems that wealthier school districts experience as opposed to those that poorer or more urban school districts experience.

4. Reflect on how you feel about extracurricular activities and the role that teachers are required to play as coaches and sponsors. What are the positive outcomes of teachers participating in these roles? What about negatives? Consider the angle of both the student and the teacher. Think about your experience in middle school or high school while reflecting on the impact that teachers have as coaches on students.

5. Have you ever thought about what behavior is appropriate or inappropriate with students? Think of examples that might be innocent, but could be construed as inappropriate. Does it depend on the grade level that you teach? Why or why not?

6. What do you see as the benefits and drawbacks to joining a teachers' union? Visit the two national teacher unions' Web sites (the AFT at http://www.aft.org/ and the NEA at http://www.nea.org/). Choose an important issue in education and compare and contrast the two unions' position on this issue.

Note

1. The Web site http://www.ed.gov/nclb/landing.jhtml?src=ln provides teachers, administrators, and parents with information about the No Child Left Behind Act. Remember, however, that implementation of the law and accountability by schools vary from state to state.—Ed.

Suggestions for Further Reading

De Marrais, K. B., & LeCompte, M. (1998). *The way schools work: A sociological analysis of education* (3rd ed.). Boston: Addison-Wesley.
    This book provides a critical overview of the philosophy, theory, and practice of education from historical and contemporary perspectives. The issues addressed afford the reader a background that helps to unveil the "inner-workings" of the school and educational system at large.

Noll, J. W. (2001). *Taking sides: Clashing views on controversial educational issues* (11th ed.). Columbus, OH: McGraw-Hill.
    This is a unique approach to the issues on education in that for each of the 21 topics addressed there is a "pro" and "con" discussion in the form of a debate. This presentation provides the reader with two contrasting arguments along with other readings on the topics, allowing the reader to decide for himself/herself where to stand on the issues.

Ravitch, D. (2003). *The language police: How pressure groups restrict what students learn*. New York: Knopf.

Ravitch addresses the important issue of censorship and how it affects the education of our children. The result of this act, she argues, is that our children are being misguided by the limited material that is made available to them. She also provides suggestions for ending censorship, which she maintains would be better for everyone concerned.

Spring, J. (2000). *American education* (9th ed.). Columbus, OH: McGraw-Hill.

Spring presents a variety of issues that make up the general politics of schools, starting with an overview of the purpose of schooling. Some of the issues addressed include high-stakes testing, tracking and other inequalities, the diversification of the student population, and issues of power and control at all levels. This is an excellent introduction to understanding how schools operate.

References

Bempechat, J. (1992, Fall/Winter). The role of parent involvement in children's academic achievement. *School Community Journal, 2,* 31–41.

Cochren, J. R. (1998, Summer). Teacher unions: A career educator's perspective. *Contemporary Education, 69,* 214–217.

Ravitch, D. (2003). *The language police: How pressure groups restrict what students learn*. New York: Knopf.

5

Power, Identity, and the Third Rail

Wayne Au

Tracking is an issue that raises much debate among students, teachers, administrators, and parents. Mr. Au tackles the issues related to tracking through his personal experiences as a student who was tracked and as a classroom teacher who has observed the effects of tracking. It is important that the reader note that there are many people in favor of tracking. For example, some argue that it is actually more advantageous for students to be grouped by like academic ability for their own psychological benefit (e.g., self-esteem, etc.). It is also often believed that teachers can be more effective if they teach students that are grouped in this manner. Mr. Au focuses on evidence in his own experience and in the body of literature on tracking that oppose these beliefs about tracking. The reader should sort through the arguments presented in order to determine his or her own stance on this very important issue.

◆ ◆ ◆

When I was younger, I would marvel at the murals spray-painted on the subway cars by the graffiti artists of the then-emerging hip-hop culture. It always struck me as an attempt to take something that was plain and dirty, something that appeared natural and epitomized the urban landscape, and turn it into a creative, new, and beautiful vision of a different world. The subway cars also held the mystery of motion as they clamored along their tracks, dutifully transporting the masses to their destinations. I was amazed

Author's Note: I would like to thank Mira Shimabukuro and Michael Apple's Friday "groupers" for their extensive feedback on this chapter.

at how the trains managed to move all those riders, everyday, along the tracks. Later I learned that the trains' motion was not mysterious at all, that it was controlled by a dangerous "third rail," which was shielded from the riders as protection from its high-voltage electrical charge. What I did not know as a child, and what all graffiti artists and subway commuters did know as they negotiated different lines, was that while the trains ride the tracks, it is the third rail that actually powers the system.

One day in the fourth grade after a recent family move to Connecticut, I was pulled out of my class and subjected to an inkblot test. Sitting with an adult I did not know in one of the large custodial closets of my new suburban school, I answered questions about the black and white images being flashed at me on cards. It was through this magical test, the school decided, that I was "gifted," causing a ripple effect in my life. I was catapulted headlong into the stratosphere of the perceived "smart" kids and henceforth was to receive the respect of the school and community. I had been knighted.

This was my earliest experience with what I think of as the "third rail" of education, that institutional and social power connected to different tracks in public education. As early as the fourth grade, the power of the third rail shifted my life onto a trajectory of academic and social success—a trajectory being charted *for me* based on an outsider's assessment. This was the system of tracking. It influenced my education, shaped my identity, and taught me about institutional power.

Leaving the Yard: Origins and Basics of Tracking

The origins of tracking are directly linked to the influx of immigrants during the early 1900s when it was believed that certain groups of people had more innate intelligence and ability than others. This, combined with the exponential growth in mass public schooling at the time, led to schools classifying and sorting students based on perceived abilities and occupational goals (Broussard & Joseph, 1998; Donelan, Neal, & Jones, 1994; McLaren, 1994; Oakes, 1985). In her critique of tracking, Chunn (1987–1988) found four rationalizations undergirding it as a system:

1. Students learn better when grouped with academically similar students.

2. "Slower" students develop high esteem for themselves and their schools if not placed together with more "capable" students.

3. The sorting process is "accurate and fair" and mirrors previous achievement and "innate abilities."

4. Teachers can more easily work with homogeneous groups of students.

Evidence suggests that these rationalizations may, in fact, be irrational when placed next to empirical evidence in tracked schools. Gamoran (1992) found that the heterogeneous grouping of students produces relatively similar overall achievement as ability grouping. Furthermore, he pointed out that within-class grouping for math and cross-grade grouping for reading increased overall achievement in elementary schools. The adverse psychological effects of tracking on "lower" track students are so pronounced that Broussard and Joseph (1998) argued that tracking essentially "stunts" schoolchildren and is a form of "educational neglect" in the least and is possibly a form of "educational child abuse" at its worst.

That the sorting process is "accurate and fair" is also highly suspect. Tests and teacher/counselor observations are used to determine what tracks students fit in to, but research has shown that standardized test results are volatile and inaccurate measures of student abilities (Heubert, 2001; Kane & Staiger, 2002; Karp, 2003; Madaus & Clarke, 2001; McNeil & Valenzuela, 2001; Neill & Gayler, 2001) and that teachers' own expectations play a large role in student performance and differential teaching strategies (Broussard & Joseph, 1998; Chunn, 1987–1988; Gamoran, 1992; Oakes, 1985). Additionally, Oakes (1995) argued that there is an inherent economic rationale to tracking that plays out the logic of public school education. Schools train the workers that the nation needs. This rationale has historically been part of the broader struggle over curriculum in the United States (Kliebard, 1995), and has recently taken on a more "race-friendly" hue as illustrated by Hunter and Bartee (2003), who advocated for closing the achievement gap between white and black students based on the country's need for a well-trained, productive, *multicultural* workforce.

In much of the existing literature, tracking is split up into two categories: "curriculum tracking" and "ability grouping"(Chunn, 1987–1988; Donelan et al., 1994; Gamoran, 1992; Oakes, 1985; Rosenbaum, 1976). In high schools, curriculum tracking is the practice of using specific educational programs, such as vocational, general, and college preparatory classes, as a means of dividing students based on their perceived intellectual abilities or potential occupational futures (Donelan et al., 1994; Gamoran, 1992). Ability grouping is commonly used to determine which level of a particular subject a student takes or is used to create small ability groups within a heterogeneously grouped classroom (Broussard & Joseph, 1998; Gamoran, 1992). It should be noted, however, that both types of tracking have similar outcomes of grouping similar students together by ranked abilities (Oakes, 1985; Rosenbaum, 1976).

In terms of educational outcomes, a substantial body of research agrees that while tracking provides little benefit for "high" tracked students, it does an enormous amount of damage to "low" track students' education (Broussard & Joseph, 1998; Chunn, 1987–1988; Donelan et al., 1994; Gamoran, 1992; Oakes, 1985, 1994, 1995). "High" track classrooms generally spend more time on actual instruction and less time on daily routines and discipline. "High" track teachers, likewise, are usually more energetic, positive, and upbeat in their teaching and often have better organization and lessons planned. Conversely, "low" track classrooms exhibit more disciplinary measures, and large portions of the instructional time are spent on teachers' efforts to exert control, attempting to make students follow directions and sit quietly, all of which adds up to the perverse reality that "low" track students, even though they effectively need more instruction, end up getting less of a lower quality (Broussard & Joseph, 1998; Gamoran, 1992; Oakes, 1985, 1994). Although recent research has found that most formal tracking systems, where students are actively placed into a preprogrammed series of vocational, regular, or college preparatory classes, have diminished greatly (Lucas, 1999), other forms of tracking still exist in public schools.

Because of these historical developments, I will refer to what I call "ability tracking" and "schedule tracking" to distinguish the two forms for the purposes of this chapter. These distinctions serve to describe the more "unofficial" ways that tracking now takes place in schools, as opposed to the earlier, more blatant programmatic curriculum tracking. Further, to simplify the discussion, I will use the terms "high"/"honors" and "low"/"regular" to refer to the two main tracks present in schools, but I do so knowing that some school systems use up to six different tracks, including special education, to label and categorize students' classes.

Riding the Black, Brown, and White Lines: Racialized Outcomes of Tracking

The most common form of tracking I have observed first hand as both a student and a teacher is *ability tracking,* which, although it varies, creates the distinction between "honors" or advanced placement (AP), "regular," and "remedial" courses. Loosely, this translates into (a) elite, four-year college students hopefully bound for professional occupations and (b) everyone else. To be sure, students who take "regular" and "remedial" classes may continue their education after high school, but the expectations are different and can imply attending no college at all or "settling" for a vocational school, two-year junior college, or less prestigious state university—something that neither "honors" students nor their parents would likely consider. Data from the 1991 National Longitudinal Survey of Youth support my personal observations. Using these data, Broussard and Joseph (1998) found that while almost 50 percent of students who take academic, college preparatory, tracked courses received some post– high school education, only 14 percent of those in nonacademic tracks did the same. Even more striking is that they found that 86 percent of students in the general and vocational tracks ended their education upon graduating from high school.

While ability tracking may be the dominant and visible form of track- ing, student differentiation takes place in other ways. *Schedule tracking* is less explicit and more transparent than ability tracking. Many times "honors" or advanced placement students are signed up for the same series of courses, whether it is advanced math, AP physics, or any other "high" track class, and because of scheduling limitations (limited numbers of sec- tions offered during limited periods), these students end up being grouped in and around the same teachers at the same time of the day, regardless of whether their classes are formally tracked or untracked. Schedule tracking also manifests itself around particular subjects. For instance, while most students in high school take a foreign language, only a very particular and narrow group of students enroll in Latin. Latin is a language that is held up as one of the intellectual peaks of student achievement, and it is associ- ated with being "smart." The most intensely college-bound students I've known, the ones determined to attend an elite, Ivy League school, all took Latin. Not only did it look good on their applications, it gave them a leg up on their vocabulary for the Scholastic Aptitude Test (SAT). Conversely, many classes such as beginning art, choir, study hall, or vocational educa- tion, become "dumping grounds" for less affluent students. These classes are viewed as less rigorous than others, and therefore are good places for those who are not oriented toward college. In addition, all students are required to have a complete schedule and these "dumping grounds" make for excellent schedule fodder, filling in the gaps for low-track students who need to be kept busy for a full school day.

The academic/nonacademic split of both ability and schedule track- ing produces racial segregation. This first became apparent to me in high school. Beginning in the ninth grade, I had "honors" courses lined up, top to bottom, on my schedule. In my classes were the students with their eyes firmly set on going to college, where every last grade counted as if it were life or death. We were "honors" students, smarter and harder workers than the rest, and whiter than the rest, too. This might not be remarkable save for the fact that we were at Garfield High School, the flagship school of the district both because of its advanced placement courses and top-notch science magnet program, and because it was, and still is, at the heart and soul of Seattle's inner-city, African American community of the Central District. Garfield had a mix of African American students from the neighborhood, white students who were bussed in mostly from other parts of Seattle, and a few Asian Americans sprinkled in between.

I was not actively conscious of tracking as a *system* per se, even though I was aware of the racialized classroom patterns. The matter appeared on the surface to be one of, "certain types of students don't take certain types of classes," almost as if it were a natural occurrence that only one or two African American students were in the average AP class, or that most of the African American and Latino students were clustered in the "regular" and "remedial" classes. This phenomenon of tracking, essentially creating two racially segregated schools in one building, has been documented by many researchers (Broussard & Joseph, 1998; Evans, 1995; George, 1993; Noguera, 2001, 2003; Oakes, 1995; Slavin, 1990; Slavin & Braddock, 1993). At Garfield, this meant there was the "honors" school with its National Merit scholars, AP exams, and dreams of Ivy League colleges and the other school with its alienation from the system of education, diminished visions of future possibilities, and overall disquiet about inequality in society.

As my ambivalence about high school steadily increased, I slowly but consistently began dropping my "honors" classes. Doing so allowed me to see the other Garfield High School. One class in particular—African studies—exposed the reality of just how racially tracked my world had become. Actively Afrocentric in its content and openly challenging of the historical and very Eurocentric assumptions of the other teachers and other history classes, African studies at Garfield spat in the face of the other, more traditional history classes. Based around a curriculum of resistance, our African studies instructor insisted that knowledge had been kept from us and that we had been blatantly lied to in the past. Developed specifically to nurture black identity and self-esteem, African studies had only African American students, except for one white student and my mixed Asian/white self. I was in a position of cultural outsider, interacting with the African American students very much on their turf and on their terms, and although it got tense at times, I loved it. We learned about African history through an Afrocentric lens, we argued about political and social issues, and we conferred with each other about who were the best hip-hop artists of the time. And I learned. I learned about the African American community in Seattle. I learned about the varying African American perspectives on history, society, and the world. And between the lines of the course material, the African American students were picking up that not all non-black folks were ignorant of racism, injustice, or history. It was real-life learning that was more valuable to me than any other class I took at Garfield, and I never would have had the experience had I not strayed from the "honors" track.

The El Train: "High" Track Power and the "Honors" Identity

Obviously, tracking did not go away after I graduated high school. Ten years later I became a teacher at Berkeley High School (BHS) in Berkeley, California, and was confronted with the exact same situation. BHS has been the subject of books (Maran, 2000), popular articles (Brown, 2002; Glionna, 2002; Maran, 2001), educational research (Bancroft, 1973; Groves, 2000; Honigsberg, 1995; Mahiri, 1996; Manley, 1979; Marascuilo & Dagenais, 1978; McCready, 2002; Noguera, 2001, 2003; Parker, 2001), and the focus of an episode of PBS's *Frontline* titled "School Colors." Roughly 3,000 students comprise the student body, which is about 40 percent African American, 40 percent European American, with Asian Americans and Latinos making up parts of the remaining 20 percent (Noguera, 2003). Shockingly similar to my high school alma mater, BHS places students in the "honors" or AP classes that are made up predominantly of upper-middle-class, affluent, European Americans from Berkeley's hills. Not surprisingly, if you look into the other tracked classes, you'll find students from the "flats" of Berkeley, which are predominantly poorer, working class, African American and Latino (Maran, 2000; Noguera, 2003).

During my time at Berkeley High, a particular battle over tracking that illustrates the power of the "honors" identity was waged in the history department. One set of teachers, who made up less than a fourth of the department (an unfortunately all too stereotypical combination of older, white, males), was actively working toward creating a special small school-within-a-school for AP students. The overwhelming majority of the teachers were against it, and a clear decision was made against this programmatic shift by the department as a whole. We wanted to teach classes that had all students of the school represented, where we could make use of everybody's relative skills and abilities to create classrooms that mirrored the diversity of the world we knew was out there. But in the end it did not matter. With the help of the all-powerful Berkeley hills parents, four teachers applied pressure with the district and got their way with complete disregard to our local decision-making power as trained, professional educators. The issue is not so much whether or not the parents from Berkeley's hills have the right to assert their input and control over the educational experiences of their own children. Local parental involvement is one part of an effective, functional educational system. However, given the vast differences in social, economic, and cultural power residing in the school and the school community, do the "hills" parents have the right to enforce a system that essentially privileges the educational experience of their children over that of the others? More simply put, if a system creates and/or maintains educational inequality, why do we end up listening to the voices of those that the system benefits?

These questions around the relative power of parents are more than just rhetorical. Ethnographic research has found that privileged parents often intervene advantageously on behalf of their children regardless of whether their intervention is in opposition to school personnel (Lucas, 1999) or whether it may prove academically harmful to other children (Brantlinger, 2003). Oakes, Welner, Yonezawa, and Allen (1998) framed schools as "zones of mediation" between community norms/tolerances and education policy. In their research, white middle- and upper-class parents balked at "equity minded" school reforms such as heterogeneous grouping because they wanted their children to be treated differently and were angered that their children might lose the power identified with high-level classes. A certain amount of institutional power lies with being labeled as "honors" that stems from the community around the school, and it becomes part of the identity of both "honors" students and "honors" parents (Smith, 2001). Generally speaking, the "honors" parents are the real players when it comes to local educational politics because they have access to resources and a sense of entitlement that the school will work for them. In the case of Berkeley High, it was clear that certain groups of parents banked on their status within the community to maintain the status of their children within the school.

In this sense, the power of the "honors" identity is both economic and cultural. The "honors" parents know how to negotiate the institution. They know the customs and norms, the language and structure, and they are confident enough to intervene. "If you mess up dealing with *my* kid, I will call my lawyer . . . I will write an op-ed to the local paper . . . I will not help with fundraising money." And this power is sometimes wielded in seemingly benevolent ways. Recently, when Berkeley was faced with tremendous budget cuts—like all districts these days, it seems—some parents offered to write personal checks to save an individual program for their children. One parent attempted to personally pay for an advanced music program because his child participated in it. While this act may be seen as a valiant individual effort, it reeks of individual economic privilege and demonstrates a lack of commitment to the school in general. All caring for education gets translated through the individual wants and programmatic needs of *my child* only.

In my experience, high-track teachers adopt the elitism of the "honors" identity, too. Certain groups of "honors" teachers at Berkeley and Garfield—where I later returned as a teacher—constantly looked down at the rest of us. I cannot relate the number of times I've heard "honors" or AP instructors wax about how qualified they were to teach their classes—the implication being that the rest of us were not—or how often students relay that a particular, untracked class is worthless according to Mr. So-and-So. Tracking plays itself out like this in the realm of department politics where newer teachers and younger teachers often get "stuck" with the "regular" classes, and bad classrooms, like a punishment or a way of paying their dues. Among teachers, tracking supports a culture of haves and have-nots, where some teachers are allowed to use their power in their own self-interests, often to the detriment of other teachers (Gamoran, 1992).

"Honors" students feel the power of this identity, too. They are in college preparatory classes, and they exude academic confidence. They know how to negotiate the school system and make use of and sometimes manipulate its rules, and they know that their "honors" teachers and their "honors" parents will do what it takes to keep them on track. This is somewhat of a generalization because all students experience differing levels of alienation in their lives, and some "honors" students, like myself, end up rejecting this system or are thrown off track by personal problems. The real issue, however, is resources and who has access to them. And when those resources are in danger, who flexes power at the school level? Whose parents put the fear of God in their teachers and administrators? Who can pay for tutors and SAT preparation classes as a standard part of their education? Who has the power to change department policy on behalf of their children?

The "honors" identity can also cloud a student's ability to recognize certain styles and content of instruction/learning as effective. Some "honors" students in my untracked ethnic studies class thought my instruction was poor because it was not structured around the traditional "honors"/AP, teacher-centered format of lecture, note taking, memorization, and testing. For them, real learning was the teacher-centered, direct instruction that dominated other classrooms in the school. The "honors" students just wanted me to shove all the information into their heads à la Freire's (1990) description of the "banking" style of education. Shor (1992) explained this as the socialization of students into a "traditional curriculum delivered to them, not created with them," where a serious classroom is defined as "one where the teacher does most of the talking and gives lots of tests." This socialization of students was also embodied in what they value as legitimate and "official knowledge" (Apple, 2000) worthy of study. Many of my "honors" students viewed the ethnic studies class as full of soft content that was not a necessary part of a real, college prep education.

Students of color who are on the "honors"/AP track are forced to negotiate particular social and cultural questions within the "honors" identity. One African American student who intended to enroll in AP classes laughingly quipped to me, "Yeah, I'm gonna take AP classes in the fall. So what if I'm the only black person in the class." Will solitary students of color have to give up some of their friends, culture, or language to fit in to the higher tracks? Are they confident enough to function as an extreme minority in high-track classes, often times being the only African American or Latino student in an AP or "honors" class? Do they feel somewhere inside that they may not quite belong in that setting or are unworthy of attending "honors" classes? How will students of color handle being accused of "acting white"?

This is not to say that students of color necessarily reject their racial or cultural identities to be successful in school. Some research has found just the opposite. Many academically successful African American students embrace very strong Afrocentric identities and find support among some of their peers (Horvat & Lewis, 2003; Spencer, Noll, Stoltzfus, & Harpalani, 2001). But as Tatum (1997) pointed out,

> Certain styles of speech, dress, and music, for example, may be embraced as "authentically Black" and become highly valued, while attitudes and behaviors associated with Whites are viewed with disdain. The peer group's evaluation of what is Black and what is not can have a powerful impact on adolescent behavior. (p. 61)

While it may be true that many academically successful African American students embrace a strong black identity, it may be equally true that some of their race- and class-based peers perceive their success in terms of "acting white." Parallel issues of self-esteem and identity arise for working-class students who take "high" track classes as well.

Jumping the Turnstiles:
"Low" Track Power and Systemic Resistance

The working-class students who predominate the "regular" classes do not get the same institutional, social, or economic reward and value for doing well in school as their "honors" counterparts. The system is just not geared toward their success in the same way. The "regular" students are not sure if they are going to college, if they have the money, or if they can even get in. As a means of negotiating their diminished institutional power, "low" track students develop strains of resistance to the academic and cultural norms of schools.

The biography of noted literacy scholar Mike Rose provides particular insight into the structural effects tracking has on individual students and the resistance it develops. In Rose's case, there were two Mike Roses in his high school, and the school incorrectly placed him in the vocational track as a case of mistaken identity. It wasn't until his junior year that the mistake was discovered, and by that time his writing and reading skills had decreased dramatically. He had essentially been transformed into a vocational-track student in the process of three high school years. Meanwhile, it took a concerted effort by several people in his life, including a very forgiving and supportive college, to effectively teach Rose how to read, write, and survive in his postsecondary education.

Rose related his lived experience as a lower track high school student and discussed one form of resistance beautifully in his essay "I Just Wanna Be Average" (Rose, 2001). He wrote about the psychological pulls for working-class students to define themselves as the "Common Joe" because it "neutralizes the insult and frustration of being a vocational kid" and provides a means of defense against an educational system that dumbs them down. Shor (1992) echoed Rose when he described two forms of student resistance to school-defined norms and authority as "playing dumb" and "getting by." He asserted that "[f]ake dumbness originates as a way to keep the teacher and domination at bay, to prevent authority from invading their cultural space or erasing their identity" (p. 138). Additionally, those who merely "get by" or "just want to be average" do a minimum amount of work to get the teacher to grant them a mediocre, but passing, grade. Shor used these ideas to illustrate that "bad" students are actually "resourceful and resilient," even if they are disruptive in the classroom environment.

As part of their resistance, "regular/remedial" track students choose to reject and resist an institution that does not value them for who they are and what they have to offer. These "regular" students often devalue the kind of education they are given by the school. Although some of his conclusions have been critiqued for being too essentialist and racially wide sweeping (Horvat & Lewis, 2003; Spencer et al., 2001), Ogbu explained this process as the development of identities that are "oppositional" to what the institution of school represents (Dance, 2002). The development of resistant or "oppositional" identities should come as no surprise since "lower" track students have bad educational experiences and react accordingly. Shor (1992) discussed this in terms of the socialization that the working poor receive and is worth quoting at some length here:

> Working people did not create for themselves overcrowded and underfunded schools, subordinated tracks in education, and vocationalized community colleges. These lesser experiences were invented for them by elite policymakers. No one volunteers to become a third-class citizen. Average people don't go out looking for bad education, low-paying jobs, crowded neighborhoods, and less political influence in society; they want for themselves and their children the resources and choices available in the best schools, residential areas, and jobs. But schoolchildren from poor and working homes receive the limited learning and shabby treatment which confirm their lower status. Unequal funding, inadequate staffing and facilities, and weak curricula—all decisions made from above—dominate the socializing experiences of students from below. (p. 115)

Shor's perspective recalls the earlier work of Bowles and Gintis (1976), shifting the burden of responsibility away from the students (who have been victimized by the educational system) and toward political and economic leadership and processes. It also makes a commonsense point that I think educators and policymakers often forget: Human beings do not actively seek to be mistreated.

Given the "shabby treatment which confirm[s] their lower status," many students find the education that they are presented with to be alienating and completely inapplicable to their lives and futures. Many students I have worked with had a hard time finding value in education if that education did not visibly lead to a profitable or "successful" future. Willis (2003) talked about the implications of linking school success with the concept of individual economic success:

> Individual logic says that it is worth working hard at school to gain qualifications to get a good job. However, this cannot be the case for all working-class individuals, even though all are asked to behave as if it were so. Only a substantial minority from the working class can hope for mobility, and their cultures and dispositions are adapted accordingly. . . . (p. 394)

For the "regular" and "remedial" students, whose parents may or may not have college degrees, may or may not have professional jobs, there are diminished opportunities for success. The schedule tells them that the right train is going to come, but instead they are forced to wait—and hope.

One way that "regular," working-class students counterbalance their overall lack of academic and social power is through their access to the power of popular culture. This cultural power is often expressed in their particular embodiment of "cool"—how they dress, how they walk, how they talk, and how they carry themselves. And it is not cool to be smart, particularly if smart is defined by a vision of submitting to school authority and potentially sacrificing your cultural values and practices. From the "regular" students' perspective, one who is "smart" speaks proper, standard English, dresses conservatively, behaves "well," and exudes certain cultural norms that the school recognizes as valuable and rewards accordingly. This kind of smart is not "cool."

This is not to say that there are not other types of smart to identify with, but that these other types are not supported by the institution in the same ways. Most of the "cool" students I've taught were quite intelligent, but they worked hard to negotiate their identities within the classroom and school. They did not like to be seen carrying books or speaking up in class. And they would resist talking with the students who were openly acknowledged as "honors." So while my intelligent-cool students knew that they were smart, they did not wear it on their sleeves for fear of being perceived as an L7 (a square), a nerd, or a geek. Willis (2003), in his work with the "lads" in the United Kingdom, similarly found that working-class schoolboys "resisted the mental and bodily inculcations of the school and rejected students who showed conformist attitudes to the school authorities" (pp. 392–393). The school's conception of just what and who constitutes "smart" did not fit with the students' conception of who they wanted to be.

While being cool does not necessarily pay off in the classroom, it certainly holds enormous capital in the hallways. In the highly tracked educational settings I have been in, many "honors" students walk in personal fear between periods, trying to avoid contact with the perceived riffraff of the school. They keep to themselves and quietly go about their business because they don't want to get "punked" or harassed by some street-tough "regular" student who might cross their path. Undoubtedly, schools need to be physically safe environments, and intimidation should not be a part of any educational experience. However, given the context and power dynamics created by our school system, I cannot help but question how the social and cultural hallway interactions are related to power differences expressed in school. When the "regular" student purposely provokes fear in the "honors" student, which is most often done with a potentially menacing look, it has to be seen as an act of self-definition and self-empowerment—almost an act of resistance to the power structure imposed by the school. Whereas inside the classroom the "honors" student is comfortable and relaxed and regularly demonstrates how smart he or she is, outside the classroom the "regular" student demonstrates just how little that kind of smart matters on the street—and maybe makes up for insecurities about intelligence and worth enforced by that same classroom.

Willis (2003) addressed this form of resistance as the embodiment of "assertive masculine style," which he described as being "predicated on being able to 'handle yourself' in a fight" as part of their school identity. Dance (2002), in describing working-class students in Boston, explained this process in terms of urban culture and students creating identities around being "hard" or street tough in rejection of the "softness" that school represents. I raise this issue not to condone the fear, threat, and violence found in schools. Rather, by looking at the issue of tracking and power in the school, we can use this perspective to understand better how our own systems aid and possibly even promote individual expressions of empowerment through these behaviors, especially when disempowerment is taking place in the classrooms. Unfortunately, playing dumb, wanting to be average, acting hard, and being cool, are all forms of resistance that reproduce existing educational inequities (Broussard & Joseph, 1998; Shor, 1992; Willis, 2003). Students who are socialized to resist school, often those who are in "lower" tracks, end up not being successful in or out of school and are subsequently left to wallow on the lower rungs of the socioeconomic ladder.

Murals on the Trains: Critical Detracking and Social Justice

For teachers deep in the trenches of increasingly underfunded public schools, tracking creates a context that forces them to make a choice: either be complacent, and therefore complicit in perpetuating this inequality, or strive to resist it and create something better. How do teachers who want to detrack their teaching, who seek to denaturalize this system and create classrooms of possibility rather than limits, actually teach? Admittedly, it is difficult but not impossible. Bigelow (1994) posited that we need to develop an "anti-tracking pedagogy," which he described as being

> more than just a collection of good teaching ideas strung together in a class-room with kids of different social backgrounds. . . . An anti-tracking pedagogy should equip educators and students to recognize and combat all inequity. Its organizing principle should be justice—in the classroom, in school, and in society at large. (p. 65)

Critical detracking, then, is more than just reorganizing our classroom practices; it is about reorganizing society as well.

The act of critical detracking has played a particularly important role in my experience as an educator. As both a teacher and a director of a small school for "dropouts" in Seattle, I participated in a program of critical detracking among the most alienated students in the district. There at Middle College High School, we had a diverse student body with very divergent educational experiences: highly skilled students who felt alienated from their schools, and less skilled students who had personal and educational needs their large high schools could not meet. What these students had in common was that they all felt "pushed out" because of the institutional inflexibility and social and cultural constraints their previous schools embodied.

At Middle College, my colleagues and I embraced our students' alienation and created classrooms that exuded cultural and political resistance to traditional school norms. In our team-taught, integrated humanities class, we built on our students' view of the school system and society by offering them the idea that their embattled perspective was justified, because they lived in an unjust world filled with inequality. Not only were our activities oriented toward a multiplicity of student skills and abilities, but we also were able to offer an "anti-tracking" pedagogy that focused on how they, as students, were in our classes both as "dropouts" and as representatives of real race, class, sexuality, and gender disparities in society. For instance, we used Howard Zinn's *A People's History of the United States* (1995) as our main U.S. history textbook, which appealed to our students because it challenged the canonical history they had learned throughout their previous public education. Zinn (1995) highlighted the experiences of people of color, women, and the working class throughout U.S. history and sided with their experiences as those who have been historically oppressed in our nation. Our students identified with those experiences and made connections with their own lives. While it would be misleading to say this leads to unequivocal success for all of our students, I stand firm behind the idea that this model provided a meaningful and critical educational experience.

I also had profound and meaningful experiences as a teacher of the critically detracked "Identity and Ethnic Studies"(IES) classes, too. Berkeley Unified School District is kind of magical in that it has an ethnic studies graduation requirement, and this requirement has been fulfilled in ninth grade through the IES course. IES is actively constructed as a nontracked class. It is the place in school where the full race, class, gender, and sexual diversity of Berkeley High's student body is present, and the course's whole purpose is to explore issues surrounding identity and power in our society. We were given small class sizes (which has now been changed because of budget cuts), and students interacted and engaged with each other through powerful content. For instance, we worked through a unit on the history and concept of "race" in the United States. We broke down the origins of racial terms and categories and examined the chameleon-like variations of how race was defined through the courts. The unit culminated with a critique of racial stereotypes perpetuated by the media. The class relied on its very diverse experiences to share perspectives and draw out meaning as we deconstructed what race was and how it impacted our lives.

While the critical detracking as presented here is only an individual solution to a much broader social problem, it provides educators an opportunity to recolonize their classrooms and teaching on behalf of educational and social equality. Critical detracking can be used to create a space that speaks to social justice and a vision of a better, more equitable world. Through it, we can challenge the factory-like structures of education and take on an "endeavor that confronts deeply held cultural beliefs, ideologies, and fiercely protected arrangements of material and political advantage in local communities" (Oakes & Wells, 1997). Further, critical detracking raises questions about what the purpose of public education is. Is it mainly upward mobility? Is it job training? Is it socialization? Is it to foster positive social change and social justice? How do we define what is valuable and necessary in a public education experience?

Mass Transit: Social Reproduction in Education

There is a tacit assumption in my position on tracking in public education: that public schools essentially operate as a reflection of the social stratification and power hierarchies generally found in U.S. society and economy, and by extension, tracks in education are physical expressions of relative privilege and access to resources. To be sure, public education can and does create opportunities for people to expand and grow and overcome the limits of their economic, social, and cultural circumstances, and throughout U.S. history, public education has been the site for struggle over inequality in our society. However, looking purely at its outcomes— who graduates, who does not, who goes to college, who does not, who "succeeds," who does not—it is hard to deny that the predominant trend is to reproduce many of the racial, economic, and gender inequalities we see in the status quo (Broussard & Joseph, 1998; Chunn, 1987–1988; Gamoran, 1992; Oakes, 1985, 1995). And even though not all students want to go to college, what is at issue is *choice*. All students should be in a position to make an active choice about their futures, rather than having the educational system make that decision for them.

As in society, powerful tracks are deeply embedded in our current system of public education. We see it in the top-down power structure of our schools: Teachers hold power over students, principals over teachers and other staff, district administration over principals, and on up, through the county, state, and federal governments (Bowles & Gintis, 1976). We see it in our assessments: quantifying student achievement through competitive, high-stakes, standardized tests, and student and school rankings. We see it in our departments, where veteran teachers have privilege over new teachers. We see it in course content, where certain knowledge is privileged over others as serious and worthy of study. We even find it in education's most entrenched assessment: the grade—where students cannot be assessed against their own individual development and learning but are forced to be compared to other students with standards set by teachers, states, and other outside forces. And our students embody these hierarchical power relationships in the social norms found in most schools, where ninth graders fear hazing, and every student is aware of who's cool or who's not, and "in groups" and "out groups" are defined dynamically and powerfully through competing gangs, cliques, sports squads, and clubs. It is a top-down organization of power, and in this system, we all are taught our places within its structure.

The fundamental question might not be whether tracking is good or bad, but rather, how we want our world to work. Do we value intercultural, interclass, intergender, international, interlingual, intersexuality explorations and all of their complex interrelated overlapping as part of a meaningful, worthwhile educational experience? Or is it better if we stay in our own worlds both in and outside of the school setting, quietly reproducing the inequality that exists in society? As the editors of *Rethinking Schools* stated, "We can teach for the society we live in, or we can teach for the one we want to see" (Bigelow, Christensen, Karp, Miner, & Peterson, 1994). And to do that, we must first reveal the third rail and examine how and why power is so unequally distributed in education and society.

What Do You Think?

1. Reflecting on your own personal experience, how has tracking impacted your education positively and/or negatively?

2. The author asserts that tracking is really an issue of power and access to resources. How has this assertion been supported or challenged within your educational experience?

3. How are issues of social and cultural identity wrapped up with the system of tracking?

4. Describe any experience you have had with untracked or critically detracked classes. What were the benefits of that experience? What did you find challenging?

5. What is your perspective on the author's claim that hallway interactions are shaped by the differential power relationships caused by tracking? Include your own personal experiences from your days in the school system.

6. If the author is correct, and much of the prevailing research demonstrates that tracking produces segregation and reproduces social and economic inequality in society, then why do you think tracking persists in public education?

Suggestions for Further Reading

Bigelow, B., Christensen, L., Karp, S., Miner, B., & Peterson, B. (Eds.). (1994). *Rethinking our classrooms* (Vol. 1). Milwaukee: Rethinking Schools.
This book presents a collection of pieces written by classroom teachers describing ways that they have strived to create a learning community with their students. There is a collection of many materials that teachers might find useful for promoting a sense of equality and acceptance of all students.

Maran, M. (2000). *Class dismissed: A year in the life of an American high school, a glimpse into the heart of a nation.* New York: St. Martin's Griffin.
Maran recounts the experiences of three students at Berkeley High School. Each of the students comes from a different background and walk of life. The data indicate that despite these students attending the same school, there appeared to be multiple schools coexisting within the same building that are determined by socio-economic and racial status.

Noguera, P. (2003). *City schools and the American dream: Reclaiming the promise of public education.* New York: Teachers College Press.
The primary argument in this book is that demanding higher standards and giving students more tests will not increase their academic performance. Based on research in many urban school settings, Noguera claims that in order to improve urban schools and help students in these schools succeed, communities must invest in them. Many issues that affect the urban student's performance are addressed.

Oakes, J. (1985). *Keeping track: How schools structure inequality.* New Haven, CT: Yale University Press.

This is an excellent book exposing the dangers of tracking in today's schools. The author maintains that tracking merely perpetuates discrimination and prevents students from reaching their potential.

References

Apple, M. W. (2000). *Official knowledge: Democratic education in a conservative age* (2nd ed.). New York: Routledge.

Bancroft, A. (1973). On the case at Berkeley High School. *California Journal of Teacher Education, 1*(4), 66–74.

Bigelow, B. (1994). Getting off the track: Stories from an untracked classroom. In B. Bigelow, L. Christensen, S. Karp, B. Miner, & B. Peterson (Eds.), *Rethinking our classrooms: Teaching for equity and justice* (Vol. 1, pp. 58–65). Milwaukee: Rethinking Schools.

Bigelow, B., Christensen, L., Karp, S., Miner, B., & Peterson, B. (Eds.). (1994). *Rethinking our classrooms: Teaching for equity and justice* (Vol. 1). Milwaukee: Rethinking Schools.

Bowles, S., & Gintis, H. (1976). *Schooling in capitalist America: Educational reform and the contradictions of economic life.* New York: Basic Books.

Brantlinger, E. (2003). *Dividing classes: How the middle class negotiates and rationalizes school advantage.* New York: RoutledgeFarmer.

Broussard, A. C., & Joseph, A. L. (1998). Tracking: A form of educational neglect? *Social Work in Education, 20*(2), 110.

Brown, P. L. (2002, October 13). Health food fails test at school in Berkeley. *The New York Times,* p. 22.

Chunn, E. W. (1987–1988). Sorting black students for success and failure: The inequality of ability grouping and tracking. *The Urban League Review, 11*(1, 2), 93–106.

Dance, J. L. (2002). *Tough fronts: The impact of street culture on schooling.* New York: RoutledgeFarmer.

Donelan, R. W., Neal, G. A., & Jones, D. L. (1994). The promise of Brown and the reality of academic grouping: The tracks of my tears. *The Journal of Negro Education, 63*(3), 376–387.

Evans, C. (1995). Access, equity, and intelligence: Another look at tracking. *English Journal, 84*(8), 63–65.

Freire, P. (1990). *Pedagogy of the oppressed* (32nd ed.). New York: Continuum.

Gamoran, A. (1992). Is ability grouping equitable? *Educational Leadership,* 11–17.

George, P. S. (1993). Tracking and ability grouping in the middle school: Ten tentative truths. *Middle School Journal, 24*(4), 17–24.

Glionna, J. M. (2002, September 4). Top-notch school fails to close "achievement gap"; Learning: Berkeley High tried to lift urban black and Latino pupils to the level of high-performing Asians and whites. But a sizable divide persists. *The Los Angeles Times,* p. 1.

Groves, S. (2000). A high school women's studies seminar. *Women's Studies Quarterly, 28*(3/4), 293.

Heubert, J. P. (2001). High-stakes testing and civil rights: Standards of appropriate test use and a strategy for enforcing them. In G. Orfield & M. L. Kornhaber (Eds.), *Raising standards or raising barriers? Inequality and high-stakes testing in public education* (pp. 175–194). New York: Century Foundation Press.

Honigsberg, P. J. (1995). A Barbie doll story. *Phi Delta Kappan, 77*(3), 252, 254, 256.

Horvat, E. M., & Lewis, K. S. (2003). Reassessing the "burden of 'acting white'": The importance of peer groups in managing academic success. *Sociology of Education, 76*(4), 265.

Hunter, R. C., & Bartee, R. (2003). The achievement gap: Issues of competition, class, and race. *Education and Urban Society, 35*(2), 151–160.

Kane, T. J., & Staiger, D. O. (2002). Volatility in school test scores: Implications for test-based accountability systems. In D. Ravitch (Ed.), *Brookings papers on education policy 2002* (pp. 235–284). Washington, DC: Brookings Institution.

Karp, S. (2003). Let them eat tests: NCLB and federal education policy. In L. Christensen & S. Karp (Eds.), *Rethinking school reform* (pp. 199–213). Milwaukee: Rethinking Schools.

Kliebard, H. M. (1995). *The struggle for the American curriculum 1893–1958* (2nd ed.). New York: Routledge.

Lucas, S. R. (1999). *Tracking inequality: Stratification and mobility in American high schools.* New York: Teachers College Press.

Madaus, G., & Clarke, M. (2001). The adverse impact of high-stakes testing on minority students: Evidence from one hundred years of test data. In G. Orfield & M. L. Kornhaber (Eds.), *Raising standards or raising barriers? Inequality and high-stakes testing in public education* (pp. 85–106). New York: Century Foundation Press.

Mahiri, J. (1996). *African American and youth culture as a bridge to writing development* (Final Report). Berkeley, CA: National Center for the Study of Writing and Literacy.

Manley, J. L. J. (1979). *Community high school: An historical study of an arts-oriented, student centered alternative public high school.* Unpublished doctoral dissertation, University of California, Berkeley.

Maran, M. (2000). *Class dismissed: A year in the life of an American high school, a glimpse into the heart of a nation.* New York: St. Martin's Griffin.

Maran, M. (2001, August/September). Damage control. *Teacher Magazine, 13,* 24.

Marascuilo, L. A., & Dagenais, F. (1978). *Social integration and school violence in a multiracial northern high school.* Berkeley, CA: Urban Education Clearinghouse.

McCready, L. T. (2002). *Making space: Querying the marginalization of Black male students in a segregated urban high school.* Unpublished doctoral dissertation, University of California, Berkeley.

McLaren, P. (1994). *Life in schools: An introduction to critical pedagogy in the foundations of education* (2nd ed.). New York: Longman.

McNeil, L., & Valenzuela, A. (2001). The harmful impact of the TAAS system of testing in Texas: Beneath the accountability rhetoric. In G. Orfield & M. L. Kornhaber (Eds.), *Raising standards or raising barriers? Inequality and high-stakes testing in public education* (pp. 127–150). New York: Century Foundation Press.

Neill, M., & Gayler, K. (2001). Do high-stakes graduation tests improve learning outcomes? Using state-level NAEP data to evaluate the effects of mandatory graduation tests. In G. Orfield & M. L. Kornhaber (Eds.), *Raising standards or raising barriers? Inequality and high-stakes testing in public education* (pp. 107–126). New York: Century Foundation Press.

Noguera, P. (2001). Racial politics and the elusive quest for excellence and equity in education. *Education & Urban Society, 34*(1), 18.

Noguera, P. (2003). *City schools and the American dream: Reclaiming the promise of public education.* New York: Teachers College Press.

Oakes, J. (1985). *Keeping track: How schools structure inequality.* New Haven, CT: Yale University Press.

Oakes, J. (1994). Tracking: Why schools need to take another route. In B. Bigelow, L. Christensen, S. Karp, B. Miner, & B. Peterson (Eds.), *Rethinking our classrooms: Teaching for equity and justice* (Vol. 1, pp. 178–181). Milwaukee: Rethinking Schools.

Oakes, J. (1995). Two cities' tracking and within-school segregation. *Teachers College Record, 96*(4), 681.

Oakes, J., & Wells, A. S. (1997). Detracking: The social construction of ability, cultural politics, and resistance to reform. *Teachers College Record, 98*(3), 482.

Oakes, J., Welner, K. G., Yonezawa, S., & Allen, R. (1998). Norms and politics of equity-minded change: Researching the "zone of mediation." In M. Fullan (Ed.), *International handbook of educational change.* Norwell, MA: Kluwer Academic.

Parker, J. (2001). Language: A pernicious and powerful tool. *English Journal, 91*(2), 74.

Rose, M. (2001). I just wanna be average. In G. Colombo, R. Cullen, & B. Lisle (Eds.), *Rereading America: Cultural contexts for critical thinking and writing* (5th ed., pp. 162–173). New York: Bedford/St. Martin's.

Rosenbaum, J. E. (1976). *Making inequality: The hidden curriculum of high school tracking.* New York: Wiley.

Shor, I. (1992). *Empowering education: Critical teaching for social change.* Chicago: University of Chicago Press.

Slavin, R. E. (1990). Effects of ability grouping in secondary schools: A best-evidence synthesis. *Review of Educational Research, 60,* 471–499.

Slavin, R. E., & Braddock, J. H. (1993). Ability grouping: On the wrong track. *College Board Review,* 11–18.

Smith, K. A. (2001). *Literacies, identities, and interdisciplinary curriculum.* Unpublished doctoral dissertation, University of Wisconsin, Madison.

Spencer, M. B., Noll, E., Stoltzfus, J., & Harpalani, V. (2001). Identity and school adjustment: Revisiting the "acting white" assumption. *Educational Psychologist, 36*(1), 21.

Tatum, B. D. (1997). *"Why are all the Black kids sitting together in the cafeteria?" and other conversations about race.* New York: Basic Books.

Willis, P. (2003). Foot soldiers of modernity: The dialectics of cultural consumption and the 21st-century school. *Harvard Educational Review, 72*(3).

Zinn, H. (1995). *A people's history of the United States: 1492–present* (Rev. ed.). New York: Harper Perennial. (Original work published 1980)

Part III

Programs

6

Hong Kong's Shifting Classroom Narrative

Betty C. Eng

In recent years, education has been put in the spotlight in many ways, especially concerning the development of curriculum and the instructional approaches employed in the implementation of the curriculum. Ms. Eng presents a personal account of her experience in working with preservice teachers and their expectations of the instructor through a collection of narratives. While the focus is on preservice teachers, the narratives provided demonstrate what was (is) important to them as students. These narratives address issues that are important to these preservice teachers as they begin thinking about their careers as teachers. This chapter is based on experiences in Hong Kong, providing an international perspective to the issues addressed, yet undeniably similar to the situation in North America and, undoubtedly, elsewhere in the world.

◆ ◆ ◆

A Hong Kong Introduction

"Good morning and welcome to the Hong Kong Institute of Education!" I say, first in English, then in Chinese, to my beginning teacher education students on the first day of our class.

The Hong Kong Institute of Education (HKIEd) is a major provider of teacher education training for initial and professional upgrading in

Hong Kong that was established through an amalgamation of colleges of education in 1994. The students I am meeting for the first time are in Adolescent Development, a compulsory class for first-year preservice students majoring in English. The class is composed of about 40 students, almost all women who are 18 or 19 years of age. Based on my records, all the students have recently graduated from a Hong Kong secondary school or high school. I hold their attention and I sense their interest to know the teacher.

> "My name is Betty Eng," I continue, and I say in Cantonese, "my Chinese name is Ng Ying Lan. My family name, Ng, is like the Chinese character for the number 5," I say, as I count out the numbers in Cantonese: 1, 2, 3, 4, 5. "Ying," I continue, "is the character for heroic or fearless as used in the character that forms the name for England, Ying kou. This is followed by the character Lan as in the orchid flower."

I am speaking primarily in English, weaving my Chinese into the introduction of my name. By this time, the students are on an alert that there is something different about me and that I may not be the "usual" Hong Kong Chinese teacher that they might expect. My physical appearance suggests I am Chinese, but given the way I speak my English and the way I speak my Cantonese, the students can't quite place me. They appear perplexed, curious, and, perhaps, uneasy, if I am reading their facial expressions accurately. I sense they are trying to figure out where I come from and who I am. I do not speak an English that they can readily link to the countries they have commonly come across. My English is not the English of the British, an English that dominated Hong Kong for over 155 years as a British colony until the return of sovereignty to the People's Republic of China in 1997. Nor does my English seem to be from Australia, Singapore, or Malaysia. My Cantonese also tells them that it is not the Cantonese of Hong Kong and that I am not a local "Hong Konger." To their hearing, my Cantonese probably lacks clarity and sounds fractured. My students continue to be puzzled but probably think it inappropriate or impolite to ask me where I am from or to ask me about my background.

> "I will be discussing the aim of this class, its topic contents, and assignments," I say. "But before we get to this, I think it would be helpful to introduce ourselves to each other. After all, we will be spending a good deal of time together during the semester, three hours per week for 12 weeks. It seems we often forget the most basic of personal amenities, such as a simple introduction. You may also

be curious about where I am from and who I am. Let me introduce myself further in an introduction activity in which we can all participate," I say in a carefully worded and well-paced English.

I have experienced this first-day introduction in my classes in much the same way over the past seven years as a teacher educator at HKIEd. My students have later shared their thoughts and feelings in their reflective journals of how they experience meeting me for the first time. Based on these journals, some of my students describe the experience of this first-day introduction:

"Since it was my first day of classes at HKIEd, I did not know what to expect. But you surprised me! At orientation, the week before, I had been prepared to have Chinese and non-Chinese teachers for my English major classes. At first glance, I thought you were Chinese, though your appearance was somewhat 'different.' I cannot describe this difference, just that it was different. Perhaps the round and black stone earrings you wore were a clue that you are from overseas. I have never seen these kinds of earrings in Hong Kong before. And when you spoke, I was certain you were not from Hong Kong."

"Your speech was different and made me think you are not from Hong Kong. You spoke English in a way that was unfamiliar to me and your Cantonese sounded strange. But it was when you asked us to pair up and introduce ourselves to someone we had not met or would like to know better that astonished me. I had never experienced this kind of class activity before in school. It seemed too informal and personal to be an activity to expect at a tertiary level institute like HKIEd. You asked us to introduce ourselves by telling our partner our name, why we wanted to become a teacher, and sharing some personal experiences such as what we did for fun and to describe the last time we were happy or cried. When you told us that we did not have to share anything we felt uncomfortable, that made me feel more relaxed about what to say. When we had completed our introduction, the whole class got together in a circle to introduce the person we have just met. I found everyone in the class keen to hear everyone's introductions. I felt somewhat uncomfortable with it because it was a new experience for me but then I found it fun to meet a new friend."

"The introduction activity was a new experience for me. I found I had to be a careful listener since we were not allowed to take notes to remember our partner's responses and since we only had about 5 minutes each to introduce ourselves when we met in pairs. I was so nervous about not remembering my partner's answers that I almost forgot my partner's name when I introduced her to the whole class! Others had similar difficulties but we all laughed about it together so it was a relaxing and fun way to begin the class."

As the teacher, I also participate in the introduction activity, and I ask my partner to guess where I might be from. Rarely do they guess that I am from the United States. I reveal where I am from and a little of who I am to my partner:

"I am a Chinese American and I have lived and worked in Hong Kong for over 13 years. I was born in Toishan, a county located in China, about 106 miles west of Hong Kong and raised and educated in California since the age of 6. I enjoy the wonderful Chinese food here! I have eaten Chinese food all my life but have since discovered so many new dishes and variety of ways of preparing Chinese meals. I also appreciate the traditional Chinese celebrations such as the public holidays of 'grave sweeping,' where the family goes to the cemetery to clean the grave sites to honor our ancestors; the annual Moon Festival, which some say is a celebration of the harvest; and, of course, the Chinese Lunar New Year. Our family celebrates such events in the United States, but it is a very different experience when I am participating in these holidays while living in the midst of a predominantly Chinese culture. Celebrating these holidays here seems more real and festive since it is an important part of a culture. Living in Hong Kong has really improved my Cantonese and my understanding of Chinese culture."

The student who is my partner says,

"Ah, I see! That explains your English and Chinese speech. I have never been to China myself even though it is nearby. I think the Toishan dialect must be very similar to the Cantonese we speak in Hong Kong. Your English is spoken so smoothly and fluently so you sound like a native English speaker even though you are Chinese. How should I call you when I introduce you to everyone in the class?"

"You may call me by my first name, Betty, or Professor Eng, as my students in the universities in the United States call me. Or, if you wish, you can call me by my Chinese family name followed by my title of 'teacher,' as most Chinese teachers are called, or merely Miss Eng."

The student who is my partner appears somewhat startled by the choices I present her and seems momentarily confused and unable to make a selection. Having the opportunity to make such a choice comes unexpectedly, I have learned, for this is an unheard-of practice in Hong Kong schools. Though bewildered, the significance of each choice is not lost on my student. Each choice that I have suggested presents its own special, complex meaning that expresses the status I should be accorded and our teacher-student relationship. I have discovered that in my students' minds, "Betty" sounds too foreign and too familiar. I have learned that it is improper for students in Hong Kong to call their teachers by their Chinese "given names." Instead, Hong Kong students commonly call their teachers by their family name followed by the title of "teacher" with a bowing nod to show their respect and deference. In Hong Kong's primary and secondary schools, it is the usual practice that at the beginning and conclusion of each lesson, the students get up from their desk, nod their head, and greet or say good-bye to their teachers as a sign of respect. Inviting my students to call me "Betty" had been intended to represent the shared and reciprocal roles that I believe we play as learners and teachers in the classroom. However, for many of my Hong Kong students, they find calling me "Betty" inappropriate and are uncomfortable with its usage. But my students who are English majors have come to expect and feel comfortable calling their overseas and non-Chinese teachers at HKIEd by their first name. In conversations with me, one student says,

> "They are Westerners and not Chinese, so calling them by their first name is okay. You, on the other hand, are Chinese even though you are from the United States. It would be improper and a sign of disrespect to you if I were to call you 'Betty.'"

Another student tells me,

> "I was confused by what to call you. You are definitely not a Westerner. You are Chinese, but not really since you did not grow up in Hong Kong but in the United States. You do not fit into being Chinese as I understand it."

More often than not, my students call me "Missee" as an informal salutation. I discover that calling me "Professor" is also inappropriate

since, in the Hong Kong context, this title is reserved as an honorific title
for those of senior rank, a title that does not match my status as a lecturer.
The use of the title "professor" in the United States is accorded all university faculty, regardless of their rank, and is used in the same way Hong
Kong uses the title "teacher." Status and rank, I have learned, are very
important, and the titles that are used signify one's identity and place in
Hong Kong society. Inadvertently, I discover that I have crossed the line,
violated a social rule, and offended some with my invitation to call me
"Betty." I find myself on a heightened sense of awareness as to how I
might be imposing a view or a set of values upon my students as I navigate my classroom experience as a teacher educator in Hong Kong.

The ambiguity that is presented by my students' description of me,
"*Chinese but not,*" and the tensions that arise, are similar to what He
(2002) called being in the "in-between" space between cultural boundaries in her study of cross-cultural lives. He, as a Chinese student from
China studying in Canada, "felt neither Chinese nor Canadian, a place
where the world passed us by. It was as if we were caught in a backwa-
ter as the river flowed past us" (p. 303). As a Chinese American living and
working in Hong Kong, I find myself situated in the margins of cultural
boundaries and am aware of the surprises, confusions, and, sometimes,
tensions that my identity and culture pose. The introduction activity experience that I describe with my Hong Kong students is but one instance
that reflects the cultural crossings I encounter on a regular basis during
the course of my classroom teaching. The milieu or context may be different depending on the setting or circumstance of where your classroom
is located, but, I believe, we all experience such cultural crossings in our
own unique ways in our classrooms.

An Evolving Curriculum: Hong Kong's Educational Reform

I also invited my students in American universities, where I had previously
taught for over 10 years, to participate in this introduction activity in
much the same way. Some of my American students also remarked that
they were surprised by this activity since it seemed such a personal and
informal way to begin a class. And, of course, not all American university
professors invite their students to call them by their first name. Some
American students may also feel it is inappropriate to call a teacher by his
or her first name.

My Hong Kong students' surprise and discomfort, however, holds a special significance, given Hong Kong's past educational system and its recent dramatic educational reforms. Until recently, Hong Kong has viewed the primary role of education as one of transmission or "funneling" of information. This funneling process in education is evidenced in a curriculum that is driven by testing. Recent major educational reforms have sought to transform Hong Kong's educational system from one that emphasizes what Sweeting (1990) described as an examination-driven curriculum with rote learning and memorization as the primary approaches to teaching and learning to one that promotes critical thinking and self-reflection. At the very beginning stages of a child's education in Hong Kong, his or her placement and advancement to the next grade are determined by the results of examinations taken at the end of each school year. Whether a Hong Kong student pursues a mathematics or science program or is given the opportunity to enroll in a school that uses English or Chinese as a medium of instruction is dictated by the results of examination. These regular exams are like taking a "mini" Scholastic Achievement Test (SAT), the test taken by high school students in the United States as they prepare for admissions to the university. The preparations for the exams are enormous with intensive drilling by teachers and parents hiring private tutors for additional lessons that are held after school and on Saturdays. Needless to say, the pressure and stress place a heavy toll on the student's emotional well-being. A significant number of suicides by youths in Hong Kong can be attributed to the pressures of the examination system.

High schools or secondary schools are ranked and identified by a "banding" rating system that has recently been reduced from bands 1 to 5 to bands 1 to 3. The reduction is a result of the recent educational reforms that, if not intended to eliminate the rating labels, are intended at least to minimize the possible number of ratings. A band 1 rating represents the top ranking and is achieved through a variety of factors, including the examination results of its students, its designation as a school that uses English as a medium of instruction, and the number of its graduating students' admission to the limited and competitive places in Hong Kong's universities. Primary schools are not formally ranked and labeled with a banding, but similar rating designations seem to be commonly understood among teachers and parents.

The recent major shifts in Hong Kong's educational policies can be traced, in part, to the inaugural address by Tung Chee Hwa, Hong Kong's chief executive, on July 1, 1997. In this address, he stressed the importance of education and pledged to draw up a comprehensive plan for improving the quality of education. Of significant importance for HKIEd, Chief Executive Tung emphasized the need to improve teacher education preparation and upgrading. Subsequent reforms in Hong Kong's educational policies have redirected their orientation from rote learning, memorization, and examination-driven curriculum to one that promotes a student's "all-round development" and a "learning to learn" approach in Hong Kong schools. According to Hong Kong's Education Commission, an advisory body to the government on the overall development of education,

> To meet the needs of society in the 21st Century, the Education Commission in 1998 embarked on a two-year comprehensive review of the overall education system in Hong Kong. . . . Students are the focal point of the entire reform. By creating space for schools, teachers and students, the reform is implemented to enable every student to attain all-round development in the moral, intellectual, physical, social and aesthetic domains according to his/her own attributes so that he/she will be capable of lifelong learning. It is also hoped that each student will develop the ability for critical and exploratory thinking; be innovative and adaptable to changes; be filled with self-confidence and a team spirit; be willing to put forward effort towards the prosperity, progress, freedom and democracy of society; and contribute to the future well-being of the nation and the world at large. (Education Commission, 2002, p. 3)

Teacher Knowledge/Knowledge for Teachers

Hong Kong's educational reforms present opportunities to attend to the personal and social development of its students in the school curriculum. This shift makes possible the introduction of personal experience, narratives, reflections, and critical thinking that provide a place for the voices of its learners and teachers. For my teacher education students at HKIEd, this is particularly significant as it provides an invitation to consider a "teacher knowledge" rather than a "knowledge for teacher" approach. Berk (1980) and Connelly and Clandinin (1991) described these approaches in educational studies as a teacher knowledge approach that asks "What does it mean for a person to be educated?" versus a knowledge for teacher approach that asks "How are people educated?" Clandinin and Connelly (2000) described the shift from teacher knowledge to knowledge for teacher in this way:

> The questions to be asked about preservice teacher education . . . begin with questions about what knowledge is held by preservice teachers and what knowledge is found in professional practice. This shifts the source of expertise from those situated in universities and policy making bodies to

preservice teachers and those who live in schools. In a program of teacher education designed around a view of knowledge for teachers one might ask "What should a teacher be taught?" and "What have you learned about teaching that can be taught to teachers?" In a program of teacher education designed around a view of teacher knowledge, one asks, as Schon (1987) asks of the professions more generally, "What does it mean to be a practitioner?" and "What may we do to help you to improve your practice?" This represents a shift in thinking about the education of teachers. Instead of beginning in theory we begin with practicing teachers' knowledge and pre-service teachers' knowledge. (pp. 99–100)

Grounded in the thinking of teacher knowledge is the recognition of experience as central to understanding education. The primacy of experience is recognized in the educational philosophy of Dewey (1938) who held that to study education and life is to study experience. According to Dewey, to understand why teachers do what they do is to understand their experience.

Schwab (1973), the curriculum theorist, translated these "bodies" of experience into the "commonplaces" that he believed are central to curriculum deliberations. He identified the four "commonplaces" as the learner, teacher, subject matter, and the milieu as essential bodies that should hold an "equal" voice in curriculum deliberations. In the Hong Kong context, the voice of the subject matter has dominated the curriculum with the voices of the learner and teacher often subsumed and made invisible. Hong Kong's educational reforms for "all-round development" of its students and a "learning to learn" approach provide opportunities for an inclusive classroom that invites a diversity of voices. The opportunities for inclusiveness and diversity that are presented are richly grounded in traditional Chinese thought as represented in the Confucian philosophy that promotes educability for all and perfectibility for all. According to Chinese tradition, it is possible to educate anyone who desires to learn and the intrinsic motivation of learning is for self-realization or the perfection of self (Lee, 1996).

With the opportunities that the recent educational reforms in Hong Kong provide, how might a teacher education curriculum introduce teacher knowledge to balance and complement the knowledge for teacher approach? How might we translate into practice the shift to a curriculum for our students that provides for "all-round development" and a "learning to learn" approach? In addition to the introduction activity that I have discussed earlier, I provide some examples of my practice that reflect this educational shift with personal narratives and the use of reading logs that provide opportunities for critical and reflective thinking.

Beginning With Ourselves: Personal Narratives

"But, teacher, I have no experiences to tell. I am just a recent secondary school graduate in my first year as a preservice student and not a qualified teacher. How can my personal experiences matter?"

"Teachers talk, students listen. Teachers are supposed to tell us how to be a teacher by giving us solutions and answers. It is the student's role to listen, follow, and obey the teacher. This is what I have been taught by my teachers in primary and secondary school."

These are statements made by one of my first-year preservice students, who, when asked to share a meaningful or important personal experience, claimed she had no experience to share with the class. We had just heard a talk on the place of experience in education and how it informs and shapes teacher knowledge. As a follow-up to the talk, I invited my students to share their personal experiences. At first, I thought my student's response might be attributed to being too shy or apprehensive to share a personal experience in class. I called on other students but received similar responses.

I puzzled over my students' remarks and sought to understand their responses. Might I have asked the question differently or provided a different approach to stimulate a fuller class discussion? After class, I spoke with a number of the students personally and discovered that it was not that they were shy or apprehensive but that they were genuinely baffled by what my question represented. My students' bafflement was grounded in their own experiences as learners in Hong Kong's classrooms.

I discovered that my student's response expressed an absence of authority to recognize the value of her experiences and how they are connected to shaping her professional identity and teacher knowledge. Unless the experiences, my preservice student reasoned, were experiences that occurred as a qualified or certified teacher in the classroom, her personal experiences were not related to her future career as a teacher. Her personal experiences did not have a valid place in the classroom.

Rarely too, it seems, are students asked to express anything personal or to initiate a question or a comment as succinctly expressed by my student's remark, *"Teachers talk, students listen."* My students' view of their place within the curriculum is understandable. Their voice as a stakeholder is rarely heard or acknowledged in Hong Kong where decisions regarding the curriculum are dictated by government policymakers in a process that has been characterized as a "consultative autocracy" (Cheng, 1997).

Hunt (1987) believed that understanding oneself is essential and is the beginning of becoming and being an effective teacher. Hunt (1987) proposed an "inside-out approach to begin with our inner feeling and beliefs" rather than starting with formal theories of education. As teachers, we need to understand where we came from, where we are in the present, and how the past and the present shape our future. And, in turn, by understanding ourselves, we are able to facilitate our students' journeys of self-understanding.

My Hong Kong students have rich and educative narratives of experience to share that become embedded in their developing pedagogy. When asked to describe the most memorable or significant personal experiences as an adolescent, my students write:

"When I was about to go to grade 6 in primary school, we moved to another school district. I found myself attending a primary school where all the pupils had very good English because the school used it as the medium of instruction. Since my previous school did not, I always failed the weekly English dictation. The teacher became very angry with me and she would physically punish the students who did not do well in their studies. I couldn't avoid being beaten by her. So, I made up my mind to catch up with the other students. I worked hard and learned all the English I needed in one month. That's the first time I realized I could be so powerful!"

"When I was in my junior middle school, I felt deeply sad. I was sad because I thought I was very physically ill. I wanted to tell my parents but did not because I did not want to bother them because they were so busy with their work. They did not realize anything was wrong with me. I could not talk about this illness with anyone. I had a lot of private things to bear in my heart. I wanted to share my feelings with others but I didn't trust anyone even though I had friends. I felt very lonely and alone and cried to myself in my bedroom listening to the sad music. I didn't understand what was happening to me and thought I would commit suicide."

"My most significant personal experience as an adolescent was in form 6. It was when I put a lot of effort working on an essay assignment, 4,000 words in Chinese. I had been working on this assignment for weeks. I wrote the characters neatly and tidily on sheets of paper. But when I found that I've used the wrong type of paper, it was too late to re-do the essay. I handed the essay in anyway. But when my teacher saw my mistake, she tore up the essay and threw it in the rubbish bin without a glance at the essay. This is the most significant experience for me because this incident helped me learn a lot in understanding and accepting consequences when I've made a mistake."

"The most memorable personal experience is the year I repeated form 7 and had to re-take the A-level exam that is required for admissions to the universities. I have to choose between continuing my studies with an associate degree or to re-sit for the A-level exam. I was so afraid that I could not get an offer from a university. If I did not get admitted to a university, I was afraid people would look down on me and I would disappoint my parents."

Attending to the personal experiences that are expressed in these narratives begins the process for the students' "all-round development" by recognizing the complex emotional, personal, and social dimensions that make up who we are as individuals. Based on these personal narratives, which are first begun in the early weeks of the term by my students, the topics that form the curriculum for Adolescent Development are developed. Through the students' experiential histories that are expressed in their personal narratives, topics such as "cognitive development of adolescents," "emotional and social factors," "peer influence," "family pressures," and "coping with stress" surface. The personal narratives that form the students' *teacher knowledge* are accompanied by the supporting theoretical framework that may be adapted and contextualized in order for Hong Kong schools to provide the *knowledge for teachers*. In this process, experience informs the theory and the theory is informed by the experience. This approach provides a basis for discussion of our experience and theoretical framework that is fluid and relevant to the Hong Kong milieu.

Learning to Learn: Reading Logs

"I do not want to be spoon-fed by my teacher. I am tired of the rote learning and memorization that I have experienced in schools. I want to develop my own thinking, make my own decisions, and be an independent learner."

This type of statement is expressed frequently by my Hong Kong students who are attempting to establish a new personal and professional identity as they enter their teacher education training. This statement can be attributed to the politics of post-1997, following the handover of Hong Kong from British colonial rule to the sovereignty of the People's Republic of China. This period calls for more liberal and democratic policies and is reflected in the recent educational reforms that have provided the shifting direction of teaching and learning in Hong Kong. More often than not, my students express this statement as an exploratory declaration of independence as much as a declaration of refutation of their past learning experiences in Hong Kong.

I have found that there are tremendous gaps between the reforms and the realities of our classroom as represented by my student's statement. My students' desire to reject the culture of "spoon-feeding" to become independent learners requires, I have learned, a period of transition and concerted guidance. The contradiction between what my students desire and the realities that have been shaped by their past educational experiences can be seen in the following narrative.

> "Wai Ming, can you give a brief review of our last lesson? Then, can you tell us what was an important or the most meaningful aspect of the lesson for you? There is no right or wrong response to this last part of the question. It focuses on what was important for you and the answers can be many and can be different for everyone in this class."

These questions, which I ask at the beginning of the class, create quite a surprising stir among my students. This is how I might describe the reaction from the students that my questions seem to have aroused:

Wai Ming looks confused and somewhat alarmed. But before replying to me, she quickly turns to the classmate to her left and, speaking in Cantonese, checks her understanding of my question. In the meantime, her classmate to her right and behind offers instructions and advice. Fairly quickly, a circle of students around Wai Ming are in a huddle, whispering in a rushed and escalating pitch, suggesting points of clarification and giving instructions on how to respond to the questions. Other students in the class are seen flipping through their notes or through their reading materials in search of a response to my questions. Others are head to head in conversation, presumably about my questions. I wait patiently and this exchange goes on for about five minutes before I interject with my own question that reflects my own genuine confusion.

"Wai Ming, what are you talking about with your classmates?"
I ask. "I am curious and bewildered by the stir my questions have
seemed to have caused."

Wai Ming hurriedly looks up from her consultation with her classmates and finally replies, "I can't catch your meaning and I don't
know the answer. I am sorry about that."

"I see. You seem to have some very helpful and supportive classmates. But why don't you turn to me with your questions?" I ask.

Wai Ming answers with, "I am unaccustomed to asking a question.
In my past experience at school, I am expected to have the correct
answer. There is no room for asking a question if I am confused. If
I answer incorrectly, I would receive a demerit point. My classmates
were trying to help me avoid receiving a demerit since I was unable
to answer your question."

"I see. I am beginning to understand. Well, in my classroom, I do not
penalize with a demerit. You can respond with an 'I don't recall the
last lesson to give a review' or 'Let me try to remember and respond
later.' I see many of you referring to your notes and reading materials
for the answer. Remember, the second part of my question, 'What
was an important or the most meaningful aspect of the lesson for
you,' is answered within yourself. The 'answer' lies in your own
thinking and, sometimes, your heart to reflect on what was important
or meaningful for you. The answers cannot be found in the reading
materials. This is an answer that cannot be given by rote or through
memorization. Let me move on to someone else who might respond."

This classroom interaction occurs frequently, and the first time I
experienced it, I marveled at the collective group support that my Hong
Kong students seemed to provide each other. This, I thought, was an act
of caring and group cohesiveness that I had rarely experienced among
my American university students. My HKIEd students' responses may be
attributed to traditional Chinese practices that place a high value on the
group and the family. I discover that my HKIEd students have established
their "family" within the classroom that provides them with a network of
mutual support.

But this reliance on the group may also be a competing tension in
developing the students' independent and unique growth. Developing

independent learning that promotes self-reflection and critical thinking to create a culture of "learning to learn" embraces a new way of thinking that requires a process of transition. Using "reading logs" is one such activity that I have found particularly helpful to promote guided independent learning, reflection, and critical thinking.

The reading log is an activity I first learned in a class in my doctoral studies and is based on the work of Adler and Van Doren (1972). I have personally found this activity helpful in my research work and have adapted it for my teacher education students in Hong Kong. The reading log asks the students to think of the different ways reading can occur and write reading logs for the materials they read. The framework for reading is composed of the following: (1) Recovery of meaning. This way of reading asks: What is the author saying? Read the material uncritically, without opinions or interpretations (2) Reconstruction of meaning. With this way of reading, ask yourself why you are reading it and what meaning you draw from the reading. (3) Reading at the edges. This way of reading invites readers to pose questions, raise issues, or discuss tensions that might emerge.

My HKIEd students read class materials and provide a reading log for each reading, addressing the three ways of reading. I found that while my students could readily understand what was meant by a "recovery of meaning," they initially struggled with the "reconstruction of meaning" and "reading at the edges." Their learning by rote and memorization posed a challenge to them to rely on their own thinking and to feel free to develop and express their own opinions. More important, I found they were not only uncertain of their own abilities for reflection and critical thinking but also wary of my response to their answers. Could they trust me as the teacher, as some have shared with me, to not judge, evaluate, or punish them with a demerit for a "wrong" answer? But gradually, when they discovered that there would not be such punishments and that, in fact, they were rewarded with praise for their "reconstruction of meaning" and "reading at the edges," these dimensions flourished in their writing.

A Dialectical View

Recently, I attended a seminar at HKIEd presented by visiting scholars from the United States where the topic was the current education reforms affecting teacher education in the United States. The scholars pointedly criticized the U.S. federal legislation known as No Child Left Behind by characterizing it as No Child Left *Unassessed*. They argued that the reforms subject children to assessment in the name of accountability, which, in turn. shifts the orientation of teaching and learning to assessment. Moreover, the federal policies include reliance on subject matter knowledge or a "knowledge for teacher" approach for teacher preparation that threatens to bypass the traditional undergraduate and postgraduate faculties of education completely. The scholars also pointed out that this policy is not new and that it was first begun in the 1980s by the Reagan administration with the introduction of A Nation at Risk and has gained momentum with the present Bush administration. The visiting scholars viewed the educational reforms in the United States as cyclical and dependent on the political and economic agenda of the administration in power.

Personally, I was disappointed to hear of these developments in the United States and reflected on the shift in direction that the educational reforms were taking in Hong Kong. In comparison, Hong Kong's educational reforms seemed to be more progressive in their efforts to cultivate critical and exploratory thinking for lifelong learning and to rewrite our curriculum to be less exam driven. Based on my past experiences as a teacher in the United States, my understanding of its current educational reform, and my role as a teacher educator in Hong Kong, I see lessons to be learned from the reforms from a cross-cultural perspective. Despite the educational reforms in Hong Kong, "teaching for the exam" remains a common practice, and the emphasis on assessment continues to dominate and have a stronghold. However, this emphasis on assessment co-exists with the recent educational reforms of "learning to learn" and enhancing the students' "all-round development." This appears contradictory and, when viewed dialectically, they are seen as opposing forces or factors that interact with each other and offer a way of viewing how their differences or tensions can be resolved. Viewed dialectically, the experiences of Hong Kong education can be seen as fluid, in a state of transition, and contested. In Hong Kong, there are opposing and competing practices and beliefs that have their roots in traditional Chinese culture and British colonization, which give context to this era of decolonization and liberalization in post-1997 Hong Kong. These historical roots serve to shape the Hong Kong classroom experience that embraces the recent educational reforms of "learning to learn," on the one hand, and "learning for the exam," on the other. This contradiction is not unlike my HKIEd students who strive to be independent yet continue to assert a reliance on a familial community composed of their peers in the classroom. I see this as an improvised blending of Western and Eastern values and beliefs that offers a creative resolution to tensions and conflicting positions.

Continuing the Conversation

The introduction of educational reforms in Hong Kong poses challenges along with opportunities. Many of the issues and dilemmas that my teacher education students in Hong Kong face as a result of these reforms are fundamental concerns shared by students and teachers in other countries. I have found that as a teacher educator in Hong Kong who is Chinese by birth and American by experience, I enter the class-room filled with my own values and beliefs that are not necessarily grounded in the theories of teaching of learning but in my personal expe-riential history. I find myself entering a fluid and shifting classroom land-scape, as I do at HKIEd in the middle of its dramatic reforms. In the same instance, my students are also engaged in this fluid and shifting land-scape. I have discovered through my teaching in Hong Kong that my ability to adapt, improvise, and create new ways of teaching and learn-ing are imperative for my participation in this fluctuating landscape. And I believe each narrative holds what Conle (1996) described as resonance, a "way of seeing one's experience in terms of another" so that others might continue the conversation that my Hong Kong narrative has begun.

What Do You Think?

1. How might you write a personal narrative that describes a mean-ingful or significant experience growing up?

2. How might your personal experiential history inform and shape your practice and your professional identity as a future teacher?

3. As a student, how have you experienced shifts or changes in the curriculum as a result of educational reforms?

4. What might be cultural diversities in your classroom and how are they represented in the school's curriculum?

5. How might teaching and learning through a cross-cultural per-spective be implemented in the curriculum?

6. Compare and contrast the issues in Hong Kong as described in this chapter with what you have experienced or learned about here in the United States.

Suggestions for Further Reading

Armstrong, D. G. (2002). *Curriculum today.* Upper Saddle River, NJ: Prentice Hall.

Armstrong addresses the issue of curriculum development from various angles, considering appropriate theories and foundations, as well as how politics affects curriculum. In addition, this book provides the reader with suggestions for developing and implementing curriculum.

English, F. W., & Steffy, B. E. (2001). *Deep curriculum alignment.* Lanham, MD: Rowman & Littlefield.

This book focuses on how flawed standardized testing has affected curriculum. The authors propose a "deeply aligned" curriculum which they believe will be more advantageous to all students.

Hamilton, R. J., & Ghatala, E. (1994). *Learning and instruction.* Columbus, OH: McGraw-Hill.

The authors compare various current theories on how students learn and then provide a section on applying these theories to real situations through case studies focusing on selected learning outcomes.

Strong, R. W., Silver, H. F., & Perini, M. J. (2001). *Teaching what matters most: Standards and strategies for raising student achievement.* Alexandria, VA: Association for Supervision and Curriculum Development.

With the expectation that students meet all of the required standards established, the authors propose four primary standards on which teachers should focus in order to be successful at fulfilling the mandated standards: rigor, thought, diversity, and authenticity. They also provide examples for implementing these standards.

References

Adler, M., & Van Doren, C. (1972). *How to read a book.* New York: Simon & Schuster.

Berk, L. (1980). Education in lives: Biographic narrative in the study of educational outcomes. *The Journal of Curriculum Theorizing, 2*(2), 88–153.

Cheng, K. M. (1997). The policymaking process. In G. A. Postiglione & W. O. Lee (Eds.), *Schooling in Hong Kong.* Hong Kong: Hong Kong University Press.

Clandinin, D. J., & Connelly, F. M. (2000). *Narrative inquiry: Experience and story in qualitative research.* San Francisco: Jossey-Bass.

Conle, C. (1996). Resonance in preservice teacher inquiry. *American Educational Research Journal, 33*(2), 297–325.

Connelly, F. M., & Clandinin, D. J. (1991). Narrative inquiry: Storied experience. In E. Short (Ed.), *Forms of curriculum inquiry.* Albany: State University of New York Press.

Dewey, J. (1938). *Experience and education.* New York: Simon & Schuster.

He, M. F. (2002). A narrative inquiry of cross-cultural lives: Lives in China. *Journal of Curriculum Studies, 34*(3), 301–321.

Hunt, D. (1987). *Beginning with ourselves.* Cambridge, MA: Brookline Books.

Lee, W. O. (1996). The cultural context for Chinese learners: Conceptions of learning in the Confucian tradition. In David A. Watkins & John B. Biggs (Eds.), *The Chinese learner: Cultural, psychological and contextual influences.* Hong Kong: Comparative Education Research Centre.

Schwab, J. J. (1973). The practical: Translation into curriculum. In I. Westbury & N. J. Wilkof (Eds.), *On curriculum building.* Chicago: University of Chicago Press.

Sweeting, A. (1990). *Education in Hong Kong pre-1841 to 1941: Fact and opinion.* Hong Kong: Hong Kong University Press.

Wong, R. Y. M. (2002). *Progress report on the education reform (1): Learning for life, learning through life.* Hong Kong: Education Commission.

7

Reflections on Compassionate and Transformative Education

Chris Carger

W ith each passing year, our classrooms are becoming more and more diversified. Future teachers must be prepared to receive this diverse body of students into their classrooms. There has been an assumption in years past that all students should be treated the same, when, in reality, each student is unique with different needs. Dr. Carger addresses the issue of diversity in the classroom by sharing her own personal experiences in an effort to encourage the reader to spend time getting to know his or her students individually. While this chapter is not a methods chapter in teaching nonnative speakers of English, it is a piece designed to challenge the preservice teacher to begin looking at teaching as an opportunity to "cultivate humanity" by stepping out of the four walls of the classroom and seeing students in the context of their world.

◆ ◆ ◆

Paolo Freire wrote, "To be in the world necessarily implies being with the world and with others" (2000, p. 33). As a teacher, I have always been drawn to be with the world and with my students in their worlds, students often considered "other" by the majority population. Just recently at a university faculty meeting arranged to encourage partnership with local school districts toward the goal of good teacher education, I was thanked by some colleagues for speaking up and sharing my perspective "from the trenches." "I've never had a problem with being in the trenches," I answered. "I think teacher educators need to be connected to the field." How unfortunate that participating with children and teachers in real school situations is referred to in terms of embattlement. Nonetheless, in many circumstances, as an educator of diverse students, I do feel that we are clawing our way up dirt walls, trying to get out of holes and head for open air in order to find, at the very least, an even playing field for all children. Entrenchment is imposed upon us, as layers of stereotypes and new, misguided patriotism bury immigrant students in cultural misunderstanding and inappropriate instructional approaches.

My own childhood, punctured with loneliness and self-doubt, was that of a student on the margins of a white-collar world. Education afforded me glimpses of something wonderful, fine, and fulfilling, something my parents never knew and that my mother, in particular, envied. From as early as kindergarten, the role of teacher and the setting of school appealed to me, the daughter of parents whose careers were spent in factories and shops that other people owned.

"Stone school" was a favorite pastime for youngsters in the neighborhood, and we would recruit "students" to sit in a row on the bottom steps of our porches. The "teacher" would stand in front of her queue of pupils with hands tightly cupped closed—one hand empty, one holding a stone. The students' job was to tap the hand they thought was concealing the stone. If they chose correctly, they moved up a step. Whoever reached the top step first "graduated" and won the game. In our zeal to play stone school, our hands would sweat and moisten the small rocks we held, leaving dirt in the creases of our palms.

I remember cherub-faced Richie, the tail end of a family of six children who lived next door, and how he fretted and carefully examined and reexamined the "teacher's" hands before he made his choice, which was usually wrong despite his sincerest effort. Long ago, I wished Richie could win just once. I wished the youngest boy with the stutter and constantly smudged face would beat the bigger kids who made more savvy guesses. Amid accusations of cheating, I would try to give Richie hints as to the correct hand with one hand held slightly tighter, raised just a bit.

As a teacher and teacher educator for almost 30 years, I feel I have seen variations of "stone school" over and over again: children trying their best to make a good guess and, hopefully, please the teacher who clamps her hand around the curriculum. Recently, I have seen educators' hands wrap themselves around standards-driven, skill-based curricula that, in my opinion, squeeze the life out of learning. They frustrate the Richies of the world but never see their own dirty palms as the problem.

As children in Prospect Park, New Jersey, my best friend Patty and I played out our futures on the wooden front porches of a small town that was part of the greater New York City megalopolis. We lived on North 9th Street, the lower, less prestigious end of our northern New Jersey suburb. The city of Paterson, largely filled with government "projects" and cheap apartments, ended on 5th Street. Just four blocks away, our world changed to a poor urban area replete with economic, race, drug, and crime problems. During the 1930s and 1940s, Paterson was a booming town on the Passaic River with a lucrative silk manufacturing industry. In fact, my grandfather emigrated from France via Canada to the "Garden State" because he knew how to build and repair silk looms and that skill was very marketable in Paterson. Another friend's father came from Syria to work in the Paterson silk mills, and his daughter translated for me her dad's memories of Eddie Martel as being the best "loom man" in town. With the advent of polyester fabrics in the 1950s, Paterson's economy withered and died. "Silk City," as it was once called, was a thing of the past, and empty factories lined the river's edge like soot on a windowpane.

Patty and I weren't too concerned with Paterson in the mid-1950s as we crafted worlds of play on our porches, perched on a hill overlooking the city's smog. We alternated between playing school and playing house. We would grow up to realize those roles, teacher and homemaker.

Patty would marry young and stay close to Prospect Park. She kept a perfectly clean house, as carefully organized as the home she created with dolls and strollers and cribs on her front porch. I would move away to upstate New York, study Spanish there and in Puerto Rico, and earn a master's degree in bilingual education.

I taught mostly Puerto Rican children all year long, taking summer teaching positions in a special school for juvenile delinquents from New York City who had had run-ins with the police. The school was nestled in a beautiful country setting on the Hudson River about two hours north of the Big Apple. I taught reading to small groups of high school freshmen sent there. We never had large classes because of the fear of violent behavior on the part of our students. Some were accused of assault and murder and were awaiting trial. At the hint of aggressive behavior, we were told to go immediately into the hallway and call for support. I hoped I never would need to make that call. But one day, a boy in my second-period group came into my room from shop class, proudly carrying a wooden gun he had created. He confided in me, in Spanish, that he was "in" for one murder but that he had actually committed three. "When your gang leader tells you to knock off someone, you just do it," he said, "or you'll be the one floating face down in the river the next day." The girl he sat next to in class had scabs from cuts covering both her arms from an attempted suicide and cutter incidents. That day she mumbled something to Tito with the wooden gun and within seconds they both were poised with wooden chairs aimed at each other's heads. I stepped into the hall and managed to say "Keegan!" loud enough for my teacher neighbor to hear. He immediately shouted down the hall for help in the library and in a few more seconds, veteran teachers retrieved the chairs and separated my students. I began to learn that day that even if you have good rapport with your students and you are a well-liked teacher, peer interactions and pressures can explode in your room. Another student at Good Samaritan, whom I had spent many extra hours tutoring and who confided in me, didn't show up for class one day. I heard that he had set a fire in the dorm and was immediately sent to jail. I could hardly believe it and took it as a personal failure. Students you reach out to can disappoint you. I am still learning that lesson.

While at Good Samaritan, Eva, one of my female Puerto Rican students, asked me to come to her Sweet 16 birthday party in the Bronx. She and her girlfriend, Lucy, another student I knew, had a weekend pass. My parents' home was only about a half hour away from the Bronx and so I accepted Eva's invitation and traveled to her apartment in my first car, a secondhand powder blue VW bug. Thirty years later, I vividly remember how the sidewalks where she lived were covered with broken glass. It crunched under my best beige sandals, like strange summer snow, as I hurried to her building in party attire, carrying gifts. We all sat in a small kitchen, with crepe paper streamers strung across the room. Eva's mother was cooking *pasteles*, a Puerto Rican dish made with plantains and cooked in banana leaves or their New York City substitute, cooking parchment. *Arroz con gandules*, rice with peas, was cooking in a large heavy pot on the stove. Punch spiked with alcohol was being passed out to the adults, and it was clear that Eva's mom had been drinking long before the guests arrived. Her speech got louder and louder and more and more slurred as she began to argue with Eva and anyone who tried to help her with the preparations. In less than half an hour, Eva left the party in tears, amid screams and curses. Lucy and I followed her out. Lucy consoled her friend who lamented that it always turned out like this at family gatherings. "Let's go to my place," Lucy suggested. I was glad to escape from the sad scene that unfolded before me at Eva's as we headed down the street. Little did I know what awaited us at Lucy's. Her apartment was in the rear of a partially abandoned building. We passed through dark concrete hallways stained with dirt before we reached her door. "Ma," yelled Lucy. *"Estoy aquí,* I'm here." We sat in a very dim living room. "Ma, ma!" Lucy continued to call. "I'm here with my friend and my teacher." We heard muffled voices, and a shadowy figure in a silky nightgown appeared in a doorway. There were hushed, angry words exchanged, and Lucy rushed us out cursing under her breath. In her accented English, she snarled, "She got a john in there, again. I can't believe it. She told me she'd stop." Now it was Eva's turn to console her friend as tears spilled from her eyes down her cheeks onto her nicely ironed blouse. To say that my heart ached for these young girls is a gross understatement. To say that I gained a new understanding of their lives also minimizes the impact these home visits had on me and on my future teaching. Lucy and Eva walked me back to my car, all of us crushing down on ghetto glass, discussing the night's disappointments. Eva's dark black hair pulled tightly against her neck, Lucy's red-tinted curls framing her tan face; they walked arm in arm to my car, alternating apologies for their mothers. I promised to see them at school the following Monday and hugged them good-bye. As I pulled away in my powder blue bug, I realized that I didn't know how to get back to the Henry Hudson, the highway I needed to return to New Jersey. But Eva and Lucy were in no shape to help me figure that out. The city's subways were their only mode of transportation, and they were unfamiliar with routes to the surrounding highways. It was dark and I found myself driving on a nearly deserted street, a level below the neighborhood I had just left. This was not a good place for a *wuera* (white woman) by herself, at night. Suddenly, I noticed a police car with two officers, parked on the grass under an overpass. "Thank God," I thought. I pulled over and asked them for directions. "What the hell are you doing here?" one officer demanded. "I'm a teacher," I stammered. "I was here at a birthday party for a student of mine and I got lost." He walked toward my car and said to his partner, "Jesus, Joe, I think she's telling the truth." He was looking at the back seat of my car, which was covered with English books. "Look at this stuff," he pointed with the beam of his flashlight at my books. It was then that I saw a woman who was leaning into the window of the police car. She was dressed in a miniskirt and a tight leather jacket with a bright scarf around her neck that was blowing in the wind. She walked over to me and while snapping her chewing gum loudly said, "Oh, don't worry, honey, they'll help you." The two officers began to give me directions to the highway then looked at each other and one of them said, "Cripes, we can't send her through here alone."

"Uh, just a moment, ma'am," the officer said to me. "As soon as we take care of this, uh, young lady," he said, pointing to the gum-chewing, miniskirted woman, "we're gonna help you." "Bye, sweetie," she waved and went back to her pose at the police car window." They talked animatedly with her a bit longer then drove up to my car and said, "Just follow us. We're gonna escort you out of here, ma'am. You know, teach, it really isn't safe for you to be around here alone." With that, they turned on their siren and red flashing light and motioned for me to follow. We swerved through intersections, ignoring traffic lights and stop signs, until we got to a ramp onto the Henry Hudson. The officers motioned for me to turn, blasted their siren, and waved good-bye. I will remember that night for the rest of my life, my police escort out of the Bronx, out of a world I had only seen from the highway until Eva's Sweet 16 party.

After visiting their homes, I found myself much more reflective about the materials I chose for Eva and Lucy to read in class. I am sure that their mothers, both single immigrant parents, had heartbreaking stories of their own, but I only knew them through their daughters' eyes. I looked for literature that might mean something to them in their real-life situations, and I continued to be there for them after classes. I discovered that Piri Thomas's *Down These Mean Streets* (1967) was a book that resonated with Good Sam students who frequently shared his Puerto Rican/African American heritage and inner-city experiences with poverty, crime, and drug addiction. In the 30th-anniversary edition, Thomas opened his searing autobiography with a foreword explaining that, because of current crack and cocaine dealing, the streets of Spanish Harlem have not improved much in the past three decades.

When summer ended, I went back to teaching elementary school–aged children in a dual-language program. My first full-time teaching position was in Beacon, New York, about 75 miles north of New York City. I had completed my student teaching there and substitute taught for them while I earned my first master's degree, then returned to be hired as a fifth-grade teacher in the district's dual-language program. Beacon was a small industrial city on the Hudson River with neighborhoods of comfortable, middle-class homes, and nice, newly built condominiums and apartments, where the mainstream half of my class lived. There was also a little barrio of older, low-income apartments and small houses, which my Spanish-speaking Puerto Rican students called home. The river's banks hosted several gritty factories that hired unskilled laborers. One such factory, which manufactured women's handbags, gave work to Marta Rodriguez, a single parent of Mexican origin, whose son found his way into my first fifth-grade classroom. Fernando joined my room late in the year and was my only Mexican student in a room with half mainstream children and half Puerto Rican students. It was a hot spring with many days in the 90s, and I noticed that Fernando always wore a clean white turtleneck and black trousers to school. He insisted that he was not hot, despite the sweat that beaded upon his upper lip and forehead. I asked if I could meet his mother some day, and Fernando excitedly returned to school to tell me that his mom invited me to visit that week. In my college-learned Spanish, Señora Rodriguez and I exchanged stories of how we landed in Beacon, New York. Marta had waded across the Rio Grande in the dark with her five children, dodging searchlights and praying to the Virgin of Guadalupe for help after she was abandoned by her husband for a younger woman. Through a relative, she had heard of work in a local handbag factory and managed to find her way to upstate New York. She and her children smiled as we sat on the one bed in her small, two-room apartment. The children were eating canned peaches for dinner, anxiously waiting for their mother's and older sisters' paychecks from the factory. The white turtle-necks Marta's three boys wore were the only shirts they had, and she washed them by hand every evening.

Señora Rodriguez was full of hope and brimming with stories of Mexico. As I returned for many other visits, she taught me about their foods and holidays, customs, and religious faith. With off-color skeins of yarn she bought on sale from another factory, she taught her two daughters and me to crochet basic stitches and enjoyed doing other art activities with the meager supplies she and her children owned. I was able to put her in contact with the local Episcopalian minister who gave her a garden plot to sow seeds. He also found friends to supply them with rice and meat for holiday meals. I remember the kindly old pastor who told me that I had to be his feet and help him to reach the people that needed the few resources he had. Soon the Rodriguez table was filled with golden ears of corn, tomatoes, and frijoles, along with the always-present cans of peaches. My friend Edwina, a young music teacher who began her career when I did, helped me to find more furniture and clothes for Marta's children. I, in turn, helped her by painting scenery for the school's production of *The Wizard of Oz*, which was enthusiastically sung in the Latino accents of our many bilingual students.

Eventually, I transplanted my teaching career from New York to Chicago and continued a lifelong interest in immigrant children, particularly those of Latino origin. In Chicago's Pilsen neighborhood, a barrio on the near west side of the city, I fell in love with the Mexican culture I had begun to learn about from Señora Rodriguez in Beacon. The Sandoval family, the Melgozas, and the Chavezes, among others, would open their homes to me and teach me about their native land, their values, and share with me their dreams for their children.

The Juarez family would generously allow me to look closely at the educational struggles of their oldest son, Alejandro, whose story would become my dissertation for my doctoral degree. I would learn to share narratives of teaching that seemed to help students of education to cross social boundaries and to cultivate compassion for the pedagogical plight of students like Alejandro who was lost between the borders he tried to navigate between his home and school worlds.

All of the families who opened their homes to me, *la maestra*, educated me in the funds of knowledge they nurtured in their everyday lives. My role as teacher gave me immediate entry into their households for the profession of teaching is often held in high esteem by Latino groups and, in my experience, by immigrant families in general. The skills I saw varied from farming and horticultural knowledge to oral poetry recitation. Home and machinery repair, sewing, crocheting, cooking, and knowledge of natural herbal remedies for various ailments were other skills I saw flourishing in families. Luis Moll and his associates in Arizona researched these funds of knowledge in working-class families, "the cultural resources of local communities" (Moll, 2001, p. 16) and integrated them into the curricula. It is often very easy to build a thematic unit around local funds of knowledge once discovered (Moll, Amanti, Neff, & Gonzalez, 1992). For example, I had a friend who noticed that a young, struggling English language learner (ELL) student, José, became alive with interest when corn crops were mentioned in a social studies class. She discovered that José's grandfather had owned a cornfield in Mexico and that it was his job to sleep among the corn plants and chase away the birds, a typical task reserved for younger children. My friend Sue allowed José to become the expert on corn for the class and developed an engaging unit around that crop. Mayan creation stories involving people of corn, science connections regarding corn's great versatility and utility, and corn recipes in reading became benchmark investigations and activities in her class and José grew in credibility with his peers.

I now include a home visit and interview as an assignment for my students in my bilingualism and literacy college course. Those who fear a home visit to students always ask if they can meet parents in school or at a local coffee shop. But once the reports begin to trickle into class about the warmth with which teachers are received in diverse home settings, even the most reluctant teachers try out the assignment. Most return with touching stories, curricular ideas, and wonderful insights that help to break down stereotypes they have built up for years. In reflection papers, I often read statements like Jill's: "I was very anxious and nervous about going on this home visit. I felt I would be intruding on this family and I would feel out of place. Quite the opposite happened! I felt very welcomed and thrilled about being there. I learned so much about them as a family that I would not have." Or Jayne who simply wrote, "I could not believe what a wonderful experience this home visit was for me."

I realize that I am asking my adult students to do something extraordinary (yet fairly simple) in many cases. I am asking teachers to take the transformative Christmas morning walk of Scrooge, to see what the world outside their classroom walls contains. And with the excitement of Dickens' irascible but ultimately loveable character, run down the streets of neighborhoods near their worlds but previously unknown and even feared. I am asking them to see, really see, their fellow citizens for the first time, with new eyes. I am encouraging them to grab the goose from the shop window and feed the children in their care, like Scrooge finally fed the Cratchit family. Nourish students with a curriculum that means something to them, that has the power to move and motivate them rather than feed them with bland, standards-driven mush. Be unapologetically concerned for the Tiny Tim they may discover within their reach and then embrace him. I believe that being a multicultural teacher requires a lifelong stroll in the snow with eyes that can appreciate the array of strengths that a world of students affords and a heart with the capacity to care about them. "Citizens who cultivate their humanity need an ability to see themselves not simply as citizens of some local region or group but also, above all, as human beings bound to all other human beings by ties of recognition and concern. The world is inescapably international," philosopher Martha Nussbaum (1997, p. 10) wrote. Referring repeatedly to classic educators such as Socrates, Nussbaum invites present-day teacher educators in colleges across America to help the pupils they teach to learn to cultivate humanity, a phrase penned by the first-century teacher, Seneca.

I believe that teachers, above all, need to cultivate humanity. They need to be able to think for themselves rather than defer to popular "authority" on best practice. They need to toil in the fields of imagination and empathy rather than bury those characteristics in objective, deficit-driven, test-centered language. A very practical place to start the process of becoming really student centered is to learn about the homes and communities from which pupils come. Learn about them not through rumor and hearsay but face to face, in their houses, in their neighborhoods. "I can't visit 30 kids," or "I see 90 junior high kids a day in my biology classes" are familiar early concerns I have heard over the years. My response is that even one or two visits a year or a single trip to an ethnic neighborhood grocery store with an ethnographer's eye, closely observing and participating in what unfolds, will make a dramatic difference in most teachers' understanding of diverse background experiences.

Another way for teachers to build their own background knowledge about diverse students is to read authentic accounts of school experiences written by the people who went through them.

I was recently observing a colleague teaching graduate students at the university and quizzing the students on their reading. He and his class were attempting to define the concept of caring education. "Does it mean to coddle a student or to protect them?" he asked. He then proceeded to answer his own question, "No, it doesn't mean to protect and coddle them." I thought back to my days of teaching in a self-contained bilingual classroom and I realized that I certainly did protect my students. How can you say that you care for someone and not feel protective of that person in difficult situations? How can you determine never to face a time when a child needs some coddling, like the day Billy in my first classroom decided to threaten to jump from our second-floor classroom windows because his father, once again, had missed his visitation day. Though my colleague was trying his best to encourage his students to reflect on the concept of a caring educator, one who both challenges and is sensitive to students, an inauthentic discussion of journal articles and professional book chapters fell far short of a meaningful educational experience. I believe that narrative accounts of teaching or of being taught in which the voice of the educator or the student in concrete, everyday situations is heard can be far more valuable than traditional classroom, college of education discourse. Narrative has been a powerful tool for centuries. Literature, I believe, has a place in teacher education programs, whether it be the formal curricula of universities, the professional development plans required by school districts, or personal agendas for career growth and understanding. Nussbaum extended her vision of the role of curriculum to world citizenship where she feels that "literature, with its ability to represent the specific circumstances and problems of people of many different sorts, makes an especially rich contribution" (1997, p. 86) to understanding differences and varied ways of looking at the world. Maxine Greene has appreciated the voices of those often marginalized and distanced as "other" throughout her distinctive career. Almost 40 years ago, she was connecting literature to education in *The Public School and the Private Vision: A Search for America in Education and Literature* (1965). She has continued to seamlessly integrate literature, from the classics to modern masterpieces from diverse authors, into the fabric of her thought on education in America. I want to add my small voice to theirs and others' that encourage the integration of narrative as yeast for raising compassion and sensitivity in the mix of preparation and development efforts that teachers receive.

Reflecting on my past teaching experiences and the literature that impacted my own professional development helps me to recapture the ideals that led me to and through the career of teaching. Educators' paths to teaching are varied. As a former student of Bill Ayers, I once worked with him as a supervisor of emergent teachers in their first field placement. An early assignment Bill gave was to make a visual representation of our path to teaching on the folder used to organize course reflections. Some students drew; some used collages of photographs and realia that meant something special to them as they traveled their particular journeys toward teaching. A simple assignment, it nevertheless revealed a great depth of feelings and dreams and beliefs associated with the profession.

I would like to extend that assignment and ask teachers, new and experienced, to pause for a moment and reflect upon their journeys as practicing educators. Do they resemble at all the paths they initially visualized or dreamed of? Or have they lost control of their journeys, trapped in packaged curricula and school climates that restrict rather than inspire? Have they rolled off their roads completely, entrenched in routine and shallow practices that disregard caring interactions with students? Do they find themselves behind barriers to dynamic teaching that is involved, as Ayers imagined, "in the wider world of children and families, of communities and neighborhoods, of society . . . struggling alongside others to improve society" (1993, p. 132). Is their journey toward the ideal of the transformative education that Freire (2000). envisioned beneath his mango tree or have they been sidetracked down a narrow path prescribed by standards-driven demands and burdensome testing mania.

I recently attended a workshop given by a facilitator who repeatedly mentioned her postdoctoral work at Harvard. She recommended that teachers write the state standard they are currently working on every day across the top of their classroom chalkboards. This will ensure high scores on testing, she assured the audience of urban educators, because children will know exactly what they are supposed to be learning. Her talk was directed at teachers of diverse students. The audience wrote copious notes, asked for her flyers, and did not challenge a word she said. This advice was given near the end of the program, and I admit that I also did not question the presenter who never allowed audience participation time. But I spoke of my disappointment in her directives to the group with whom I sat when the program concluded. I will not be led quietly down the road she recommended. I find it confining, restrictive, and detached, not to mention burdensome. No one else seemed to feel that way. The promise of high test scores had made a big impression. As I thought more about it, I decided that I wanted to write my own single standard to put across the chalkboards of American schools for the entire year. It would sound something like this:

> To live, learn, and think with respect and compassion and to engage positively with the world around us (with the hope of transforming it in a thousand small ways)

I may be pushed into educational trenches with the children who are often undervalued in this world, but I will not lose sight of my personal view of meaningful, great education. My path as a teacher has not been a romanticized one, winding blithely down a fairy-tale countryside road. I have walked on the crushed glass of mean streets and know the importance of challenging students and maintaining high goals for them without losing my ability to be compassionate. I have heard their stories and seen their settings. And I have learned that a pressing desire of all students is to be recognized and cared about as they navigate their own educational journeys. May we, as educators, strive to walk a mile in our students' shoes, hear their stories, and those of others in our profession, and realize that we do not have "jobs" but rather vocations, calling us to action and lifting us to envision attainable transcendent goals.

What Do You Think?

1. Careers are often forged by the values of a family and the early emotional events in our lives. How have your family values encouraged you, or perhaps hindered you, in pursuing a career as a teacher?

2. Think of a beloved teacher you have had. What was it about that teacher that you most remember, qualities that you would like to emulate in your own teaching?

3. What would you consider in your common practices or points of view as being part of your culture (i.e., assumptions about "the way things should be" that are actually culturally driven rather than driven by necessity)?

4. What frightens you about working with minority students? What excites you? Explain.

5. Do you think the author was acting "professionally" in visiting her students in their homes and witnessing the hardships of their lives? What would you do? Explain.

6. Do you think that the author stepped over the line by visiting her minority students, witnessing the hardships of their lives, and finding sources of food and clothing for them? Explain your answers. How would you achieve an ethos of caring and concern in your classroom?

7. The author does not specifically articulate her philosophy of education. Can you suggest from the chapter what her philosophy might be? How would her philosophy differ from yours?

Suggestions for Further Reading

I ask my adult students to read Francisco Jiménez's *The Circuit: Stories from the Life of a Migrant Child* (1997) and its sequel *Breaking Through* (2001) for an eye-opening account of a Mexican child's struggle for an education under the challenging circumstances of migrant life. Panchito, a character Jiménez based on his own experiences as the son of migrant workers in California, finds himself feeling anxious with headaches in classrooms where he cannot understand the language, where he feels turned "inside out" (p. 14). In *The Circuit*, he relates beautifully ordinary stories of teachers tutoring him on their lunch hours and noticing his intellectual ability through his artwork, and of a principal helping his brother find a nonagricultural job to support the family. There is hardly a dry eye in the classroom when Panchito relates the loss of his *librito*, a small notebook he keeps to study English vocabulary while working in the fields. Or when, while doggedly practicing an assignment to recite the opening of to the Declaration of Independence, Panchito is picked up by *la migra*, the Border Patrol, as his history class begins. *Breaking Through* follows Panchito and his brother Roberto into high school where he confesses that he loved gym class because it was the first time in his life that he could take a shower. When his gym shoes are stolen, a resourceful Panchito finds a pair in the city dump so that his teacher stops "taking off points" because his gym uniform is incomplete. Eventually, Panchito "picks up" English and, in a triumph of perseverance and conscientiousness, graduates from high school with a college scholarship.

In *Crashboomlove* (1999), a novel in verse by Juan Felipe Herrera, we meet another child of migrant workers whose father, unlike Panchito's hard-working dad, abandons the family. César Garcia is turned off to school and spirals downward into a world of punitive procedures for failing students in the San Joaquín Valley's academic administrative process. In a piercing diatribe, filled with inventive word crafting, Herrera writes, "Erase everything after school . . . erase the yearbooks that are too expensive . . . erase the English handouts on Shakespeare that don't make sense . . . erase the front row . . . I am going down . . . we are the after school stars . . ." (pp. 27–28). César dabbles in gang activities and eventually crashes his car while drag racing. The accident helps him to turn his life around and spurs his mother, intimidated by school officials earlier, to become involved in her son's education. The poetic story gives teachers a glimpse into the world of a student who feels alienated by the curriculum he is offered and angry at the blows life has dealt him.

In another book by Herrera for young children, we see a migrant student who refers to himself as *The Upside Down Boy/El Niño de Cabeza* (2000), who gets everything mixed up in a school that does not use his language. A young African American teacher ends up taking him under her wing, and he dedicates the storybook to her with actual photos in his afterword.

Alma Flor Ada in *My Name Is Maria Isabel* (1993) and S. Yamate in *Ashok by Any Other Name* (1992) write poignant stories of how immigrant students feel, one Mexican, one Asian Indian, when their names are not accepted in mainstream school situations.

Sandra Cisneros, in her vignettes from her childhood on Chicago's north side, includes stories of her feelings of embarrassment in schools callous to her needs.

All of these books can instruct teachers with their concrete, personal stories of marginalized students' school experiences. Readers see both wonderful and disturbing portraits of various teachers' responses to diversity in their classrooms.

In addition, there are teachers' stories of working with diverse students. I remember being moved as a young reader by a biography of Helen Keller describing the tenacity of her teacher, Ann Sullivan, in working with her. Later, when I was a teenager, *The Water Is Wide* (Conroy, 1972) told me the dramatic story of a white teacher dedicated to the African American children of Yamacraw Island off South Carolina. These stories helped me, as a young reader, to envision the role of teachers, particularly of a teacher of non-mainstream students.

In *Of Borders and Dreams: A Mexican-American Experience of Urban Education* (1996), I tell my own story of working with Alejandro Juarez in Chicago's public and private schools with the hope that it will encourage teachers of Latino students to try to look more holistically at the lives their students live. Greg Michie's *Holler if You Hear Me: The Education of a Teacher and His Students* (1999) tells with compassion, hope, and humor of his experiences as a teacher of Latino and African American adolescents. His writing is grounded in his teaching and learning experiences and gives teachers a wonderful example of the power of careful observation and a willingness to see and hear students and change something that isn't succeeding. Jonathan Kozol's refusal to accept the invisibility he saw blanketed over children of poverty in the United States, particularly in New York City, is piercingly related in *Savage Inequalities* (1991) and *Amazing Grace* (1996). Vivian Gussain Paley of the University of Chicago shows teachers her in-depth, insightful descriptions of very young preschool children in her classrooms over the years. William Ayers in *To Teach* (1993) writes about a team approach to close observation with thick descriptions of students in a method created by Pat Carini as well as his own journey as a caring educator. These narratives of teaching experiences offer compelling classroom vignettes and useful models of activities and approaches to students of teaching. They provide realistic yet compassionate glimpses of teaching in America.

References

Ada, A. F. (1993). *My name is Maria Isabel*. New York: Atheneum.

Ayers, W. (1993). *To teach: The journey of a teacher*. New York: Teachers College Press.

Carger, C. (1996). *Of borders and dreams: A Mexican-American experience of urban education*. New York: Teachers College Press.

Carini, P. F. (1979). *The art of seeing and the visibility of the person*. Grand Forks: University of North Dakota Press.

Cisneros, S. (1984). *The house on Mango Street*. Houston: Arte Publico Press.

Conroy, P. (1972). *The water is wide*. New York: Bantam Books.

Freire, P. (2000). *Pedagogy of the heart*. New York: Continuum. (Originally published in 1997 in Portuguese as *À sombra desta Mangueira* [In the shadow of the mango tree]).

Greene, M. (1965). *The public school and the private vision: A search for America in education and literature*. New York: Teachers College Press.

Herrera, J. F. (1999). *Crashboomlove*. Albuquerque: University of New Mexico Press.

Herrera, J. F. (2000). *The upside down boy/El niño de cabeza*. San Francisco: Children's Press.

Jiménez, F. (1997). *The circuit: Stories from the life of a migrant child*. Albuquerque: University of New Mexico Press.

Jiménez, F. (2001). *Breaking through*. New York: Houghton Mifflin.

Kozol, J. (1991). *Savage inequalities: Children in America's schools.* New York: Harper Perennial.

Kozol, J. (1996). *Amazing Grace: Lives of children and the conscience of a nation.* New York: Harper Perennial.

Michie, G. (1999). *Holler if you hear me: The education of a teacher and his students.* New York: Teachers College Press.

Moll, L. (2001). The diversity of schooling: A cultural-historical approach. In M. de la Luz & J. I. Halcón (Eds.), *The best for our children: Critical perspectives on literacy for Latino students* (pp. 13–28). New York: Teachers College Press.

Moll, L., Amanti, C., Neff, D., & Gonzalez, N. (1992). Funds of knowledge for teaching: Using a qualitative approach to connect homes and classrooms. *Theory into Practice, 31*(2), 132–141.

Nussbaum, M. (1997). *Cultivating humanity: A classical defense of reform in liberal education.* Cambridge, MA: Harvard University Press.

Thomas, P. (1967). *Down these mean streets.* New York: Knopf.

Yamate, S. (1992). *Ashok by any other name.* Chicago: Polychrome.

Part IV

Practices

8

Positive Relationships for Effective Teaching

Teresa Rishel

Paul Chamness Miller

This chapter is unique compared to the others included in this book in that it was written by two people with different professional backgrounds. The first author has experience as a principal and the second author as a classroom teacher. This combination will afford the reader an opportunity to gain insight from both perspectives. In order to help the reader follow the narrative of the teacher and the narrative of the principal, I have divided each section of the chapter into two parts, one for the former and one for the latter. As is the case with the majority of the chapters, this work is not exhaustive in regard to the topic. I encourage the reader to consider what other relationships might be important in striving to be an effective teacher.

◆ ◆ ◆

Introduction

We have learned in our careers as educators that one of the important keys to success, whether it be in the classroom or the administrative offices of the school, is establishing effective and positive relationships with all those involved in the educational experience of the students. Effective teachers realize that the social and academic success of the students is dependent on the forging of relationships between students, parents, and the community. In forming and maintaining these relationships, interesting dynamics are at play, particularly from the differing viewpoints of a teacher and a principal. However, while one may assume that there is little commonality between the two perspectives, in reality, a common vein runs through both. This common vein is the students, because the relationships that we establish in our profession are to meet their needs, regardless of preconceived notions of our respective roles.

Relationships With Students

A TEACHER'S PERSPECTIVE

I had the opportunity to teach in an urban school in Houston, Texas. This particular school was the largest of the city schools, where the majority of the students were nonnative speakers of English. The largest population was Spanish speakers, most of whom came from Mexico and El Salvador. The next largest group was Vietnamese. This particular job also happened to be my first teaching assignment, and I immediately discovered how little I really knew about establishing relationships, especially with students whose cultural and linguistic identity was unfamiliar to me. Many of my students were still in English as a second language (ESL) classes, and I was expected to teach them French! I knew that if I was going to be effective, I would not be able to rely on their knowledge of the English language, something that I took for granted when completing my student practicum in an upper-middle-class suburban school. But in order to understand how to reach these students, I knew that I would need to spend time getting to know them in order to build relationships. I first decided that I would need to understand more about their cultures and languages as a whole, and from there attempt to work on relationships with the individual students. This would not be an easy task since I had nearly 180 students.

There were many opportunities to get to know the students as individuals. An effective technique that I use regularly begins on the very first day of class. I ask each student to write me a letter describing a little bit about himself/herself. I specify that I want to know what interests they have in music, food, sports, and other activities. I also ask them to tell me why they want to learn French. In addition to writing about their own lives, I like to ask the students to think about what they expect from me as their teacher and what they will expect from themselves as the students.

This is a simple task that I learned from my mentor teacher, but an activity that I use at the beginning of every course that I teach, whether in high school or at the college level. Based on the responses from this activity, I am able to plan my lessons to include that which interests them. It also helps me keep up with what is "cool" for the age group. Throughout the course, I attempt to draw more personal information from the students as appropriate. This information not only helps me understand the students on an individual level, but I am also able to discuss topics with the students that I know they find interesting. These simple steps allow me to create a two-way street in my classroom; it is a mutual time of sharing with one another, thereby establishing those crucial personal relationships that contribute to the positive learning environment that I strive to create.

An example of this two-way street came from my experiences as a beginning teacher. Many of my students felt that since I was teaching them "my language" they should teach me theirs as well. So as I taught my students French; they taught me Spanish and Vietnamese. My interest in their language and culture demonstrated to them that I valued them as individuals, opening the door for an even greater experience in my class-room. It was at this point that I began to understand the importance of a reciprocal relationship with my students.

There were also opportunities for me to get to know my students on an individual level. I remember one student from my time in Houston, who still holds a special place in my heart. From her letter, I was able to learn of her religious beliefs. Her religion was really important to her in all that she did, and she loved to talk about it. I expressed to her my own interest in religious issues, which opened the floodgates for conversations throughout the entire year. She often came to me before or after school to ask my thoughts on religion. While this is a very sensitive topic in public schools, I knew that if I dismissed her because of my fear of addressing her concerns, I would have lost the opportunity to have that relationship with her. Instead, I let her ask whatever she wanted. I also knew that she did not have many friends at school, perhaps partly of her own choice. Once our relationship was established through the discussions of religion, she trusted me enough to confide in me when dealing with other problems.

I knew that eventually the inevitable would come, and it finally did; she invited me to come to her church. I was reluctant to go because I knew that I did not share in her beliefs, and the services were in Spanish, a language that I did not speak. But if I did not go, I knew she would be disappointed. So I went, and despite my ambivalence, she was the happiest girl there that night. While many teachers may draw the line at going to church with their students, I was certain that, in this instance, my student would have somehow felt dismissed.

My second teaching experience was in a small, rural school where the dynamic was completely different from what I experienced in the urban community of Houston. My classes were small and there were few students of color. Once again, I started the school year by asking my students to write me a letter of introduction with the same litany of questions so that I could get to know them as quickly as possible. Despite the largely homogeneous exterior of my students, I quickly began to see their individual interests and personalities surface. We also began to establish our own relationship that existed only within the walls of my classroom, with our own running jokes and stories.

Something that I learned very quickly in teaching is that students want their teachers to like them and to value them. I had one student who commented one day that she thought that I did not like her. This comment took me aback because I have never disliked a student, although I have disliked some behaviors that surfaced in particular students. I knew, however, that if I did not address the issue quickly, this student might never give me her best effort. I asked her to stay after class one day and we sat down and talked about her feelings. We were able to work out the issue and move on.

In addition to what occurs in the classroom, it is interesting how students want their teachers to see them excel elsewhere. Many of my students were involved in drama, music, or athletics; often they asked me to attend their performances or events. Not only did my attendance at these important occasions build the students' morale, it also gave me a better picture of these students as individuals. I was able to use these opportunities to further strengthen the relationship I had with them.

I remember one student in particular at this school to whom I had taken a particular liking. He was a "gothic" student, dressed frequently in black, and was labeled by other teachers and students as "weird"; many were even intimidated by him. Despite his eccentricity, I discovered the intelligence this young individual possessed. Once I knew that he was fascinated by medieval history, I was able to grab his attention by including information in my lessons that interested him. He was also particularly gifted in language learning, despite his aversion to traditional teaching methods. He commented one day that I was one of the few teachers who appeared to feel comfortable around him and he appreciated how I treated him as an individual. As a result of our mutual respect, we developed a relationship that provided an environment that was conducive to his learning French. This positive relationship even sparked an ambition in him to consider going to college (something which was out of the question just a few months earlier) to become a French teacher.

A PRINCIPAL'S PERSPECTIVE

One of the greatest joys in my 17 years as an educator was the time I spent as an elementary principal. I had the opportunity to interact with students of all ages, getting to know them in a variety of situations. The best part was not having to be responsible for grading what they said or what they did; for the first time, I was able to just enjoy them. My administrative experience took place in an elementary school (K–6) in a small, rural community in the Midwest. Of the three elementary schools in the district, mine was the largest with a student population of about 350. Diversity was defined mostly in terms of social class, with low-income families and the extremely poor juxtaposed with the middle class and a few professionals (e.g., doctors, lawyers, a judge). The community had a high unemployment rate, mostly skilled labor employment, and little economic growth. Industries had left the community over the years, providing the residents with few options to work locally. A main focal point of the community was the school, the only place where many students could interact with adults outside of the home and have the opportunity to participate in clubs, sports, and activities. In light of the importance placed on school, community members held school officials and teachers in high regard.

As principal, opportunities for me to get to know the students were endless. There were always students engaged in activities somewhere in the school, unlike my seeing them only in the context of the classroom. One way that I established relationships with students was to go to the cafeteria twice a week while they ate lunch. I visited with them, announced upcoming events of interest, and encouraged them to participate. I also used this opportunity to announce the names of students who had successes in academics, extracurricular clubs, sports, and exemplary behavior; this public acknowledgment of their successes brought applause from everyone. However, the best and most memorable moments were when I announced the students having a birthday that week. The birthday students stood as I led the rest in singing, while simultaneously motioning the words in sign language. Students quickly learned how to sign the birthday song and would often request that we omit the vocal portion of it. It was invigorating to watch a room full of students, silently and in unison, using sign language to communicate. This activity sparked their interest in learning more sign language as the year progressed.

During inclement weather, recess was held indoors. Because students and teachers alike grew quickly frustrated from the confined quarters, and student behavior worsened, I started a yo-yo club at noon recess. Interested students would bring a yo-yo to school every Friday and extras were available for students who could not afford one. Since yo-yos were prohibited at school, the noon club became very appealing to them. The only rule was that the yo-yos had to remain out of sight the remainder of the school day and on the school bus. If students breached the rule, they were no longer allowed to participate. Within a few weeks, and with no problems from breaking the rule, the gym was packed with students playing with yo-yos. Laughter filled the gym as students first impressed each other with their yo-yo expertise, and then taught others how to perform the tricks. As the club supervisor, I had to block out an hour each Friday, which is a major accomplishment for a principal. However, because the mental and social health of the students was important to me, I made every effort to make sure the club met. As a result of the weekly club, which eventually became a good-weather event also, I was able to establish good relationships with the students. It was a time for fun.

One of the most significant relationships I established was with a fourth grader, Chris (pseudonym), who struggled with the transition from his reputation of poor behavior. Chris held the "bad boy" image and wanted desperately to change it. Through his transition, he lost many friends and gained few new ones. Former friends found his new demeanor less attractive, while the other students did not trust the new version. Chris struggled to find a level of acceptance and often shared how difficult it was to keep trying. One Monday, Chris came to me and asked if I would attend his baptism at church the following Sunday, because his mother refused to go. As he shifted nervously from side to side, exhausting his explanation of why he wanted me to attend, he looked up with hopeful expectation. I felt I couldn't refuse his invitation even if it meant crossing a boundary that I was hesitant to cross. Chris was trying to improve, and he needed my support regardless of what may be predefined "as appropriate." That Sunday, I attended the baptism and the reception that followed. Chris introduced me to everyone, proudly announcing, "This is my principal!" while they looked at me with surprise and disbelief. I felt uncomfortable at first, but soon remembered the importance of connecting school to students' personal lives.

I took advantage of every opportunity to be with the students. Since much of an administrator's job is filled with problem solving, discipline, and management, I welcomed the chance to interact with the students in a positive way. I knew that if I was feeling the pressures of the daily routine of school, they must be also. Undoubtedly, one of my favorite activities was one that I adopted from my former principal mentor. Each month, 20 to 25 students were chosen to go into town for pizza as part of the "Pizza-with-the-Principal" program. Students, ranging from small kindergarten children to adolescents, were chosen for displaying outstanding or improved academics, behavior, citizenship, or other areas where recognition was deserved. Our conversations over pizza were not usually about school, but about things that mattered most to them. Each month, I returned to the school with a more heartfelt realization of what was truly important to these students, and believe me, it was not about academics.

Other interactions included visiting students who attended a summer academic camp that was three hours from the school, teaching a sixth grader how to use sign language for a song she was performing at her church, and paying the college exam fee for a highly qualified high school student whose parent did not have the money. Obviously, each of these situations fell outside of the traditional responsibilities of a principal. The point of each was not to regale myself as an exemplary principal, but to find ways to connect to the students in order to make school a better place for them. These methods were successful for me as a principal, and would be applicable for teachers as well.

Relationships With Parents

A TEACHER'S PERSPECTIVE

Establishing relationships with parents is equally as important as the relationships built with students in order to ensure the success of the academic year. As previously mentioned, I spent my first year teaching in an urban school in Houston, Texas, where the majority of the students were English language learners. This usually indicates that the parents are also nonnative speakers of English, and in many cases my students' parents spoke very little English and relied on their children to help translate when it came to issues with school. Because I did not speak Spanish or Vietnamese, it was a challenge for me to establish strong relationships with parents. I usually resorted to asking a colleague who spoke the parents' language to do the speaking on my behalf in order to ensure that my message was understood and received. I felt distanced from the parents because of my lack of ability to communicate in their language, but was fortunate to have colleagues to whom I could turn in my time of need.

In the second school district where I taught, developing relationships with parents was easier because I was able to communicate directly with them. One of my first experiences with the parents at this school was at our open house. This was an evening sometime during the first month of the school year when the parents came to the school to have dinner with the faculty and then follow their child's daily schedule in an abbreviated format. During the parents' visit in each classroom, we talked about our curriculum, discussed the kinds of activities and projects we had planned for the academic year, and answered the parents' questions. One of the primary purposes for this event was to provide the teachers and the parents with an opportunity to meet and begin developing relationships.

These relationships that I developed were vital to my success as a teacher. For example, if I was experiencing difficulty with a student, having already established a relationship with parents made dealing with the situation easier. I remember a particular student in my classroom, whom I'll call "Nate," who started the year out on a strong note. I had met his parents at the open house earlier in the fall where we were able to get to know each other and where I was also able to learn more about Nate and his particular situation. As the semester progressed, however, their son's performance began to decrease in quality, to the point where he did not do any work at all, despite my efforts to get him back on track. I arranged for a meeting with his father and his counselor, who were adamantly opposed to his dropping French. I learned from my previous contact with his parents that Nate enjoyed developing Web sites and, in fact, had his own business designing Web sites for local businesses. His father and I decided that what might be a good way to help him get through my class was to use his skills in Web design for French purposes. I, therefore, asked him to create a Web site that his classmates could use to review for their final exam. This worked out really well, providing a medium for me to instruct Nate in French, but in the context of Web design. This enhanced his motivation to learn French in a situation that was more familiar to him, thus resulting in a considerable increase in his performance in class. Having established a prior relationship with his parents afforded me the opportunity to come up with an alternate plan to help Nate succeed in my class.

Another part of teaching a foreign language is providing the students with exposure to the language or culture outside of the classroom. I was fortunate to have restaurants nearby that prepared the cuisine of France and other francophone countries. To ensure the safety of my students, I always insisted on having parents serve as chaperones. In addition to the supplemental adult supervision, these events provided me with opportunities to get to know the parents and for them to get to know me, developing a relationship that would prove to be beneficial in the future. One year, the Spanish teachers and I organized a trip to Europe with our students. We had more students interested in the planned excursion than we had anticipated, and thus required several chaperones to join us. Having spent time with parents prior to these special events provided me with contacts to whom I could turn for help. I appreciated how much time many parents were willing to contribute for the sake of their children's education. All I needed to do was ask.

A PRINCIPAL'S PERSPECTIVE

Early in my professional career, I learned the importance of establishing and maintaining positive, or at the very least, communicative relationships with parents and guardians. I cannot emphasize enough the impact that substantial and consistent communication with parents has on a successful school year. Administrators and parents working together are essential to student success; it is not two distinct groups working separately. Some principals have difficulty accepting this, and often admonish parents for their supposed lack of interest, responsibility, or support. Too often, a principal's values and beliefs about good parenting interfere with accepting that parenting is not an exact science or an absolute. Communication breaks down when principals and parents get caught up in an "authority versus authority" struggle, where each positions herself/himself as the "true" authority in the child's life. The adults engage in a contest based on what they each believe to be in the best interests of the child.

My beliefs about the most effective treatment of and attitudes toward parents are based on years of learned experience. In the beginning, I, too, found that it was often difficult to put aside my own ideas and beliefs of what should be expected from parents. However, when I failed to do so, power struggles ensued and the absence of collaboration between the parents and myself resulted in a lack of support for the child. Although I thought I was correct in my assumptions, for example, that caring parents always attended school events, I quickly learned otherwise. I found that the parent's form of caring must be accepted and appreciated by the principal, not devalued or deconstructed. As I began to be more accepting and open to a variety of parenting styles, I started to understand the importance of our relationships, even when we did not always agree. Similarly, some of the biggest problems I saw as a principal were when teachers viewed parents as intrusive in the educational system, yet the same educators were astonished when parents did not respond to teacher requests for conferences and meetings. Students were caught in the middle like pawns in a power play.

From my experiences as a teacher and administrator, I formed some basic beliefs about parents. Parents must be treated with respect at all times. This sounds simple, but true respect is often lost in the midst of conversations where one side is attempting to get the other side to agree to an arrangement, method, placement, and so on. The lifelong role that parents play in the child's life is often overlooked when the emphasis is on a particular moment in the school year.

Conferences, whether they are parent-teacher conferences or meetings with the principal, should be a time of sharing what each adult knows about the child and how this knowledge can be merged to allow the best possible situation for student learning. As the consistent adult in the child's life, a parent's knowledge of the child must be valued by the school. Often, the conferences end up feeling like a bashing session to parents, where they are held captive to hearing a barrage of negative aspects about their child. It is important to recognize the alienation and confrontational stance that results from conferences such as this. Parents should be treated as significant partners in the child's education.

As guests in their child's school, parents should be treated with honor. They should feel welcome, with the classroom and school as common ground, and they should not feel as though they are walking into an arena that belongs to someone else. Shortly after the beginning of each school year, it is customary for schools to prepare for call-out or open-house night, where parents visit their child's classroom and become familiar with school and classroom rules and procedures. In schools where I taught, students were not invited to attend, but many did anyway. I find it interesting that this event usually resulted in parents being treated as students themselves in that they are asked to sit, listen, and learn, followed by a period of question and answer. Papers are handed out containing information the parents will need to know for the school year and the parents are then dismissed. This method works well for certain parents and teachers, in part because most parents who attend are the ones who liked and enjoyed school, so they find this format familiar and acceptable. Additionally, parents who attend these school events are typically the parents of the academically and behaviorally successful students. However, for parents who struggled in school, did not like school, or had bad experiences at school, call-out nights and open houses are not welcomed and enjoyable events.

I found myself struggling with this recurring issue and felt there was surely a more inviting way to treat parents as guests, as well as offer the students an open invitation to attend. My struggles led to the establishment of the "Sundae Sunday" event, where the teachers and PTA (Parent Teacher Association) worked together to make call-out night a welcoming event for everyone. For Sundae Sunday, ingredients to make ice cream sundaes were available to parents and students throughout the evening, which began with an open forum in the gym. I introduced myself and the faculty, talked for a few minutes about the excitement a new school year brings, and encouraged their involvement in the school. As was customary when I was a classroom teacher, I gave them the following advice: "If you don't believe everything your child tells you about me, then I won't believe everything your child tells me about you." This was always met with a roar of laughter and nodding of heads, but also with an understanding of the truthfulness in it. Sundae Sunday was held on a Sunday evening, not only for the purpose of using the catchy title, but to allow a larger portion of parents and students to attend since most parents are not working and students are not involved in extracurricular activities. We also planned call-out night around evening church activities, therefore minimizing as many hindrances to attendance as possible. By making all parents, as well as students, feel welcome, yearly attendance and involvement grew at the call-out night and, later, at the parent-teacher conferences.

Another way that I established positive relationships with parents was to invite them to participate in planning school activities or to sit on committees they usually would not have been invited to serve on. For example, parents who otherwise would not have been considered were asked to assist on the textbook adoption committee. Parents with particular skills or talents (i.e., playing an instrument, crafting, singing, etc.) were invited to share at school events. The goal was to link the parents to the school in an interesting and participatory manner, where they could be actively involved, not just passive participants. They also had access to the "open door" policy, which was both literal and figurative in meaning. One door of my office led to the main office, while the other door opened to the school entranceway, where parents, students, and visitors entered the building. From the first day I arrived, I left the door to the entranceway open as a gesture of welcoming parents and students to my office. Several comments were made by parents who noticed the open door. One parent in particular told me that her children had been going to the school for eight years and she had never seen the door open. She said it made her feel welcome—and she liked it. Growing up, I always wondered what went on behind "the principal's door!" and imagined all sorts of torture that occurred there. By literally opening the door to the entranceway, it signaled that parents were important. The figurative open-door policy meant that parents did not have to make an appointment to see me, and if I was available, they could stop by anytime.

Most important, I worked closely with parents whose children were having behavioral or social difficulties at school. In many cases, when it became apparent that a student had recurring discipline problems, I took the extra measure of establishing a good relationship with the parents early on. In many disciplinary situations, tempers flare easily, attitudes quickly emerge, and situations escalate. When a good foundation has already been established with parents, it is easier to communicate with them if the student's behavior becomes more serious. I had learned this with a particularly aggressive parent during my first few years of teaching, but there had been no further incidents. However, during my first year as a principal, an episode occurred that brought about a new perspective for me in dealing with parents.

Repeatedly, a student named Ryan (pseudonym) was sent to my office for poor behavior, ranging from covert bullying to physically harming other students. His aggression would lay dormant for several weeks, then emerge and remain for sustained periods of time. As his aggressive acts became more violent in nature (at the same time the zero-tolerance policies were implemented), I invited Ryan's parents to help me brainstorm a solution. I was caught totally off guard when his parents revealed that they endorsed, in fact encouraged, his behavior. Ryan's father was adamant that Ryan would not "be a wimp" or avoid confrontation out of fear of breaking a school rule. It was also suggested by his parents that I would be held responsible for any discipline Ryan received at school because of his need to protect himself. Astonished and frustrated, I shared that Ryan would be held to the same standards and rules as other students, regardless of the circumstances. The meeting ended with a harshness that I had not anticipated or desired. I was worried about Ryan.

A few months later, Ryan hit a student in the face with his fist at noon recess. The student, bleeding from his nose and mouth, was taken to the hospital. Ryan was detained in the office and his parents were contacted. Ryan's father showed up soon, and on discovering that I was busy, paced the main office like a tethered bulldog. I could hear his steps, back and forth, and his repeated questions to the secretary, who had phoned my office to announce his arrival. When I buzzed the secretary to send him to my office, she came instead. Quietly, she warned me about the father's violent reputation in the community, of his being known as the town bully since he was in junior high when he was continually expelled for fighting. She shared further that he had been raised by an alcoholic father who had also been the town bully. She warned me not to "mess with him or tick him off," and suggested that I have a male teacher attend the meeting, or leave the door open so she could hear if I needed help.

Shaken by her words, I asked Ryan's father to my office, closing the door behind him. It was still the middle of the afternoon of a typical school day. Parents, teachers, and students would be wandering in and out of the main office, so there was no way that I could keep the door open and maintain student and parent privacy. Ryan's father did not pause to listen to what had happened, but began ranting and raving about Ryan being in trouble. Pounding his fist on my desk, he reminded me that he supported Ryan's right to defend himself, and that if Ryan didn't, he would punish Ryan himself. At first, I became agitated at the way Ryan's father was handling himself, then I decided it would be best to let him vent and avoid interrupting him. It was one of those moments where I had to let the parent react in a manner that was best for him, instead of my ideas of what a parent should do. Ryan's father continued without any words or arguments from me, until he finally sat down and just looked at me in anger. I simply stared back and allowed the silence. He slowly began explaining that his father had expected him to be a bully and because of that, he was never accepted at school, nor did he like school. He said he wished he could do it over and that he thought he could have done a good job at school. Tears ran down his face as he finally released what seemed like years of pent-up frustration over what had happened to him. He apologized to me for his actions and thanked me for listening. Then he vowed that he would support the school rules and that Ryan would also. This incident brought to light, once again, that parents often act and react, not out of willful violation of school policy, but as reflective of past life experiences. The role of the educator is to be patient and understanding, cognizant that there may be hidden reasons behind others' actions.

Relationships With the Community

In addition to establishing relationships with parents and students, it is also crucial for teachers to establish relationships with others in the community. The communities in which I taught had much to offer the schools as a way to contribute to their students' education.

A TEACHER'S PERSPECTIVE

I have always made an effort to locate people in the community who are able to contribute to my students' learning process. As I was a French teacher, it goes without saying that I would have guests come to my classroom who were native speakers of the language. I have had many friends from French-speaking countries come to the classroom to talk about their culture and to give my students opportunities to practice their language skills. We also had a student from Haiti in our school who came to my classroom on a regular basis to speak with the students. Several of my colleagues also sought out opportunities to involve the community in the learning process by soliciting the expertise of individuals as guest speakers.

In my experience as a teacher, involving the community meant more than having visitors in my classroom. As previously mentioned, in organizing our trip to Europe, we knew that many of our students who wanted to participate did not have the financial means to do so on their own. As a result, we approached several members of the community to help us raise funds for those students who needed assistance. A local photographer also provided a discount for students who needed passport photos. Other community members assisted in a variety of ways to make this trip feasible for so many students. It was largely because of the contributions of the community that this learning experience was possible. I learned that even though I teach in a room with four walls, learning should include the incorporation of outside resources and opportunities.

Establishing relationships with the community is more than asking members of the community to come to or contribute to the school. It is also about bringing the students outside the classroom into the community itself. For example, I was fortunate to have a large midwestern university with a department of hotel and restaurant management near the second school where I taught. Part of the program was to prepare a series of international dinners throughout the academic year, some of which were French and Caribbean. Because of my connection with the university community, I was able to arrange to bring a group of students to these dinners on a regular basis. This benefited the students because they experienced a culture other than their own through the food that was prepared. It also brought them to a college campus, which might have in some small way nudged them to consider higher education.

Professional organizations have also helped me establish ties to the community. These organizations continually informed me of various community activities related to French, which afforded my students other opportunities to experience francophone culture outside of my classroom. For example, I took my students to see plays in French, hear music written by francophone composers, among others. These activities demonstrated to my students that the community provides many occasions to use what one learns in school outside the confines of the classroom.

Relationships with the community are not one-way streets. In other words, it is not just about what the community can give to the school or the students. It is also about what the students can give to the community. For instance, by taking my students to eat meals or attend plays, the school is supporting these cultural venues by providing business, while the restaurants, theaters, and symphonies are educating the students. In one school where I taught, I chartered a French Honor Society. We decided that part of our society should be providing service to the community, and one way to do that was to sponsor a poor Haitian child through a nonprofit organization. The members of the society raised the funds to sponsor the child and then we contacted the organization to make the donation. There were other organizations within the school that engaged in similar activities as a means for giving back to the community.

In working with the community, I have learned that I can bring French to life and avoid the "you will use this someday" syndrome that is a common mantra heard in the classroom. In essence, community relationships enhance the teacher's effectiveness and the students' education. These relationships also provide much needed support to the community as a whole.

A PRINCIPAL'S PERSPECTIVE

Good relationships with community members are as important as those made with students and parents. The community is the backbone, the support system of the local schools, not only financially, but also in providing resources to help with the needs that would not otherwise be met. Many community members have attended these very same schools or have children who did; they are familiar with what goes on in the life of the school district. Although hidden at times, they have tremendous influence on what occurs. Community members, who possess a wealth of knowledge, talent, and resources, want to be involved and should be as much as possible. They are usually waiting to be approached.

One of my first connections to the community was through the Pizza-with-the-Principal program that I described earlier. I explained the idea to the owner of the local pizza establishment, realizing that he was probably approached by the schools on a regular basis. We negotiated an agreement and the deal was set. As I drove away, I realized that in my excitement to start the program, I forgot to take into account how I was going to pay for it each month. As a teacher, I never had to consider the cost of what I wanted to do or how to find the money to support it; the principal sorted that out and gave me a yes or no on ideas that I submitted. It was strange to be on the other side of the situation. I had established a good relationship with the officers of the school PTA when I first arrived in the community, having learned from my teaching days that this organization was always willing to help make things happen for the students. I was fortunate, too, because this project included students from each grade, not a specific one, which was always better when working with a parent organization. I explained the program and they agreed to help with the costs, but not until after three months, because their budget was already set and approved for that time period. Because I was new to the district (and new to the position), I had not been involved in submitting budget requests for that school year.

Because I was so excited about the program, I went ahead with my plans and decided to pay the expenses myself until the PTA could do so. After the first month, as word of the program spread throughout the community and after the newspaper and school letter came out describing it, I began receiving calls from local businesses offering their financial support. I was astonished at the outpouring of interest, and by the second month of the program, it was fully funded by the community. When the PTA took over the costs after three months, many businesses continued to help with the expenses. I was humbled at the extraordinary measures of the local people in making the program a success for the students. The relationships established during the year with the businesses involved, as well as the PTA, set the foundation for a collaborative and exciting partnership between the schools and the community.

Another program that involved building relationships with the community was the creation of the Kids Care reading program, where students were bussed to the local nursing home to read to the residents. Each month, teachers chose two or three students to participate in the Kids Care program. Prior to reading aloud at the nursing home, the students selected a few books and practiced reading orally so they would feel comfortable. When I initially visited the nursing home to present my idea to the director, I was worried that some type of legal issues might prohibit the students from entering the facility. The director quickly set my mind at ease and fully endorsed the program. I believe she was more excited than I was, which was motivating to me. Sometimes good ideas are squashed by the lack of enthusiasm or cooperation of others, and in this case, it was quite the opposite. We mapped out a schedule of dates for each month and decided to begin the program the following month.

A few hours after returning to the school, I received a phone call from the director. She said she had presented the idea at the board meeting that afternoon, where it was accepted unanimously and with enthusiasm because it was such a novel idea. She said that the board decided it would supply baked goods and drinks for the students and residents after they finished reading. The students would escort their residents to the dining hall with the assistance of the employees and then enjoy time to visit. I could hardly express my joy at the idea, not only because the students would love it, but also because the community was going to such great lengths to make the program even better. In a few short hours, many people had banded together to make something happen that would benefit people from ages 5 to 95. I was impressed.

The program was a great success and students began begging their teachers to let them be the "reader" for Kids Care. It was exciting to see such unusual interest in an activity that was based on reading. From tiny kindergarten students reading picture books to sixth graders who had to choose "just one chapter?" to read, it was an invigorating educational experience. With the interest and support of the community, the program was able to take place. During the fourth month of the program, a television station from a neighboring city sent a reporter to film the students and residents. Several were interviewed and were fortunate to see themselves on TV that evening. It was a great day for the community!

Probably one of the most eventful moments that resulted from of community support was the culmination of the General Mills Box Tops for Education program, which rewarded schools with equipment and supplies based on the number of box tops that were collected over a specified period of time. The PTA adopted the program, encouraged the students to bring their collected box tops to school, and rewarded the winning class each month with a pizza party. In addition, an agreement was made that if the students reached a set goal by the end of the school year, the principal would sit on the top of the school building and eat Cheerios (a General Mills product). As the year progressed, the number of box tops grew in huge proportions. The PTA president told me the increase was due to the flyers distributed in the community and to information spread by word of mouth. Churches, clubs, and other organizations were giving the box tops they had collected to the school, and continuing to collect more. It was obvious that the community wanted to see me make a fool of myself!

A few weeks before the end of the collection time, the PTA president came to me to discuss how we would organize my promised feat of sitting on top of the school if the students met their goal, which she said they definitely would. We decided we did not really want the usual "principal would sit on top of the school" idea that was so popular at the time. After some discussion, it was decided that a better plan would be for me to sit in a plastic kiddie-sized swimming pool filled with Cheerios. The students would pour milk over me to "complete" the bowl of cereal. The president and I laughed as we imagined what this would look like. She left my office with the mission of advertising the upcoming PTA meeting where the principal would be featured as a key ingredient in a bowl of cereal.

Word spread quickly and soon the staff, students, parents, and community members were expressing that they couldn't wait for the big event. On the evening of the meeting, which was in May, the weather had turned very chilly. As I sat outside in the kiddie pool, I was shivering in my light jacket, knowing that soon cold milk would be poured on my head. At one point, I almost decided to call it off, and then I looked around at all of the students, parents, teachers, and community members who had come to watch. I knew I couldn't disappoint them, so I got in the kiddie pool and faced the inevitable. Within minutes, I was drenched in cold milk, looking up at laughing children and behind them, hysterical parents. The sounds of the evening will always be forged in my memory, as I don't recall having had so much fun at a school event. The PTA and the community worked together to create this atmosphere, to offer their students a moment for out-of-the-ordinary fun, and to create a memory that would last a lifetime. The efforts put into the Box Top program affirmed my belief in the power of community spirit.

Conclusion

In order to be an effective teacher, positive relationships must be established with those who are involved in the learning process, that is, the students, the parents, and the community. We hope our perspectives described in these narratives have given credence to this importance. The goal of this chapter was to give the reader real-life examples of how relationships impact students both academically and socially. These examples have demonstrated how relationships facilitate the responsibilities of the teacher and provide a way for the community to participate in their investment beyond what is required of them.

What Do You Think?

1. In what ways do the authors' perspectives about relationships parallel each other?

2. How did the authors step outside of their traditional roles to establish effective relationships? Given what you believe about teaching and learning, are there any situations that you would have handled differently from the authors? Explain your answer.

3. Have you experienced any situation in which a teacher or principal stepped outside of his or her traditional role to help you? Describe this situation. How did it affect your relationship with that teacher or principal?

4. In reflecting on your years as a student, has there ever been an occasion where you had an experience that negatively affected your relationship with a teacher or principal? Explain your answer.

5. With a partner or in a small group, brainstorm ways that you will establish positive relationships with your students' parents.

6. In a small group or with a partner, list the necessary keys for establishing effective relationships with students? Parents? community? In what ways will you implement these keys as you develop relationships with your students? Parents? Community?

Suggestions for Further Reading

Ellis, J., Small-McGinley, J., & DeFabrizio, L. (2001). *Caring for kids in communities: Using mentorship, peer support, and student leadership programs in schools.* New York: Peter Lang.
    This book provides several models and case studies of various programs for teachers interested in helping students develop mentor-protégé relationships with adults. The authors also discuss the establishment of student-student (peer) relationships and student involvement in leadership opportunities in school.

Olsen, G. W., & Fuller, M. L. (2002). *Home-school relations: Working successfully with parents and families* (2nd ed.). Upper Saddle River, NJ: Pearson Allyn & Bacon.
    This book offers advice to educators regarding the development of relationships with both students and parents. The authors stress the importance of getting to know the students and understanding their family and home life.

Paley, V. G. (2000). *White teacher.* Cambridge, MA: Harvard University Press.
    This narrative is the account of one kindergarten teacher who learned rapidly that in order to be successful at teaching her diverse group of students, it was imperative that she develop relationships with her students and their parents. These relationships afforded her the opportunity to get to know her students as individuals.

Wright, K., & Stegelin, D. A. (2002). *Building school and community partnerships through parent involvement* (2nd ed.). Upper Saddle River, NJ: Prentice Hall.
    This book is an excellent example of how a teacher might establish relationships with students, parents, and the community. The authors' focus centers on the family, with strategies for involving parents and other family as members of an ever-diversifying community in the learning process.

9

Amplifying Student Performance by Teaching and Modeling Responsibility

Crystal Reimer

C lassroom management is an issue that haunts most beginning teachers and one with which even seasoned teachers still struggle. The goal of this chapter is not to "teach" the reader how to manage a classroom; most teacher education programs have entire courses to do that. Instead, this chapter presents the personal experiences of one seasoned teacher who has taught all levels and multiple subjects. In addition to presenting several approaches and techniques that have worked for her in maintaining a positive learning experience in her classroom, the author leads the reader to think about how to approach the learning process in order to prevent behavioral problems as well as how to address students who may challenge the teacher. Keep in mind that classroom management, like many other topics in education, is a complex issue that may seem overwhelming and that lends itself to much debate. The reader should simply begin to think about what approach to this issue he or she might like to take when it is time to enter the classroom as a teacher.

♦ ♦ ♦

Introduction

Classroom management and discipline serve as critical components of teaching, especially for the preservice teacher. This book will undoubtedly be an important resource for those who have chosen to embark on one of the most difficult professions available. Yes, it is true that as well as being one of the most rewarding jobs, teaching students means teaching younger people, teaching moral character, and modeling responsibility. Educational training and pedagogy provide reference points toward making good choices for yourself and your individual students; a strong, philosophical background based on this training serves numerous purposes. Such a background will be helpful when you are creating a positive classroom, activating students' brains, tapping into the structural framework for why you should get up day after day and meet the students in the trenches of discovery, preparing for administrative appraisal systems, developing lesson plans within the curriculum, and implementing classroom management. These may be some of the concerns that a first-year teacher has prior to the first day of school. My worthiest objective will be to connect with you, prepare you, and inspire you to efficiently manage your students by enhancing your performance and theirs.

A Relatively Short Effective History

It truly seems like 142 anxiety attacks ago when I contemplated walking through my first day of ninth-grade English I class all on my own. Don't get me wrong, I had excellent preparation at Texas Woman's University to handle, explain, and understand a highly respected textbook on classroom management. With a little luck, I could probably recall the precise course number and professor, but that is useless information for you. I am forever grateful to my alma mater for my beginning and training, but really getting into the water is really getting wet all over. In my practicum hours, I scribbled countless ideas in my spiral notebooks. I stole from the best of them, the perfect ways to do this and to do that. I loved volunteering, and I didn't have to pay for all of the cool stuff they were so eager to let me see and experience. My student teaching was a mixed bag of nuts. I had three areas of certification, so I had three different assignments in the course of one semester. My elementary physical education assignment provided a litany of things not to do, how to get a classroom started ineffectively, and promotion of organized chaos for the masses. I learned valuable lessons from a teacher who cared nothing for classroom discipline; she unfortunately blamed the students for not wanting to learn. She said to me one day, "If they wanted to hear what I have to say, they will get quiet to hear it. Otherwise I am not going to spend 10 minutes trying to get them to listen." I had a few walk-aways (intangibles to be gleaned from any experience) from that enduring experience. It was there I learned about novelty and young students. My next assignment would put me in the high school setting, assisting two coaches. One female physical education teacher/coach and one male ninth-grade English teacher/football coach were my mentors for my student teaching assignments. I learned the art of and dedication to documentation from my physical education coordinating teacher, and from my part-time English/full-time football coach, coordinating teacher how to threaten and intimidate my students. Actually, that is where this skill of managing students entered my blood and forged the authenticity of the paragraphs that follow. You see, my classroom was fine as long as coach was present, but the minute he left, I was on my own. He told the students that I was to be respected by them, or else. I realized within moments of his leaving the room that I had a problem. The students smelled it more quickly than I could cover it up, so I began marking names, checking off for each additional infraction, and so on and so forth. This was not effective. I had to dig deep, pick up my own stick, and walk tall. I would fine-tune the art of getting busy and learning. I had to gather my senses, listen to what they were saying indirectly, and own this ninth-grade English class. I had to make it work for me and for them, without making threats that I could not implement. Students must be taught a huge lesson in humanity: to respect themselves, each other, and the privileges of learning.

Teaching Is an Act of Love

Of utmost importance is realizing that teaching children is an act of love; and if you love what you are doing, your students will love being in your class. Above all, your love of reaching your students must be greater than your passion for the subject matter, although your enthusiasm for what you teach will transfer to your students. At this beginning of this new stage in your life and career, I would earnestly hope that you have chosen the right career to earn a living and that you will enjoy pouring your heart and soul into it for the *benefit* of younger people. I aim in this chapter to omit failure in the discussion of managing your students. As you read of the numerous ways children can be taught and how to keep it legal, your classroom could appear like a three-ring circus whether following a student-centered approach or a teacher-centered approach to learning.

First Self-Exam

Regardless of the subject matter or grade level you teach, you must be able to examine yourself and your methods critically. As you begin thinking about teaching, ponder these two key questions: What's worth doing? Is this working for me or for the students? (Hellison, 2003). Within the first week, establish your expectations and your rules. I floated (a term to describe a teacher who "floats" from classroom to classroom) for the first three years, and classrooms did not belong to me, so I typed all of my daily assignments and kept them readily available to see. There would be absolutely no excuses for not following the procedures of the class and being successful. Keep in mind that creating a positive learning environment includes general principles such as an environment that is warm, safe, friendly, and supportive and allows students to develop and mature in meaningful academic settings. This is especially important during community-based learning experiences (e.g., field trips) as students and parents rely on us to be in control, to plan for contingencies, and to ensure security in every setting. As I pen these words, I remember my first years: I enjoyed control and I daydreamed of being rewarded for using my power in superior ways. I did not go as far as diagramming and charting the tally marks for each student's sniffles, but I foolishly prided myself in instilling fear into my students. It was exactly where I wanted to be.

When I Discovered My Look

No one ever taught me in my college classes that a certain look could stop students dead in their tracks or strike fear in them, or even that it could build a bridge of unspoken trust. It seemed to be a natural reaction when I looked at a student with such lamented disappointment in his inability to make a good choice at that moment. A student near my desk looked at me and felt very comfortable telling me that I looked angry, and she did not like it when I showed that kind of face to her. I will reveal that I am taller than the average female, and my voice is deeper than what you might expect, too. These physical features coupled with the looks I have developed are often effective in getting my students' attention. I would like to suggest that you take a good, long look in the mirror, and I do not mean with your best Ann Taylor or Kenneth Cole jacket adorning your body. Write out a few words you feel you might use frequently in your job and practice saying them in front of your mirror. What does your face mean when you look indignant, when boundaries have been crossed, and when your student is well on the way to becoming just the kind of person you would like to live next door to. You need to learn your face, your mouth, your eyes, and your arms; learn how you respond to all reactions. Facial coding has different implications, depending on the situation. Charles Darwin revolutionized the study of our "hard wiring," which is part of our DNA makeup. In the moment of reaction, our emotional response usually occurs within three seconds. Your students' response, in essence, will be as though they are holding a mirror for you to see how you are doing. You should, therefore, predetermine how you will respond to your students. Should the eyebrows be up or down? Should your mouth be opened or closed while smiling? Your eyes are windows into your thoughts; if you think it, your students will know it. The position of your arms can also tell your feelings. Take note of your feelings when you cross your arms, put your hands on your hips, fold them, tuck them under your chin, put them in your pockets, and when you gently place them on another person.

Cruella DeVil—aka Ms. Seville

It is beyond the scope of this chapter to delve into what your body means, but you should at least take an opportunity to create the look that can stop a student dead in his or her tracks. Word will get around the school about you. I know that I developed a reputation in the high school where I taught and apparently would have had Cruella DeVil running scared. Well, it was nothing compared to the accolade I would hope to receive one day in the footsteps of my English team; a lump of them had the scariest reputations on campus. Their last names were coupled with not-so-positive names that either rhymed or had classical connotations. A few choice examples included Saber Tooth Tiger, Death Rowe, Crying with Ryan, Carson City, No Pardon with Parham, and on and on; one teacher, however, was given a friendlier nickname because of her laid-back approach: San Antonio. I could not believe these unique names informally assigned, but many a truth is spoken in jest. As I began my career, I was told from the beginning that intimidation is the answer. All I really wanted was, in as few steps as possible, to unscrew their heads, ladle out the junk that did not work for any of us, and put their heads back on straight. I thought this would be easy enough until I realized I had to capture their hearts first. In recent studies and trendy books, there has been an emergence of arguments for teachers to develop better communication skills. I have no other method more effective in maintaining my classroom than active listening, in which I keep my eyes on the person speaking. When a student finishes a thought, I repeat it and look for the reception—verbally or non-verbally. Some students do not feel comfortable doing this, so as long as I am not crossing a cultural barrier or dealing with a student who cannot emotionally connect, I pay close attention to the student I am working with in order not to be offensive. I will never forget that students are looking to me for the answers and a possible role model to duplicate.

Looking Deep

After all the content is covered, the worksheets completed, the grades calculated, I have found myself at the end of the classroom objectives mastery schedule, still enforcing acceptable moral behavior in students. What does moral character look like? It will undoubtedly appear differently in each student, but nonetheless it looks like self-guided good decisions being made. Examining yourself as a person has proven to provide remarkable results in becoming an effective teacher. "We are all teachers and students to each other, and we are never finished in either role" (Jampolsky, 1991). An actor will train up to 20 years in perfecting the craft of acting, where the most powerful work is written about in more words than are ever uttered on stage. That is to say, the least important task for an actor is to speak during a performance. Like actors, talented teachers have less to say in reacting to student misbehavior; hence, a look is worth a thousand words (adapted from the picture metaphor). Therefore, allow more time for learning and less time for words in managing the specified tasks. I realized my ability to give directions could use a more efficient technique after a series of failures with students not finishing the in-class assignment to my expectations. I became more acquainted with each task before I presented it and created a system for giving directions in a 1–2–3 format.

Less Is More

Following the "less is more" philosophy invites room for knowing one's facial expressions and utilizing them in the midst of a variety of classroom scenarios, resulting in a decrease in the negative behavior choices of your students. For example, when you love your students, it is felt when you are in the room or when you reenter the room (stepping out for brief moments should be easy). If a "ringleader" has determined it's time to strike, a pleasing smile to the students who stayed on task works well, and a look of disappointment to the students who chose to get off track, especially coupled with close proximity, can go a long way in turning that behavior around. I'll discuss a little later possible prevention and intervention techniques. Last, Lavay, French, and Henderson (1997) listed four questions that are adaptable to any learning environment. Daily, I ask myself the following questions, tweaking my positive approach to classroom management:

- Are you tuned in to your students and what's going on in your classroom?
- Are you enthusiastic?
- Are you being flexible with the day's unforeseen events or the behavior agreement?
- Are you personable and approachable to your students?

In conclusion, it seems appropriate to know who I am, what I'm capable of, and letting that little light inside of me shine.

Planning

I have found that making an informal assessment of my students' current level of behavior at the beginning, about the first six weeks of the school year, establishes a baseline score from which to plan. As I have stated previously, I take my time with students personally, and our interactions are gifts from which both they and I can learn. A roadmap of how the students are behaving at the beginning of school is an indicator of possible behaviors that could be improved. My favorite areas are responding to teacher, relating to peers and equipment (classroom furniture), effort, and self-acceptance. These are broad strokes for evaluating the students, but I realized for myself what areas are most important to me in this educational life. The old adage, "Failing to plan is a plan to fail" has an incredible amount of merit when programming for the year.

Organization

Being organized is a skill I love sharing with my students; they need to know that everything has a place to rest and an adaptable regimented sequence. Lesson plans, the desks, and the electricity—these may all disappear tomorrow, but you must be ready for it to be where you left it all, as well as a "Plan B" if the impossible occurs. Organizing, creating a daily routine, and being consistent develop predictability in the learner, accountability in the teacher, and answers to all the "why" questions students could think of. This reminds me of the younger population of students who are greatly affected by the moon, food, and barometric pressure—these are important factors to be mindful of when your best student has turned into a most undesirable class member. I remember when I transitioned from high school to elementary school and thought, "I am a brand new teacher all over again." I learned quickly the beauty of novelty, silly rules, and that being sarcastic went a short distance with these younger students. I posted my rules, expectations, and consequences on the wall and made a beeline to the bookstore, searching out books that had information on meeting children's needs and surviving kindergarteners. Organization is limitless; it knows no boundaries when helping all class members succeed. In my first year of teaching physical education to 5- to 12-year-olds, I immediately wanted to call on the physical education teachers I had as a youngster and ask 100 questions on how to manage them. I had been away from this younger group for three years, and time had had its way with me. An avoidable reason for misbehavior by students is when they sense a scatterbrained teacher taking care of their work. Important information needs a home in your room. Solidifying a consistent base in which to put daily work, homework, makeup work, and extra-credit work is not overrated. I learned many enduring attributes of working with young children; they are best won with love, spirit, and organization.

Take Care

Students are better able to enjoy themselves in a classroom when there is an absence of stress and harm. Safety should never be compromised, and creating a safe place for students to learn freely, to learn free of ridicule, free of dangerous egos, free of damaging thought patterns, is essential. Consider taking a summer improvisation class at a nearby junior college. Being a student of humor could turn into a rewarding experience for your children and add a little marketability to your résumé (in case things do not work out). Have fun, laugh at yourself, and laugh with the students.

My Failure Turned Lesson

Up until a few years ago, I would switch gears to service students as needed. Then I realized that I was a behaviorist. I zeroed in on behavior more than anything else, including perfect topic sentences and lay-ups.

What kind of disciplinarian I was really governed how I approached students and their strict following of the Student Code of Conduct. Looking back, that first year was a zinger for hard lessons learned. I had a volatile student who was old enough to be a senior taking my English I course. All year long, I emphasized his positives. Knowing how he responded to public praise was key, and I tried to do it as much as I could. I made scripts to put in my book; when reading literature as a class, I made sure that I put his name in a sentence with a positive note each week. Now, I had heard that he might be experiencing some gang activity within his circle of friends, but I was determined to win him with education and make him see his potential. All year long, there had been missing assignments, little deals made without anyone knowing, and we kept his grade in the average range. Then the dreaded research paper came, and he stayed on top of the schedule, getting things turned in on time. I was really proud of him; he picked someone to admire and possibly follow. The research paper came due; he turned it in a few days late, but in pretty decent shape from the heaviness of it falling upon my desk. I looked forward to seeing what he had retrieved for this big important paper. I was shocked when I came across what I suspected to be plagiarism and/or the prospect that someone else must have written this. The paper contained sentences beginning with adverbial phrases and vocabulary he did not use in conversation or previous assignments. The red flags/signs were there (again, taking the time to get to know this student early on). The next day, I knew that I was going to have to call him out in to the hall to figure out what had happened here. It was a huge blow for him, especially after all we had been through together; he opted to have his sister write his paper for him. That came later, when we were in the office for him choosing to shove me in the hall the day I confronted him about the research paper. I know that it ended for us there; his culture machismo was crushed, and my hand held the gavel that did it.

Keep It Positive, Silly

In retrospect, I am sure I would have handled the preceding situation differently, but how? Shaping student behavior is vital; it's the similarity of criminals and saints. The same decision base is used all day to either make continuous good choices or not. This is one of my greatest challenges as a teacher, but as Jampolsky (2000) reminds us, "No life is without challenges. Make them a part of learning to love fully instead of becoming reasons not to." I have found that along with this advice it is best to state everything in the positive. For example, "Please enjoy your drinks in the cafeteria" (instead of "No drinks allowed in the classroom") or "Participate in gum chewing outside of the school at appropriate times" (instead of "No chewing gum"). This usually sends a positive message to students concerning what they can and cannot do in the classroom. On general behavior, I like to use directives that are simple and symbolic, or a sign (nonverbal cue) and/or a replacement word (verbal cue) or phrase to guide my students. For example, if I want them in their seats and quiet, I could simply raise my hand in a fist and slowly extend each digit until the expected behavior is met. I've found that this works well when coupling the nonverbal clue with, "I'm counting to see how long it takes to get your attention. I thought we agreed it takes five seconds for you to respond to me." The older the group, the more responsibility I give them. A good litmus test is early in the year. I usually begin by challenging them and giving them a tangible reward. I gauge their response time to stop what they are doing and listen to me. Eventually, personal satisfaction will be internalized and I will no longer need a physical reward. The younger the group, the sillier I can be. Walk around using proximity to get their attention. I have used these verbal cues with kindergarten to eighth graders with pleasing results: "Apples" = stand up, "oranges" = sit down; putting my index finger straight across my mouth indicates time to get quiet. I've even used whispering to see if they could hear me, providing positive praise to those who were listening. Other teachers use signs in the classroom, such as a red, yellow, and green traffic regulator. An assignment regulator allows students to self-govern their time on task and their abilities to control themselves under pressure. An example might be using the green to indicate that the activity has begun and will continue for 25 minutes (a clock next to green is helpful). This works well for independent and group work. The arrow on the yellow might indicate that five minutes remain for this activity. I feel these methods teach individual responsibility or team responsibility in a positive way. Students need cues; part of my job is to help navigate those who struggle with time constraints. The arrow on the red might be used to redirect them to a new task or signal a transition to another subject. And at the end of the day, I am not worn out by saying, "Don't do that" and "No" to him or her. I am surprisingly more energetic by keeping positive.

Student Portrait

I like to begin early in the first week of teaching elementary physical education by having my class create together the portrait of a child who is ready to learn. Ultimately, the equipment, the lesson plans, and me are all for the students. They decide what they are capable of doing; I, as their teacher, hold them to it, hook or crook. I am accountable for keeping them motivated to learn. I have realized the benefit of intrinsically motivated students; with even just one motivated child, the whole class can rise to the level of the water. Once one student is on board, others will follow, continually growing to meet your expectations. Using positive reinforcement, that is, tangibles, intangibles, reinforcers, and privileges, is very important. What does a student who is ready to learn look like? Are his or her feet under the desk, writing utensil with paper out on the desk, lips together, etc.? Similar to artists of various kinds, it is very typical for most teachers to begin with the end in mind. I love creating the Social Contract with my classes. I know it is scary to open my rulebook wide, but students never cease to stop amazing me with their incredible voices of justice. I expect the comedians to shine on such particular days, and I let democracy take effect. Most behavior expectations are very observable and by having the students participate in creating this portrait, it is no longer the teacher mandating the rules. Rather, I have created a learning community that is working together. My more conservative neighboring teachers will be surprised at how well the students will hold each other accountable when each has been a part of the entire process.

Learning Rules

I know the rules I need in order to perform the awesome job I have undertaken as an educator. What rules will be important to you? Talking at inappropriate times or paying attention will most likely be at the top of your list. Talking while the teacher is talking has so many implications that I think it is most effective when posted in the classroom for quick reference. If one or two students are not responding to your cues to be quiet, there are several solutions. I have used an unorthodox method to get their attention by making examples out of them and by teaching them that it is impossible to listen to two people at the same time. This activity consists of inviting the "talkers" up to sit in a chair, one of three at the front of the classroom. I can choose another person who wants to participate. The person in the middle of the three chairs is the designated first listener; the two on the sides are talkers. The talkers speak simultaneously to the listener about two different subjects for two minutes. At the end of the two minutes, the listener must convey what they were both telling him or her in detail. This will prove to be an impossible task—proving my point that two people cannot talk and be listened to effectively in a room. Believe it or not, I usually repeat over and over again that life, in general, is not that much fun without rules to embrace us and help us along the way, and that is solely what rules are. I wish for my students to learn to use the rules and not rebuke them. Rules are lifelong.

Sponges

Students love learning as much as they love my consistency. Set the precedent early; the first two weeks of school is the most valuable time of the year. I start with my plan of desired behaviors and work from them, not against them. Sponge activities, warm-ups, and icebreakers help me meet many of the desired objectives. First, these activities may encourage the students to be on time. Second, they serve as transitions for my great class, and they initiate being prepared for class (utensils, paper, brain on). Last, they engage the students immediately for learning, providing individualized learning at the individual's own discovery rate. As far as the construction of these sponge or other activities, I have turned vocabulary terms into a puzzle, crossword, or game show, or used an interactive classroom approach. My all-time favorite is to pin a term or definition to the students' backs as they enter the classroom. I ask them to sit in their seat with zipped lips and to wait for me to get all the students pinned with either a definition or term. They are allowed to ask one person one yes/no question, and then must move on to someone else. So, for this activity, a student would start by asking, "Am I a term?" The answer provides a clue as to whether he or she is a term or a definition. Next, the student would ask a relative question about that week's vocabulary. The objective is for two students to find a matching term and definition. This activity is adaptable to any subject. When I engage my class with fun, meaningful, and thought-provoking activities, they seem to appreciate my ingenuity and talent for helping them learn.

Hold Students Up in the Light

Each day, I stand at the door and greet my students by name, and if they are willing, with a handshake. I speak each one's name uniquely; I notice something about each one, and check in with each one. I look each student in the face, emotionally connect, and get a feel for what is going on with that person. They know where to find their warm-up and the day's schedule listed on the board. Engaging students as quickly as possible when they enter my room aids in classroom management and transitional issues. Doing so will save a lot of time that is wasted in getting the students settled down and focused on the lesson. I do this efficiently by providing brief, clear instructions. One effective colleague passed on to me that the first two or three minutes dictate how the entire class will go. I provide or guide my students to a reasonable conclusion to be in my class each day. Varying the initial activity prevents boredom. Off-task behavior is often attributed to boredom. The feedback is evident. Patience is a must to trusting the process; so keeping the class climate somewhere between boredom and fear is optimal and finding this range gets easier with time. Teaching is beautiful in that we are free to try different approaches in order to find what works for us and the environment. I always take time at the end of each day to reflect, make notes, and make adjustments to what I have done.

Positive All the Way

Following a positive approach to classroom management means that I constantly challenge myself to state all directives in the positive. This is the number-one attention getter when I encounter a variety of behavioral issues. I focus on the students making appropriate behavior choices and proceed as an auctioneer, identifying the crescendo (domino effect) of students being good. Students love the attention. Maintaining a positive attitude fills the air like a vanilla candle and usually relaxes them, and they become self-correcting. (Student noncompliance comes later in the chapter.) As Glover and Midura (1992) noted, "Praise and encouragement are two ways we can all feel good about the team" (pp. 9–10). They also provided a list of 72 ways to say "Very Good!" Some of the phrases on this list include *Superb, Terrific, Outstanding, Good Work, Tremendous, Excellent*, and *Sensational*. It is important to remember to praise students for doing good work and to make every effort to praise *each* one.

Reinforce Appropriate Behavior

Once you have created and written out all of the expectations of your students and the possible consequences for not meeting the expectations, you are ready to become an enforcer of positive behavior, otherwise known as an effective disciplinarian. There are numerous approaches to behavior, and I identify my style as following the behavioral approach. Inappropriate behaviors are truly at the discretion of the teacher's tolerance; so I have to decide what is important. I feel that there are a few behaviors that must be addressed or a once-effective classroom will quickly come undone. Most of the time, it is the small things that slowly build up and tear the code of conduct down. Student morale is affected, my enthusiasm withers, learning dwindles, and principals or other administrators will become privy to my ineffective management style. The "theory" of allowing inappropriate behaviors to take care of themselves will destroy the learning community that I have worked so hard to establish. I have embraced the suggestions of Lavay et al. (1997) for using the behavioral approach to address behavioral problems. First, I select and define the behavior, then observe and record the behavior. Once I have pinpointed the behavioral problem, I begin an intervention and then evaluate the success of the intervention. Interventions rely on the skill of the teacher to focus on the behavior to be corrected, to use data in observations, and to determine what occurs prior to the behavior needing to be corrected (the antecedent). A cause for the inappropriate behavior will be identified as the antecedent. Linking the antecedent to the behavior and the consequences (the reaction, positive or negative, to the behavior) is the beginning of this process (Lavay et al., 1997). The consequences will either increase or decrease the targeted behavior, and you must know what the desired outcome is and make decisions accordingly. The process becomes one of trial and error in the search for the most effective consequences. Most behavior incidences will escalate before beginning to diminish. For instance, I must plan to call a student's parents at the beginning of the school year to identify myself as their child's teacher and welcome the parents to my classroom. Then if I should decide to phone the student's home and notify the parents of the behavior that is occurring in my classroom, we will have already established a positive relationship. Making all meetings positive, even if the real reason for the meeting is to address a problem, usually works to my advantage. Otherwise, the phone calls, e-mails, letters, or other communication may not be as effective, and I may not get the desired results from the parents or the student. Instead of only addressing the problem, I like to surround the negative observations with positive comments about the student. As difficult as it can be, I keep the behavior of the student as the topic, not necessarily the student in general. For example, "I'm calling to let you know that Jimmy is being bad" would be ineffective. A better statement would be, "Jimmy is coming to class prepared, he always has his supplies ready, but I'm concerned about his talking out of turn. He really expresses himself very well. However, for the past four weeks he has been talking out loud without raising his hand, and he is blurting out the answer while taking a quiz. I've had two awareness talks with him about these actions." I document the meeting, making sure I provide the parents with plenty of information, so they can help me resolve the issue. That is, after all, why I am calling them. Phoning the parents early on serves as a preventative measure. Consider the adage "an ounce of prevention is worth a pound of cure." It is more efficient if I implement preventative techniques tailored to my students in the beginning and make negotiations in behaviorally individualized contracts, known as interventions, later. For example, if a student dumps his trash on the ground, I would create a contract with the student, making him or her responsible for cleaning the area when everyone else was done.

Educator's Bank of Goodies

I have learned to be adaptable and consistent in my effort to keep students on track and eager for their journey of education. I am a teacher for all students, not just the easy ones to manage, but the difficult ones, too. I never give up on my students; it's a concession to me. My overall direction for them is to teach them to rely on themselves. Possible intervention strategies and online support can be found by accessing various resources. A favorite Web site of mine, and a valuable resource for teachers, is www.disciplinehelp.com. This site has a comprehensive list of inappropriate behaviors and possible causes. We cannot do a job of this magnitude alone; we need each other. I have established a network of experienced teachers who can give me advice when I find myself in need. There is no "I" in team, but there is a "me." Flippen (1999) suggested the following as important attributes for illuminating students:

1. Personal integrity—a model of honesty, loyalty, faithfulness and respect towards all people and opinions.

2. The ability to affirm and encourage others, motivate students in a multivariety of ways.

3. The ability to demonstrate genuine caring.

4. Professional skills in preparing meaningful lessons and teamwork with others in accomplishing tasks.

5. Teachers act as construction workers to facilitate the students to bond (teamwork), and live productive lives within their community.

6. Ethical role models—exemplify high standards in all endeavors.

A Final Look

A teacher's personal strengths are reflected in his or her students' ability to develop strengths. It was a few years back when a not-so-comical educational seminar leader defined education as a place for younger people to watch older people work. In order to change this image of the teaching profession, let's give them a clear picture of successful experiences, where strength, courage, humility, and self-acceptance are key factors that students need in order to learn to take risks and make sound decisions. The classroom is the safest place (thanks to you and me!) to practice these lifelong lessons. We are all where we are because someone decided to be a teacher; we have an amazing role to fulfill every day, and it starts with the person in the mirror.

What Do You Think?

1. Think back to your previous educational experiences. How have praise and negative phrases affected your performance in school and in the "real" world? What will you use in your classroom?

2. Do you believe children should be bribed and rewarded for proper behavior and work? Explain your answer. Think about the potential dangers in using this approach to manage the classroom.

3. The author of this chapter describes her experience in motivating students to learn through her own enthusiasm and love for learning. Do you believe that *all* students can be motivated to learn and conduct themselves appropriately in school? Why or why not?

4. What will be the basic organizational structure of your classroom? How will you make connections with your students as preventative measures of behavioral problems? Describe what is important to you for shaping your approach to classroom management.

5. Think about what body prompts and facial reactions you use. How will you use these reactions to your advantage in the classroom?

6. Identify the truly intolerable behaviors you envision surfacing in your classroom. How will you tap into the intrinsic motivation of your students to prevent these unwanted behaviors?

Suggestions for Further Reading

Burden, P. (2002). *Classroom management: Creating a successful learning community.* New York: Wiley.

This book tackles the topic of classroom management by creating a classroom environment that will prevent problems. The arguments are grounded in research but address contemporary issues. As the title suggests, an emphasis is placed on establishing learning communities that consider students of all backgrounds.

Emmer, E. T., Evertson, C.M., & Worsham, M. E. (2002). *Classroom management for secondary teachers* (6th ed.). Upper Saddle River, NJ: Pearson Allyn & Bacon.

The authors provide a very practical approach to managing the classroom from the very basic, such as arranging the desks and other furniture, to the more complex, such as appropriate communication techniques. This book also takes into consideration today's diverse classroom as well as the urban setting.

Evertson, C. M., Emmer, E. T., & Worsham, M. E. (2002). *Classroom management for elementary teachers* (6th ed.). Upper Saddle River, NJ: Pearson Allyn & Bacon.

As in the book for secondary teachers described above, this book provides the same information but with a focus on the elementary classroom.

Fay, J., & Funk, D. (1998). *Teaching with love and logic: Taking control of the classroom.* Golden, CO: Love & Logic Press.

Based on the Love and Logic approach to dealing with students, Fay and Funk provide many techniques to reduce the amount of time spent disciplining students, increase the positive atmosphere in the classroom, and gain greater cooperation from the students.

Gootman, M. E. (2000). *A caring teacher's guide to discipline* (2nd ed.). Thousand Oaks, CA: Corwin Press.

Gootman provides many ideas for approaching classroom management by teaching students to take responsibility for their own actions, rather than "disciplining" them. She provides a list of strategies for reaching this goal.

Wong, H. K., & Wong, R. T. (2001). *The first days of school: How to be an effective teacher.* Harry K. Wong Publications.

This book is especially good for the preservice teacher to read in order to begin thinking about how to address classroom management before entering the profession. As the title implies, the authors suggest that many of the techniques be implemented at the beginning of the school year.

References

Flippen, M. B. (1999). *Capturing kids' hearts*. College Station, TX: M. B. Flippen & Associates.

Glover, D. R., and Midura, D. W. (1992). *Team building through physical challenges*. Champaign, IL: Human Kinetics.

Hellison, D. (2003). *Teaching responsibility through physical activity*. Champaign, IL: Human Kinetics.

Jampolsky, L. L. (1991). *Healing the addictive mind*. Berkeley, CA: Celestial Arts.

Jampolsky, L. L. (2000). *Smile for no good reason*. Charlottesville, VA: Hampton Roads.

Lavay, B. W., French, R., & Henderson, H. L. (1997). *Positive behavior management strategies for physical educators*. Champaign, IL: Human Kinetics.

10

Maneuvering the Emotional and Social Demands of the Classroom

Teresa Rishel

A n important concern on the minds of educators across the globe is the safety of teachers and students alike. Dr. Rishel begins with a discussion of the issue of school violence and its causes. With the notion that acts of violence are the result of a student's emotional and/or psychological stress, the author focuses on a specific type of violent act, suicide. Although suicide is at the center of this chapter, other acts of violence could easily replace suicide within the same contexts presented.

♦ ♦ ♦

School Violence

A surge in the number of student deaths and injuries from school violence in the last decade, specifically the massacres at Columbine High School in Littleton, Colorado, and at Heath High School in Paducah, Kentucky, among others, has contributed to an increased concern about school safety. Not only are many adolescents wading through an erratic and volatile time emotionally, physically, and psychologically, but they also enter school with increased fears of school bombings and shootings, physical or sexual assault, theft of their belongings, and being bullied (Elkind, 1988, 1994).

School violence has affected the nation and impacted schools by generating an atmosphere of fear and worry. Highly publicized school shootings

164

caught our attention with the violence and the rapidity with which they occurred. This resulted in the establishment of zero-tolerance policies designed to decrease school violence and bullying and to provide a safer environment. Columbine ushered in a new era of thinking differently about what constituted a safe school and a new awareness of how quickly and easily the school environment can be altered; a climate of cautiousness and an increased focus on discipline was created. As a result, school safety plans have been developed or improved to protect students from toxic chemical leaks, terrorist attacks, violent rampages, bomb threats, building intruders, and anthrax. Many of these fears were previously nearly nonexistent; students today are no longer protected from the possibility and reality of their occurrence.

However, while theoretically a positive step toward making schools safer, zero tolerance in practice has done little to change school safety (Richardson, 2002). Four years after the implementation of zero-tolerance policies, many schools were found to have an increase in violence. Contributing to this increase were not the actual types of violence that were defined prior to zero tolerance, but an increase in what was considered to be violent acts according to the policies that were implemented. For example, at an elementary school near Littleton, Colorado, seven fourth-grade boys were suspended from school for using their fingers pointed like guns during a game at recess (Richardson, 2002). The boys not only received a suspension, but upon being admitted back to school, were also ridiculed as they sat in the hallway at lunchtime serving five days of in-school detention. The suspension seemed a high price to pay for their unintentionally harmful behavior. The confusion they suffered at being reprimanded was exacerbated further as they sat subject to the jeers and harassment of their schoolmates. Seemingly, one should consider that the boys were punished for breaking zero-tolerance rules, yet were subjected to the same type of zero-tolerance policy infractions by the students who harassed them.

The extreme measures with which zero tolerance is being enforced, combined with the large discrepancies in how administrators perceive and interpret the policies, only add to the distress and further veer away from the original intention to make schools safer. What is of importance here lies in how the focus on increasing the physical safety of these students resulted in inflicting a decrease in the emotional safety of the boys. One would have to consider which was safer—disciplining the boys for their inappropriate, yet innocent, behavior or subjecting them to emotional torture and humiliation.

What Is Safety?

When we think of school safety, images come to mind of backpacks and lockers being searched, metal detectors, student identification tags, policemen guarding the doors, and other protective mechanisms that ensure the physical safety of students. However, when one digs deeper, sooner or later the question of why these safety measures are needed must surface. While school safety measures have emphasized violent acts, the disregard for the causes of and reasons for violence is of particular importance and is often neglected. Violence, whether inflicted on others or self-inflicted, is situated within the context of the psychological, emotional, and social well-being of the students. The issue becomes one of student emotional health and safety in the context of the school environment. As the myriad of outward safety measures are implemented, attention should be given to the importance of addressing students' personal and emotional suffering, which has the capacity to result in harm to themselves or others.

To understand the role of emotional safety in classrooms, and the role of teachers in ensuring that safety, we must first understand the state of many students as they enter the classroom and school. I believe we need to take a serious look at what is going on in the lives of the students and how their struggles are exacerbated within the school environment, thus placing them at greater risk. We need to understand how school impacts student autonomy, how they function within that environment, and the results of negative interaction with teachers and peers. Since a large portion of their lives are in school, the environment "plays a central role in both promoting children's acquisition of knowledge and shaping the ways in which they learn to regulate their attention, emotions, and behavior" (Eccles & Roeser, 1999, p. 504). Considering that nearly all students encounter an average of 50 teachers over a 12-year span, they must learn to adjust to more authority figures than they will be required to deal with at nearly any other time throughout life. The adjustment to differing teacher expectations, attitudes, and instructional methods occurs yearly as students pass from one grade to another. The daily routine is laden with constant change.

Many students come to school each day "already victims of injurious conditions" (Dewey, 1938/1997, p. 56), with a heavy load of emotional, physical, and psychological baggage from home and their lives outside of school, causing them to withdraw and become passive at school. Family issues such as divorce, death, and illness, as well as problems with the law, severe injury, losing a job, or remarriage, can create further stress for the student in the school environment (Elkind, 1989). Student suffering also results from their living in alcoholic or abusive families, from neglect, and from poverty. Students who bear these burdens should be considered emotionally vulnerable, needing the full support of school staff. However, researchers have noted that as the grade levels increase, the greater focus on academics largely replaces concerns for students' mental health (Eccles & Roeser, 1999). Further indications of this decreasing focus were described by Eccles and Roeser as follows:

> Teachers are less likely to endorse the notion that students' mental health concerns are part of the teacher role. We suspect that high school teachers feel even less responsible for addressing the socio-emotional, in contrast to the intellectual, needs of their students. An important implication of this change is that, at a time when children need academic and socio-emotional guidance and support from parents and nonparental adults, teachers may be less likely to provide such support given the number of students they teach, their educational training, and the size of secondary schools. (p. 516)

Further, attending school has become stressful for students as they accumulate attitudes toward teachers and school, which emerge naturally from the climate and culture of the school setting (Butler & Novy, 1994; Elkind, 1989). As a support system, the school environment, combined with the quality of interactions between school personnel and students, contributes significantly to how students acclimate to their surroundings. Students learn where they fit in and where they do not, and they begin to realize that as one of a crowd, their problems seem insignificant. Part of the reason for this lies in the fact that school practices "do not support every child's autonomy, nor provide a sense of meaning, or consistent social support, which results in poor academic achievement and negative feelings" (Schlosser, 1992, p. 128).

Additionally, the social context of schooling (i.e., how students fit into the school environment in relationships, comfort, identity, and so forth) also greatly influences a student's emotional health. Peer groups become increasingly more important. Research indicates that "one of the major factors contributing to youth violence is the impact of peers" (National Institute of Mental Health, 2000). For adolescents, school is the social mechanism of relationship building and acceptance as they manage peer group situations. When students do not feel that they fit into the school environment, they experience a general sense of isolation and alienation, a contributing factor to suicide.

Why would students want to kill their schoolmates, or themselves? What creates the angst that causes a student to enter the school with a weapon? Why do some students fear for their safety at school, while constantly avoiding the bullies that exist there? And what are we going to do about all or any of it? What does this translate into, then, in the classroom? How can emotional safety be viewed in terms that are understood from a preservice or novice teacher's perspective?

The answer to these questions lies in part within the classroom walls, the place where the quality of interactions bears upon what occurs outside of the classroom. It is important to acknowledge the variety of reactions from educators to the emotional state of their students. Some see it as their duty and are responsive to it; others are more inclined to view emotional issues or problems as outside of their realm of understanding or responsibility, or both, and defer to school administrators and counselors. Teachers have a moral and ethical responsibility to maintain emotional safety for their students. When they disregard this responsibility, it "creates a hole in the safety net" (Eccles & Roeser, 1999, p. 516) for students during a time when it is needed most from adults. The safety net provided by the teacher occurs in many ways, as seen in the following story.

Brin (pseudonym), a participant teacher in my research study, shared a story that further impacted the views I already held about how the safety net is often allowed to collapse under the guise of academic success. Her student, Tyler (pseudonym), came to school looking more disheveled than usual, tired, and without his homework. Upon questioning Tyler, he replied that everything was fine and that he was just tired. As the day progressed, Tyler's behavior grew worse as he became agitated at the slightest infraction by his classmates. Further, Tyler refused to do any of his schoolwork and sat sulking at his desk. Brin, usually a strict disciplinarian, let Tyler's actions pass because it was uncharacteristic of him, until she felt it necessary to intercede. She took Tyler to the principal's office, where the three of them attempted to resolve his issues. Tyler wove the story of what happened at home the previous night. His mother and her boyfriend had been drinking at a local bar, and when she decided to return home, the boyfriend refused to accompany her. Tyler heard his mother come home and stumble around until she passed out on the couch. Awakened a few hours later, Tyler heard screaming and banging outside of his bedroom window. The boyfriend was repeatedly crashing a crowbar against the porch railings and flooring, upset that he was locked out of the house. Tyler's mother attempted to get the boyfriend to stop, but he would not listen. Hour after hour, the ranting and destruction continued, until finally, the entire porch was torn from the house. And then Tyler went to school.

Teachers are overburdened with the basic requirements of their profession regarding the academic concerns of their students and courses.

Standards-based education, emerging as the impetus behind much of the work in which teachers engage, requires full attention to ensure the success of their students and provide job security. With such a focus, teachers are left to wonder how they can address, let alone solve, the emotional problems of their students. They feel helpless in their attempts to contend with the insurmountable problems that reside within their classrooms. Teachers feel inadequate and unqualified to handle serious student problems, particularly if they are life threatening. This causes great concern and distress for teachers who do not consider themselves to be counselors or psychologists, justifiably so.

Aligned with our discussion of students' emotional safety, the increasing number of student suicides and issues related to suicide, such as depression and self-cutting, are national concerns and are the focus of my research. Problems of poor female self-perception are revealed through the development of anorexia and bulimia, and have been linked to self-punishing or suicidal teenagers. Further indications that students' emotional health remains at risk are the increasing number of students engaging in life-threatening behaviors on a regular basis, such as drinking alcohol, smoking, taking illegal drugs, and practicing unprotected sex (Centers for Disease Control and Prevention, 2003). Beane and Lipka (2000) addressed how the traditional support systems for young people— the home and school—focus more on criticism and disregard students' needs, causing an "increased incidence of drug use, eating disorders, early pregnancy, crime activity, and attempted and actual suicide" (p. 5). As we consider the ramifications of the *entirety* of these problems and the manifestations resulting from each, suicide surfaces as a key issue. Although suicide is rarely considered a viable topic in teacher education programs, my personal and professional beliefs require that it be considered within the context of classroom safety.

Suicide: The Realities

In September 1994, at the age of 20, my son committed suicide by shooting himself. Four years later, after I had resigned my position as principal, a former student poured gasoline over his body and set himself on fire, resulting in his death at the age of 14. Suicide, affecting my life both personally and professionally, remains the focus of my challenge that preservice teachers consider its importance each day as they walk into the classroom. Unfortunately, during a time when suicide has climbed to epidemic proportions among those aged 10 to 24, and the need for awareness, knowledge, and intervention continues, the term *suicide* has taken on new meanings, some of which are not identified with the type of self-inflicted death that results directly from personal or emotional trauma. Since the attack on the World Trade Center in 2001, suicide has become synonymous with suicide bombings and war. Rarely does a day pass without our hearing about the occurrence of a suicide bombing, or our hearing the perpetrators referred to as "suicide bombers." In these instances, suicide is performed as a matter of national or religious allegiance and honor.

As a result of the suicides of the perpetrators at Columbine, suicide has become associated with school shootings. In this case, popular opinion was that they deserved to die; thus, suicide was viewed as a means to a justified end. It also portrayed their suicides as acts committed by insane, unstable, and otherwise inferior people, instead of acts by two young men who suffered from being taunted and harassed at school and neglected at home. Suicidal behaviors of this type need to be juxtaposed to suicides that are not related to violent behavior. Unfortunately, with the increased rate at which the term *suicide* is becoming an everyday term, I fear there is a decline of the impact of the truest meaning of the term of taking one's life because of personal trauma. During a period when the U.S. surgeon general declared suicide a national crisis (U.S. Public Health Service, 1999) and the AIM (Awareness, Intervention, and Methodology) plan was subsequently developed to address it, much attention has been directed to the alternate meanings of suicide, risking further diversion from the morbidity rate of our adolescents and young adults. It is my belief that interest needs to remain as much on student suicide as on suicide outside the context of the school. Students who have attempted or contemplated suicide walk into classrooms everyday. There are also many students whose lives have been affected by the loss of a loved one to suicide, which affects their abilities to function within the school environment. The reality of this epidemic for educators is that every two hours, another person under the age of 25 commits suicide (American Association of Suicidology, 2003). Suicide rates are increasing at an alarming rate within the very population that schools serve. This is particularly true in adolescents, but there has also been a recent surge of suicide in young children (Centers for Disease Control and Prevention, 2002). Suicide rates for children and adolescents have increased at a rate higher than all other categories of death in a 10-year span, with one in five teenagers contemplating suicide (Butler & Novy, 1994; Centers for Disease Control and Prevention, 2002; Davidson & Range, 1999; Elkind, 1994). Suicide is the third leading cause of death in 15- to 24-year-olds, preceded only by alcohol and substance abuse and accidental death (Elkind, 1989; Jacques, 2000; King, Price, Telljohann, & Wahl, 1999). It is estimated that a more realistic count of suicides actually committed would be to consider a percentage of the alcohol and substance abuse deaths, accidents, and suicides that are covered up by relatives and coroners (Butler & Novy, 1994; King et al., 1999; Lukas & Seiden, 1987). Suicide claims victims of every class, gender, race, socioeconomic status, and intelligence level. Among adolescents, suicide occurs predominantly between the hours of 3 and 6 p.m., and it is most prevalent during the months of April and November (Davidson, 2003).

BEGINNING UNDERSTANDINGS OF THE CRISIS OF SUICIDE

Family issues can create situations that require coping skills beyond students' capabilities. During stressful times, students lose their sense of reality, ability to cope, and ability to think rationally (Elkind, 1989). They feel emotional emptiness and they no longer communicate effectively, adding to further family dysfunction and poor relationships (Butler & Novy, 1994; Elkind, 1989). Without adequate coping skills, they are prone to commit suicide as a result of the "unbearable anguish," particularly if they are self-punishing teens (Hewett, 1980, p. 29). Eccles and Roeser (1999) reported that adolescents become suicidal as problems increase with "family, friends, boyfriends or girlfriends, and school" (p. 504).

Young people who become caught in relationship problems suffer humiliation, depression, and inappropriate behaviors. The cycle further perpetuates itself when the alienated student is unable to perform well at school, exhibits consistently poor behavior, or resorts to extraneous methods (drug or alcohol abuse, sexual experimentation, eating disorders) to relieve the stress. They become socially isolated, their self-esteem plummets, and they experience further depression (Butler & Novy, 1994; Elkind, 1989; King et al., 1999), which is a key indicator that often results in suicide. Teenagers who find themselves deep into depression, or seeking release from it feel that there is "no way out . . . they are helpless, hapless, and hopeless" (Elkind, 1989, p. 172).

The moral aspects of schooling, where the actions and interactions of each individual affects others, must be recognized as significant in how the adolescent views himself within the school environment. Students quickly learn, "What's good for the group had better be good for me" (Ayers, 2001, p. 50). Educators often fail to realize the impact or importance of their role in these moral decision-making moments.

While teachers are considered the front line in handling a large variety of student problems, they feel less competent, are less competent, and are uncomfortable handling situations involving suicide (Davidson & Range, 1999; Eccles & Roeser, 1999; King et al., 1999; Oser, 1991). However, while educators may feel unskilled in handling suicide, their day-to-day choices regarding classroom management remain within their control. Ineffective teachers use frequent office referrals and classroom punishment as the usual method of discipline. When teachers use attention, approval, and grades as ways to motivate and reward students, those with behavioral, emotional, and discipline problems have difficulty surviving (Bransford, Brown, & Cocking, 1999). Consider the following journal entry, submitted by H. Lee (pseudonym), one of my preservice teachers:

H. LEE JOURNAL #6

A while back I wrote about a little girl that was going through some tough times. I first met her mother in conferences and she seemed very upset about her daughter's grades. After talking to her, I found out that she had just gone through a divorce and her daughter was not taking it well. This young girl used to be an honor student and is now failing every subject. Her mother is an alcoholic and was arrested again for driving under the influence. My student was taken out of her home and has been refused all contact with her mom. She is not allowed to call her, speak to her, see her, nor write her letters. She is left without any parents now. She broke down and told me a lot the other day when her friends started to be mean to her in class. She has much more on her mind than school and trying to find time to get together with her friends to complete a project.

You know those teachers that are stuck back in the old times when only worksheets were given out and they based the whole class on lecture and stupid rules? Well, she has one of those teachers for English. Her class is getting ready for the proficiency tests and this teacher is very strict on these tests, as she should be [but] not to the extent to where it is life or death. My student has an excused pass for any class if she feels the need to go to the counselor to talk . . . because she was showing signs of suicide. Whenever she was feeling depressed . . . she could get out of class and see the counselor. This past week, her English teacher threw a fit because this student missed her class a couple of times. She was saying that this was unacceptable behavior and that this will reflect her grade.

I could not believe this! This girl is showing signs of ending her life, her mother is continuously arrested, and God knows what else she has been through! I think sometimes people forget how it was to be a teenager and the struggles they go through. That is a rough enough time for teenagers without any problems, let alone for a child that has to go through these ordeals. I will be gone in three weeks and then I am only left with wondering what will happen to her.

One method of applying academic pressure, as a system of competition and reward, is through tracking and grouping. This separates students not only physically but also emotionally and socially, because it determines their peer group. Academic achievement becomes a limited vision for some students because of these preset boundaries, which leads them into passivity and lack of involvement. Beane and Lipka (2000) warned that educators must "stare long and hard" (p. 35) at what they do concerning forms of institutional alienation, which are proven methods of lowering self-esteem, "stripping learners of their personal dignity" (p. 21). Regardless of the intelligence level of the student, academic pressure is a significant cause of suicidal behavior (Beane & Lipka, 2000; Butler & Novy, 1994).

Further, "more serious behavior problems and violence are associated with smaller numbers of youths who are failing academically and who band together, often with other youth rejected by prosocial peers" (National Institute of Mental Health, 2000).

In my study on suicide, a participant administrator shared that focus on standardized testing creates emotional damage for many students because the school values something the student cannot have—academic success. Many students' failure to perform academically is due not to lack of ability, but to the fact that there is no need to value education. These students are not going to leave their hometowns, go to college, or enter a career; their future is already determined. Many students struggle to pass graduation exams, still failing after three or four attempts. To many, the focus on academics and testing only hinders graduation and thus keeps them from finding employment.

Upon reflecting on the lack of balance and the irregular flow between the emotional and social needs of students, it becomes obvious that academic achievement cannot be gained for those students whose lives are in turmoil. Without dealing with the core issues of human problems, test scores will not rise, and for many, academic success will remain undesirable or unobtainable. The challenge for educators is to find ways to improve students' lives and give them enough hope and direction to move forward with desire and motivation, instead of allowing them to view school as a waste of time. I believe it is often difficult for us as educators to remember that our successes are the result of enjoying school, fitting into the school environment, and valuing what it offered. Moreover, we had the notion that we could succeed, and we wanted to succeed.

While violence and aggression rise to the forefront of school concerns today, and those who perform these violent acts increasingly find a target for their anger within the school walls, students who attempt suicide, idealize suicide, or actually commit suicide far outnumber those who commit school violence (Jacques, 2000). As a result of this phenomenon, the American Academy of Pediatrics, "strongly recommends that education about depression and suicide prevention be integrated into the educational system" (Kirchner, Yoder, Kramer, Lindsey, & Thrush, 2000, p. 238). Former surgeon general David Satcher stated, "It is time for us to move from shame and stigma to support" (Portner, 2001, p. 57), declaring suicide a serious national health problem. Unlike murders and other violent crimes where we can learn about motivation from assailants, suicide leaves no solid answers to the myriad of questions that follow such a death. "Finding an answer to the riddle of self-murder is not like tracing the origins of a disease. There is no one factor that causes suicide" (Portner, 2001, p. 8). Suicide can occur quickly, with no warning signs and no apparent symptoms, and is based on a fragile state of emotions.

A STUDENT NAMED DALTON

I never expected suicide to be a part of my job as an elementary principal. It was not a topic discussed in my teaching or administration preparation. However, students who wanted to talk about killing themselves appeared on a regular basis, particularly three male students. My actions and reactions as a principal to these students grew out of my experiences resulting from the suicide of my son, Tony. As the students shared with me their desires to die, the memories and feelings of Tony's death emerged and reemerged. The students initially talked about things that bothered them, such as school, friends, and family, but on a more superficial level and within what seemed normal angst. Then, in a shift of dynamics, and possibly after feeling less vulnerable, they talked openly about their desire to die. Suicide, for them, was the answer to their problems. It was at those moments that my sympathy for them became overwhelming. I worried about how they would cope in a school environment that was not conducive to understanding these types of problems. Through intense work with two of them, their wishes to die were dissipated and they seemed emotionally safe. Dalton, however, was a different story.

I had not expected to become as involved with a student as I did with Dalton. Although he was a troublemaker, rude to teachers, antisocial, and sarcastic, and presented a challenge to nearly every staff member, particularly the male teachers, I found something intriguing and interesting about him, something hidden beneath his bravado. He seemed to enjoy life, displayed a great sense of humor and wit, and often caused a burst of laughter among his peers. School was the place where he demanded, and thus received, an enormous amount of attention; sadly, the attention was usually not due to positive behavior.

Dalton was extremely intelligent, scoring the highest possible on standardized tests; he had a way of understanding and solving complex problems that were years beyond his age group. Physically, he was an attractive young man whose smile could light up a room; alternatively, he could have a dark, sullen look that darkened the same space around him. He had a lively spirit, insight into the world around him, and an understanding of the larger picture of life. A deep thinker and amazingly verbal, Dalton's ability to engage in incredible conversations always left me wondering how he had acquired such a large body of knowledge. Dalton was a talented artist whose drawings, while usually morbid and violent, were detailed and expressive. While there was concern about the message in his art, some dismissed it as just another attempt for attention.

Dalton had a difficult life. His father left when he was young, leaving Dalton to be raised by his mother. She did not have a high school education, making it difficult for her to provide for the family. Living in a house with a dirt floor and no running water, Dalton was responsible for taking care of his younger brothers. He often complained that it was difficult to prepare food for them when there was none in the house. He frequently referred to his mother in anger, talking about the irresponsible things she did and her wild lifestyle, sometimes stating that he disliked her. Dalton referred to killing others or himself on a regular basis, but never directly referred to his mother as the target of these threats.

When I met with Dalton and his mother to discuss his anguish and suicidal thoughts, Dalton's attitude toward her was obvious, not only through what he shared verbally, but through his gestures and body language. His mother begged him to understand and forgive her for the things she had done; I felt that progress was being made and a good outcome seemed possible. The meeting reached a turning point, though, while alternating between justifying her actions and apologizing for them, Dalton's mother revealed that he had been conceived as the result of being raped, and, therefore, she found it difficult to accept him. I was alarmed at her highly personal disclosure; Dalton looked devastated, broken, and angry. He jumped from his chair and screamed that he hated her and would never love her. He cried and yelled simultaneously, with the familiar sinister look on his face. I felt helpless.

As a result of that meeting, I worked carefully and consistently with Dalton and his mother with the hope that their relationship could be salvaged. Dalton's death wishes would probably increase if he remained aloof and angry. I talked with her about my son's suicide, which was the first time I had told anyone outside of my own community. From that disclosure, we developed a closer relationship and talked often about Dalton. Sadly, after a few months, our communication became infrequent. To continue communication and ensure that I was aware of what was going on with Dalton, I allowed him to do schoolwork in my office in lieu of in-school suspensions. My office also provided Dalton a safe place to come when he needed to retreat away from the stresses of school and life.

Other teachers had a different view of Dalton. They considered him a student who refused to try, who did his best to find ways to create trouble, which was often unfortunately true. It was suggested that as a product of his family, there was little hope of changing him, which only served to perpetuate the self-fulfilling prophecy that he had inherited. Dalton was a child who needed help, as he was desperate enough to end his life. The feelings of the staff made Dalton's retreats to my office often difficult for me. I was occasionally accused of "making things too easy for him," letting him manipulate me to get out of class, and "listening to him too much," instead of telling him what to do. While I found these comments disheartening, I also realized that the role of a principal was unfamiliar to most and often misunderstood. I struggled knowing he needed the office time, yet realizing that I had to figure out a way to mainstream him into the school environment where he would be accepted.

The day before Dalton's elementary school graduation, he came to tell me good-bye and that he would not be at his graduation. He explained that he did not have anything appropriate to wear and would rather not attend than look out of place. Stupidly, I laughed and said it did not matter what he wore; it only mattered what he had accomplished. I will never forget Dalton's reply:

"Mrs. R., you just don't understand, do you? *I am not like the other students;* I am different. I do not have clothes to wear to graduation. I have never, ever, had a new shirt, pants, or shoes."

I felt foolish and embarrassed for minimizing his reality by simplifying it to fit my own. It was not as easy for him to accept that his accomplishments were more worthy than his appearance; I had failed him miserably in my remark. I convinced Dalton to come for the morning session, which he did, and I called him to my office. I handed him a bag that contained clothes for graduation and explained that he deserved to attend. A few hours later, Dalton looked happy and handsome as he received his diploma.

Two weeks before school started the following year, Dalton committed suicide by dousing himself with gasoline and lighting a match. Although I was no longer employed in the school district, I visited his mother to extend my condolences. I brought photos of him to place beside his casket, one of which included Dalton's graduation and showed him smiling in his new clothes. She had asked the school to contact me for pictures because she had none. As I pulled away from the house where Dalton had lived, guilt resurfaced as I recalled the familiar despair and help-lessness of his mother. Why did I have to witness this again, live this experience again, only through another's eyes? Old questions haunted me, pulling me into a place that I thought I had buried deeply enough. What should I have done to prevent this? Why didn't I do enough? Was this my fault?

Connelly and Clandinin (1988) noted that educators experiences are filtered through the lenses of personal practical knowledge, a "moral, affective, and aesthetic way of knowing life's educational situations" (p. 59), because they are felt, valued, and appreciated. Thus, what we do as professionals results from experiencing different types of knowing, which fluctuates within the context of the situation, where knowing constitutes not only objective knowing, but the emotionality involved with that knowing. Connelly and Clandinin extended this knowing into education where the experiences that occur outside of the educational setting are often the most important experiences that affect our lives. Thus, we can incorporate our experiences within our lives as educators, to make meaning within the context of schooling. It encourages seeing students as more than just students.

What Now?

So, where do we begin to incorporate the understanding that our roles as educators are more inclusive than our delivery of an academic-based education to our students? Now that we know the deeper, hidden issues confronting our students, and the way they are manifested and often exacerbated within the classroom and school, what do we do?

First, continued knowledge and awareness will provide ways to seek connections to our students and help them make meaning of the confusion in their lives within the context of the academic aspects of schooling. To become effective educators, we understand the need to remain current and knowledgeable about instructional methods, technological advances, and "best practice" measures. As a part of the accumulation of teacher knowledge, we must also value the importance of staying current with student social, emotional, and psychological issues, particularly as we maneuver the demands of classroom life. Psychiatric and behavioral problems remain the most prevalent health concerns in young people between the ages of 10 and 18 (Kirchner et al., 2000). We must be able to understand *why* homework does not get turned in, instead of simply recording it. We must recognize the signs of futility when a student attempts to fit in with peers, but fails. We must dig deeper to find the hidden causes and issues behind the students' lack of concentration, engagement, and success.

Self-reflection, a continual method of recalling the little, seemingly insignificant interactions and occurrences, must become part of the everyday appraisal of what took place in the classroom. It is an ongoing process that allows us to replay moments and to continually reflect on "who we are" in the classroom. As a result of self-reflection and evaluation, we reaffirm the importance of caring and empathetic relationships with our students. Reflection also allows us to consider our own attitudes toward risky behaviors, particularly suicide, depression, and other forms of self-degradation. Do we simply brush aside these facets, armed with the attitude that it is not our "job" to deal with these types of problems? Do we judge, alienate, or otherwise chastise students in spite of, or because of, their problems?

When a student comes in tardy, is the situation handled publicly, with the teacher requesting a reason for the tardiness and demanding proof in front of the class, or privately at an appropriate time away? When an assignment of poor quality is handed in, is the student chastised in front of classmates? If a student is restless, distracted, or sleepy, is attention drawn to it, ensuring that the student suffers some form of embarrassment or humiliation as a method of discipline? In each instance, and many more, it is our moral and ethical duty to help maintain students' emotional safety. To allow students to remain isolated beings, thrashing around in self-destructive thoughts and behaviors is a disregard to the commitment that is made upon deciding to be a teacher.

But we must remember that "affect" refers to a major dimension of humanness and, in the end, the one that gives education its legitimate meaning in the school context. After all, we are concerned not simply with cognition and psychometrics; neither one alone nor the two together contribute adequately to the improvement of human experience. It is the affective dimension, in all of its complexity, that finally serves the crucial personal and social ends of schooling (Beane, 1990, p. 12).

What Do You Think?

1. In your opinion, what is included under the umbrella of school safety? How do you feel about many schools' decision to implement a "zero-tolerance" policy? Is this too extreme, just right, or not strict enough? (Think back to the issue of the students who pointed their fingers like guns.)

2. Reflect on the issue of safety in schools. Are you concerned about your safety as a teacher? Have you experienced any moments in your educational experiences where you didn't feel safe? What makes you feel safe in an educational environment? How did Brin provide the emotional "safety net" for Tyler?

3. Thinking back to the discussion presented in this chapter, how can a teacher identify a student who might be on the verge of committing a violent act against himself/herself or another individual? What could you do to help this student?

4. Imagine that you were one of Dalton's teachers. How would you react to his behavioral problems? If you were his principal, how would you respond to his numerous difficulties?

Suggestions for Further Reading

Beane, J. A., & Lipka, R. P. (2000). *When the kids come first: Enhancing self-esteem.* New York: Educator's International Press.

This book is a great read for anyone who works with children from ages 10-19. The authors discuss in great detail the concerns and issues of students in the middle age range and how schooling impacts how they act and react. Beane and Lipka write in a manner that makes the reader *want* to make changes for students now, not at some point in the future. This book would be a great addition to any educator's library.

Blauvelt, P. D. (1999). *Making schools safe for students: Creating a proactive school safety plan.* Thousand Oaks, CA: Corwin Press.

In *Making Schools Safe for Students*, Blauvelt tackles the timely subject of concern about the safety of schools today. As the president and CEO of a group dedicated to school safety (National Alliance for Safe Schools), he shares his expertise and offers practical approaches that school personnel can readily incorporate into their already existing school safety plans. This book is a must for administrators or committee members responsible for remaining current on school safety.

Bluestein, J. (2001). *Creating emotionally safe schools: A guide for educators and parents*. Deerfield Beach, FL: Health Communications.

Bluestein presents a book grounded in the basic challenges for every school. Her in-depth conversations about school safety are not exclusive to violence at school, but the issues that are part of the hidden curriculum of schools. Her view of schooling offers a holistic look at what is going on in schools today. Bluestein encourages and inspires the reader to look at these deeper issues, and then to adopt a plan to begin dealing with them.

Davis, S. (2004). *Schools where everyone belongs: Practical strategies for reducing bullying*. Wayne, ME: Stop Bullying Now.

For educators interested in extending their knowledge of bullying in schools, this is an excellent resource. Davis offers bullying prevention based on research combined with practices and procedures for schools to incorporate.

Elliott, D. S., Hamburg, B. A., & William, K. R. (Eds.). (1998). *Violence in American schools: A new perspective*. Cambridge, UK: Cambridge University Press.

Current concerns in education focus on violence in the schools. This is a topic important for educators, decision and policy makers, social workers, psychologists, and others who work with young people at risk. This book takes a very in-depth look at school violence and prevention measures in terms of what has worked and why. It is direct in reporting research findings from a variety of disciplines that lend themselves to the study of violence. Readers will find a plethora of information.

King, K. (1999). Fifteen myths about adolescent suicide. *Education Digest, 65*(1), 68-71.

This article is a definite must for anyone working with the adolescent population. Awareness is the beginning understanding of the dangerous phenomenon of suicide that takes the lives of our young people every day.

References

American Association of Suicidology. (2003). *About suicide: Youth suicide fact sheet*. Retrieved December 30, 2003, from http://www.suicidology.org/displaycommon.cfm?an=1&subarticlenbr=9

Ayers, W. (2001). *To teach: The journey of a teacher* (2nd ed.). New York: Teachers College Press.

Beane, J. A. (1990). *Affect in the curriculum: Toward democracy, dignity, and diversity*. New York: Teachers College Press.

Beane, J. A., & Lipka, R. P. (2000). *When the kids come first: Enhancing self-esteem*. New York: Educator's International Press.

Bransford, J., Brown, A., & Cocking, R. (Eds.). (1999). *How people learn: Brain, mind, experience, and school*. Washington, DC: National Academy Press.

Butler, J. W., & Novy, D. (1994). An investigation of differences in attitudes between suicidal and nonsuicidal student ideators. *Adolescence, 29*, 623–639.

Centers for Disease Control and Prevention. (2002). *Suicide in the United States. Programs for the prevention of suicide among adolescents and young adults.* MMWR, 43 (No.RR-6), 22 0.54. Retrieved July 9, 2002, from http://www .cdc.gov/ncipc/factsheets/suifacts.htm

Centers for Disease Control and Prevention. (2003). *Suicide in the United States. Suicide: fact sheet.* Retrieved July 27, 2004, from http://www.cdc.gov/ncipc/ factsheets/suifacts.htm

Connelly, M. F., & Clandinin, D. J. (1988). *Teachers as curriculum planners: Narratives of experience.* New York: Teachers College Press.

Davidson, L. (2003). Suicide and season. *Youth suicide prevention education program.* Retrieved December 30, 2003, from http://www.yspep.org/season.html

Davidson, M. W., & Range, L. M. (1999). Are teachers of children and young adolescents responsive to suicide prevention training modules? *Death Studies,* 23(1), 61–71.

Dewey, J. (1997). *Experience and education.* New York: Touchstone. (Original work published 1938)

Eccles, J. S., & Roeser, R. W. (1999). School and community influences on human development. In M. H. Borstein & M. E. Lamb (Eds.), *Developmental psychology: An advanced textbook* (4th ed., pp. 503–546). Mahwah, NJ: Erlbaum.

Elkind, D. (1988). *The hurried child: Growing up too fast too soon.* New York: Addison-Wesley.

Elkind, D. (1989). *All grown up and no place to go: Teenagers in crisis.* New York: Addison-Wesley.

Elkind, D. (1994). *Ties that stress: The new family imbalance.* Cambridge, MA: Harvard University Press.

Hewett, J. H. (1980). *After suicide.* Philadelphia: Westminster Press.

Jacques, J. D. (2000). Surviving suicide: The impact on the family. *Family Journal, 8,* 376–382.

King, K. A., Price, J. H., Telljohann, S. K., & Wahl, J. (1999). High school health teachers perceived self-efficacy in identifying students at risk for suicide. *Journal of School Health, 69*(5), 202–207.

Kirchner, J. E., Yoder, M. C., Kramer, T. L., Lindsey, M. S., & Thrush, C. R. (2000). Development of an educational program to increase school personnel's awareness about child and adolescent depression. *Education, 121,* 235–247.

Lukas, C., & Seiden, H. M. (1987). *Silent grief: Living in the wake of suicide.* New York: Bantam Books.

National Institute of Mental Health (2000). NIH Publication No. 00-4706. Retrieved November 14, 2003, from http://www.nimh.nih.gov/publicat/ violenceresfact.cfm

Oser, F. K. (1991). Professional morality: A discourse approach (the case of the teaching profession). In W. M. Kurtines & J. L. Gewirtz (Eds.), *Handbook of moral development* (Vol. 2, pp. 191–226). Boston: Allyn & Bacon.

Portner, J. (2001). *One in thirteen: The silent epidemic of teen suicide.* Beltsville, MD: Gryphon House.

Richardson, V. (2002, May 13). Zero tolerance takes toll on pupils. *The Washington Times.* Retrieved December 30, 2003, from http://asp.wash times.com

Schlosser, L. K. (1992). Teacher distance and student disengagement: School lives on the margin. *Journal of Teacher Education, 43*(2), 128–140.

U.S. Public Health Service. (1999). The surgeon general's call to action to prevent suicide. *Mental health: A report of the surgeon general.* Retrieved December 30, 2003, from http://www.surgeongeneral.gov/library/mental health/home.html

11

Assessment for Learning

Its Effect on the Classroom and Curriculum

Magdalena Mo Ching Mok

A n important issue that future teachers must consider is how to determine whether or not students are learning. Throughout the world, legislative bodies have established standardized tests in an effort to make such a determination, and classroom teachers implement daily their own forms of assessment. Dr. Mok addresses many of the concerns surrounding the issue of assessment and how it affects education around the world. After this chapter was submitted, Dr. Mok brought to my attention an editorial submitted on May 3, 2004, to the Hong Kong newspaper, *Oriental Daily,* which demonstrates an issue that is often overlooked: the students' feelings about high-stakes tests. In this case, a primary 3 student, studying in a prestigious school, wrote a poem (originally in Chinese) expressing how she feels about one such exam: "Tomorrow 8 a.m., worry, worry. Do not know why, worry, worry. Tomorrow afternoon, very worried. Do not know why, very worried, Just hope oral exam, pass pass" (p. A25). Assessment involves more than attempting to measure what students have learned, as Dr. Mok discusses below.

◆ ◆ ◆

Setting the Scene: Assessment Reforms in America and the Asia-Pacific Region

I belong to a tai chi group at my workplace with around 20 members comprising teacher educators of the institute. We meet regularly every Wednesday after work to learn tai chi. Most of us are over 40 and are more aware of our health than are our younger colleagues. The venue until last week was a large seminar room, with all the chairs stacked up and put on the side to give room for our tai chi movements. The sessions were fun in general but there was, like most workplace hobby groups, no big excitement. Things have been quite different since last week, however. The atmosphere has turned noticeably more joyous. There is more laughter and chatting. Members seem to be in high spirits and are making better progress than before. Since last week, we have moved to the institute's dance room, which is equipped with huge mirrors all around and is much more spacious than the previous seminar room. Members expressed their appreciation in various ways, but the following struck me the most:

"Now I can see how I get from one leg to the other leg."

"Now I know exactly what was meant by the teacher when he said I bent too low and that might hurt my kneecap in the long run. Nobody else bent the way I did."

"Isn't that amazing! Twenty of us are in one harmonious movement as if we are just one body!"

"I didn't know that I could be so graceful (at my age) as I made the circles with both hands. Well, I did make two circles of the same size instead of a bigger circle with my right hand but that's all right, I can fix that quite easily. Just love it!"

We talked and laughed as we did when we were in our 20s. As you might have guessed, the mirrors are the miracle; they give us immediate feedback as we learn. We are able to assess and adjust ourselves as we go along. The whole process, starting from the teacher demonstrating a new movement, to us mimicking his actions, checking our accuracy in the mirrors, making adjustments, and finally grasping the right way to do the action, is uninterrupted. We no longer have to wait in turn for the teacher to notice our errors and fix them. Instead, assessment is initiated by the learners who are actually empowered by the feedback. Assessment is now integrated with, and contributes to, our learning. Nobody in the group is put down by it. Rather, the feedback assures us what we have achieved and informs us which way we should go next. This reassurance gives us confidence to learn the next movement. As a reflective teacher educator, I cannot help but think, isn't this what assessment should be? Shouldn't assessment help us to find out where we are, what we are good at, and how we can be better instead of telling us what we fail to do? Each student should be given a mirror in our educational system.

Using Feedback to Learn

The theory of giving feedback for learning is convincing enough but putting it into practice requires some careful planning. The feedback has to be relevant and meaningful to my students. I decided to use Education Projects in the module that I have been teaching for three years to try out some of my ideas. The module has two phases: The first one is a taught component whereby students learn the basics of how to do research and they have to develop a proposal, including a 1,000-word literature review on their topic. The second phase of the module uses a flexible mode of teaching. Students conduct their project in their own teaching environment.

The 13 students I have this year are practicing English teachers in primary schools. It is already the third week of class and students are still feeling their way through educational research. None of them has had any experience in independent inquiry. Traditionally, Hong Kong students are taught with a didactic approach. The teacher is the source of information and knowledge. Students listen and follow the instruction of the teacher. Feedback in this tradition carries a negative connotation and is usually in the form of the teacher telling students what they have done wrong. Feedback usually occurs at the end of learning through end-of-term examinations. My students and I were brought up in this tradition. As a teacher educator, I want my students to experience something different—that feedback can be supportive and empowering. I want them to construct the feedback themselves.

> "Your major assignment for this module is a review of the literature relevant to your own project. At our last meeting, we had some hands-on experience with Doris in the library on how to identify the literature. We had also discussed the purposes of a literature review. Today, I want us to develop a set of criteria that we can use to judge the quality of our literature review. I want you to tell me how I should judge your major assignment. What would an A-grade literature review look like?"

There is silence in the class. Might I have asked a question too diffi-cult for the students? I wait patiently. After a while, whispering begins to take place. At first the conversations are between neighboring students, then the pairs between the front and back rows join heads. The murmur grows louder and louder. I am amazed at the reaction.

> "I really want us to construct this standard for our work together and I am pleased that you are sharing your ideas. But I want to be part of it, too. It seems that you have some views. Could someone tell me what are your views about an excellent literature review?"

Hang, the student representative replies, feeling a little bit obliged to respond on behalf of the class:

> "Teacher, we are discussing why do you ask us for the grading criteria instead of just tell us. We do have some views but are you serious that we can set up our own rules for excellence?"

> "Yes, I do mean it. I want us to set up the rules so that we can use the rules for the major assignment. I want you to be able to tell what is quality work from mediocre. For sure I can just give the rules but coming from you, the criteria will make more sense."

Hang says, with more confidence,

> "Teacher, if you would permit me, quality literature review should first be relevant. It should tell us what has been done before in the area and should not be just a collection of any interest work."

> "Very good, Hang. Relevance is one of the key criteria for a good review. What else should be there?"

Being encouraged, Fun joined in,

> "Teacher, I agree with Hang but in addition, the work should be recent. The world has moved on and previous work can be dated."

> "That's right. We have to include recent work. But does that mean we should always discard work done sometime ago? How recent is recent? . . ."

Now that the class is reassured, they are happier to contribute their ideas. The discussion is scholarly and interesting. In the process of the discussion, very often students challenge each other by demanding examples or giving nonexamples. When misconceptions occur, they are soon corrected in the process of debate. The conception gets clearer and clearer with more definitions and examples. Pretty soon, we come up with a set of 12 criteria on how to judge a literature review, the criteria for their major assignment.

> "We have made great strides today. We should be very pleased with ourselves because this set of criteria on quality literature review is unique and of high standards. It is not only useful to us but also to other researchers. Could someone please help me to type it up and e-mail it to each of us before our next meeting? The criteria is to be used as standards for our work this semester."

I am quietly pleased with myself when I write my reflective journal after class. I taught in Australia for over 10 years before returning to Hong Kong. Before that, I spent three years in Glasgow, studying for my master's degree and working as a research assistant at the University of Glasgow. Hong Kong students are very different from their Australian or Scottish counterparts. I am still feeling my way as a faculty member at the Hong Kong Institute of Education. There are reasons to believe that today is a success. At today's meeting, I am not the only one to give feedback. Students give feedback to each other and in the process they learn more. Students are capable of setting up their own criteria to judge the quality of their work. The class is an "assessment" in the sense that students are being "assessed"—by themselves and by their peers—on their true understanding of what makes a good literature review. Learning and assessment go hand in hand. The process of setting up criteria for the final assignment also means that the class establishes common meaning for the assessment of the assignment.

In the next session, I bring three examples of literature reviews from the work of previous students and ask students to grade the pieces of work using their set of criteria. In the process, students modify some wording of the criteria. In applying the criteria to assessing real work, the students are able to consolidate the meaning of the literature review even further. My class is putting into practice what Jerome Bruner (1966) called "the process of knowing." He explained the learning process as follows:

> To instruct someone . . . is not a matter of getting him to commit results to mind. Rather, it is to teach him to participate in the process that makes possible the establishment of knowledge. . . . Knowing is a process not a product. (p. 72)

In this new conception of learning, assessment is part of the knowledge building process, focusing on the "how" rather than the "what" in learning. Instead of finding out what the student knows or does not know, assessment serves as a mirror to reflect the problem, and it provides an opportunity to learn from the feedback.

Getting Feedback From Students

As a teacher, I naturally want to know how my students are performing. What is their level of understanding? Are they ready to move on to the next topic? Hong Kong students are in general shy and introverted. If they have problems, they try to hide them or solve the problems themselves. They believe that they are "causing trouble" for the teacher if they ask questions. It is therefore particularly important for me to be proactive in getting feedback from them. In order to understand where my students are, I created a device called Listen-to-Me, which looks like the following:

LISTEN-TO-ME: Feedback to Lecture No. ___

1. The most valuable learning for me in this lecture is:
2. I still do not understand:
3. I want you to improve your teaching in the following way:
4. Other comments for you:

It is a one-page handout that is passed out at the end of the lecture for the student to complete and return to me. This is our fourth meeting, and by now my students can see that my style is a little bit different from the other lecturers. They have generally accepted my teaching style, but they are rather taken aback when they are asked to provide me with feedback with this form. In our tradition, teachers never consult students on how to improve their teaching. This may not be the best day to try out the Listen-to-Me. Quite a number of them were late to class, and I had already expressed my dissatisfaction with them last time. I thought my message was clear enough. After all, we spent much time on the topic at our last meeting.

"I feel obliged to speak on the topic of punctuality again although we have spent much too much time on it already. You are going to be teachers. How can you be a role model to your students if you cannot even come to class on time? I am really disappointed with you! If you have not learned from your other teachers when you were younger and if your parents have not taught you, then it is time that you learn. . . ."

I go on and on, with heartfelt disappointment. They look sheepishly ashamed of themselves, but, as usual, no one speaks up. "*I am not going to let you ruin my lecture. Let us move on,*" I tell myself. The lecture goes on, a little bit quieter than usual, but I can see that sparkle in their eyes. By the time I hand out the Listen-to-Me forms, I have already forgotten about my "speech." I expect students to give me feedback on their learning. They do, but to my surprise quite a number of them refer to the punctuality issue.

One student writes,

"Teacher, the most important learning today is that we have to be punctual and I thank you for your teaching. No one has ever talked to us like the way you do. Other lecturers only concentrate on academic work but you teach us how to be a person. Thank you."

Another says,

"I appreciate your teaching but please respect my parents. If I do something wrong, you should teach me and not shame me on my parents. This is something I want you to change."

Some students are even more direct:

"Those who are late do not hear what you say to us. They are the ones to blame. Why take it out on us? You talk about role modeling. Please role model by directing your dissatisfaction to the right people."

"Thank you for being frank with us. My classmates are wrong in coming to class late. But please know that they are not going against you. They do that for every lecture. Other lecturers dare not speak up because they are afraid we give them poor SET ratings. I am glad you are honest."

"Teacher, sorry I am late. I belong to a track and field team and there is training every morning. I cannot miss the training. I will be late again. Please forgive me. I should have come to seek your understanding first."

I collated and printed all the responses to each question and gave a copy to the students so that they would know how the whole class responded and so that they would know they were not alone in their feelings. I also wanted to empower them to be in charge of their own learning. I told them how I appreciated their being frank with me about what they had learned, the parts they enjoyed, the things they still did not understand, and the ways I should change my teaching. Then I moved to more specific topics related to the module:

"Many of you tell me to include real-life examples on making observations for research. I hear what you say. In response to what you say, I have made video footage of the children at play in the Jockey Club Primary School on campus. This is an authentic play situation. Let us use this video footage to learn how to observe."

For the whole semester, I made use of the Listen-to-Me form to collect feedback from my students. I adjusted my teaching in response to their expressed needs. With time, they became more and more sophisticated in their communications with me. The messages became clearer and more focused as they gained confidence in me that I was not going to punish them for what they wrote. In addition, my collating the responses of the whole class and providing them to the students in the following lecture heightened their metacognitive levels. Students responded to the Listen-to-Me forms in their reflective journals:

"I become more aware of where I am in Education Projects now than when I first started. Writing the Listen-to-Me responses has helped me to reflect upon what I have actually learned. It helps me to consolidate my learning."

"I am glad that I am not the only one who worries over the assignment. The others also say how they stress over it. Strangely enough, to know that there are others who share the same pressure as I do gives me strength to strive on. I am not alone."

"No wonder you are so different from the others. I did not realize you worked overseas for such a long time. Now that you explained, everything falls into place. I like your approach and I will try it with my students after graduation. I am the one who rebuked you. Both of my parents died in a car accident when I was about seven. To me, they are forever perfect. My grandma who brought me up let me have my ways. She says my life is hard enough and there is no need to give me more hardship. But I desperately want to know what is right and what is wrong. You are like a mirror. I lack a mirror in my life."

How much I want to tell my students that they are my mirrors, too! They have taught me that people learn best when they have better knowledge and awareness about themselves as learners and when they actively participate in the learning process. This experience is echoed by research findings (e.g., Boud, 1995; Gordon & Debus, 2002), which report in addition that high metacognitive levels are also associated with positive learning outcomes and self-efficacy (Butler & Winne, 1995). I believe timely quality feedback is critical to learning in two ways. First, it informs students where they are and whether the learning strategies have worked. Learning is enhanced by the provision of periodic feedback on the learning process and support in self-monitoring. Feedback is an important resource for learners to build their metacognitive skills. Second, it informs me of the extent of their learning and the effectiveness of my teaching strategies. My teaching has flourished as a result of feedback from my students.

Aspects of Assessment Reform

Assessment for learning is a major reform movement involving changes in many aspects from the conception of assessment to its implementation. At times when provision of education is limited, selection is a major function and purpose of assessment. For instance, in the 1960s, only the top-performing primary students had the opportunity to receive secondary education in Asia, including Hong Kong. Public examination served the purpose of selecting the academically best performing students to progress to secondary schools. Today, in many places across Asia, including China, Hong Kong, Japan, Korea, Taiwan, Thailand, and Singapore, education is free, compulsory, and provided to students up to around 15 years of age. The selection purpose of assessment for primary/secondary transition is no longer applicable, although for these countries competition for higher education is still intense. With the growing availability of online learning, it is envisaged that the selection purpose of assessment will diminish in importance. In the classroom, the need for teachers to prepare students to compete at public examinations has been reduced in its urgency. Instead, there is now space for classroom assessment to move from assessment *of* learning to assessment *for* learning. That is, teachers can use assessment to help each student find out where she or he is in the learning process, to determine whether the previous learning/teaching strategies have worked, and to give feedback to the student with regard to the next available learning strategies.

Assessment *for* learning differs from assessment *of* learning also in terms of its initiation. Whereas assessment of learning is externally mandated, takes place at assigned time intervals, usually at the end of key learning stages, and is used to find out what has been learned, assessment for learning is initiated by the teacher and student whenever feedback is deemed appropriate, tends to be both frequent and irregular, and is used to find out what the next learning strategies should be. Feedback from assessment for learning serves to consolidate what has been learned, to ascertain that learning is adequate, or to prepare for the next stage of learning. It may be easy to confuse assessment for learning with formative assessment. There is much overlap between the two concepts, but the latter refers to assessment while learning takes place and the former highlights the active generation and use of evidence about student performance to inform learning. Consequently, feedback and diagnostic information are key features of assessment for learning. The monitoring, measurement, and reporting in assessment for learning all have one goal: to guide continuous improvement in students' learning.

Quite different from assessment *of* learning, which tends to rely on externally mandated criteria, the criteria *for* making judgments on the extent of learning in assessment for learning can be jointly developed by the teacher and the student through a process of negotiation. The Sipaw Primary School in Taiwan allows its students to set their own goals for their individual yearly projects. Students plan their own timetable as well as set the milestones and assessment criteria to measure their own progress. Sipaw Primary (http://www.spps.hlc.edu.tw/homepage.htm) is the only school situated in the middle of the scenic national park of Taroko Gorge in Hualien County on the eastern coast of Taiwan. It had only 70 students when I visited in December 2002. Students largely come from the surrounding mountain villages. Many of them are descendants of the Atayal people, an aboriginal tribe of Taiwan. Children in the school call themselves "spirits in the mountain," and the locals fondly call the school "Kingdom of Kids in the Forest."

A Sipaw Primary 1 student set out to learn how to build paper airplanes for his yearly project because he had seen a plane flying overhead when his dad took him on a rare trip to town, and he was fascinated by this big bird. He decided to use the distance reached by the plane as a criterion to measure how good his design was. Instead of measuring the distance once for each plane, he decided to take the average of three attempts of throwing the plane from the stage down the school hall. Each week, he systematically modified his design of the plane, as well as the angle and force he used to throw the plane. He recorded the outcomes in a large chart, to indicate the dates, design details, action details, average distance achieved, his own comments on how to improve the next time, and the teacher's feedback. Another student wanted to learn German as her project; however, none of the teachers knew enough German to be the supervisor. The principal and teachers negotiated with the student to learn French instead. All were happy. Ah Mei, a Primary 2 student, chose to study clouds. She called her project "The Little Observatory." Ah Mei's project book included her detailed observations of clouds at different times of the day and year, complete with pictures and clippings. Ah Mei's mother gave this feedback:

> "Once you asked me, 'Mother, if I were clay, what would you make of me?' I was intrigued by your question, my child. In fact, children are more like clouds. They have their own shape, size, and color. Let my child be a cloud in the sky instead of a piece of clay in my hands. You fly freely and take your own shape. Whether you are a cumulus, stratus, cirrus, or even a cumulonimbus cloud that brings rain, you are the most precious gift to me from God."

Assessment for learning is assessment with love. There is genuine passion for the student to learn and excel. It is therefore sometimes called "student-centered assessment." Assessment for learning may take many formats, including projects, portfolios, journal writing, and performance. Instead of assessing each subject area, assessment for learning very often evaluates knowledge and skills across curricula, breaking the boundaries of curricular subjects. Professor Patrick Griffin of the University of Melbourne, Australia, quoted the example of the Investigative Performance Task used by the Tasmanian government in one of its public examinations (Griffin, 2003). In this assessment, students were invited to study the advertisements and articles in any 10 pages of a daily newspaper and then to respond to the four sections of the assessment. Collectively, tasks in the assessment gathered evidence on the students' capacity to understand, define, measure, compute, present, classify, reason, and apply their knowledge in solving real-life problems. Section 1 of the assessment asked the students to devise their own rules for categorizing a newspaper article as an advertisement, as news, as a feature, or as an article for information. Section 2 asked the students to measure the space devoted to each of these four categories in the 10 pages of the newspaper and present their results. In the third section, the students were to produce an article for the newspaper, classify it, and then identify its potential readers. Finally, the students had to decide where to place an advertisement for a product in the newspaper, estimate the cost involved, and justify their answer. Here, students' performance can be matched against Bloom's (1956) and Anderson et al.'s (2001) continuum of learning, comprising knowledge, understanding, analysis, evaluation, and creating.

As in the Tasmanian example, a major aspect of assessment reform concerns the reference to theories on learning in assessing the level of learning instead of making reference to the norm. Similar to a driver's license test, the emphasis is not on the number of other drivers surpassed by the candidate. Rather, the test aims to confirm the level of driving competence reached by the individual candidate. It is perhaps feasible to classify all drivers along the driving competence continuum. At the low end of the continuum, is the "nondriver" who does not know even how to start the engine of an automobile. The next level along the continuum is the "beginning" driver who mimics the instructor's actions and mechanically follows strict instructions from the instructor. The next level up is the "coping" driver who knows all the mechanical actions of driving but has not internalized the rules of driving and sometimes makes mistakes in judgment. The "performing" driver masters the traffic rules and driving skills with few errors. Near the top end of the continuum is the "defensive" driver who not only drives smoothly and politely and internalizes the traffic rules, but also anticipates dangers on the road and takes the necessary precautions.

This continuum from nondriver to defensive driver is called the "rubric of driving competence." Teachers wanting to use assessment for learning have to develop the appropriate rubric to reflect accurately the level of learning. In the Tasmanian example, a student who operates at the knowledge/ understanding level would be able to categorize articles as an advertisement, news, or feature. Another student who has reached the analysis/evaluation level would be able to analyze the placement of these types of articles in the newspaper using statistics or some other criterion, critique the pros and cons of placement of an advertisement in various locations for different groups of readers, and justify the choice of placement.

The change from norm referenced to criterion or standard referenced is key to assessment reform, but a distinguishing feature of assessment for learning is the developmental nature of the scoring rubric. Bloom (1956) and Anderson et al. (2001) proposed one developmental learning theory that can be used as a basis for establishing the scoring rubric, but other learning theories can also be used. For example, Biggs' (1995) SOLO (Structure of Observed Learning Outcomes) taxonomy can be the framework for assessing students' performance levels. SOLO describes different levels of learning from prestructure (little or no learning) to unistructure (one or several disjoint facts are known about one aspect), multistructure (several aspects of the learning task are mastered), relational (the different aspects of the task are understood as an integrated whole), and extended abstract (the integrated whole is understood at a higher level of abstraction and generalized to a new topic).

The consequence of a traditional mode of assessment designed for selection purposes is deterministic in the sense that the outcomes are unchangeable and usually have a severe impact on subsequent chances of formal learning for the student. For example, only about half of my primary 6 classmates got a place in a secondary school in 1966. The others were removed from the system by public examination. On the contrary, the new mode of assessment is to facilitate learning. Mrs. Kwong, one of my students in the curriculum and assessment module reading for a bachelor in education degree said,

> "In elitism education in the past, the main function of assessment is to categorize students into those who can and those who can't. With the advent of generalized education, assessment should support learning. Assessment, if used appropriately, can motivate learning, inform students of their achievement such that they can modify their approaches to learning, clarify learning goals for them, and identify their strengths and weakness. As a teacher, I am all for assessment for learning. But so much work is involved; I am soon going to be crushed by the reform!"

How Does Assessment for Learning Reform Affect Teachers' Work?

From the preceding discussion, it is tempting to visualize assessment reform as isolated events in classrooms with teachers fighting lone battles. Increased workload is an easy trap that teachers fall into if no deeper meaning is attached to the reform. A case in point is the failure of the Target Oriented Curriculum reform in Hong Kong. The Target Oriented

Curriculum was a major curriculum renewal initiative introduced by the Hong Kong government between 1990 and 1995 to improve the quality of primary education. The reform was well intentioned and based on sound academic principles that emphasize (a) the setting of goals to guide all instructions; (b) an all-around approach to teaching, including knowledge, thinking, skills, and attitudes; (c) contextualized teaching in the daily context of students; (d) student-centered approach; (e) equal importance on targets and processes; and (f) linking assessment with learning (Morris et al., 1996). The reform was well funded by about US$55 million for additional resources. In the implementation, however, there was inadequate consultation of and insufficient professional development for teachers.

The top-down approach resulted in a lack of understanding and a loss of ownership by teachers as well as many grievances from the teachers. In the confusion, teachers seemed to be trapped by the mechanical aspects of assessment instead of developing meaning from it. They felt that they were being coerced into the reform. Further, teachers did not see much benefit in the continuous detailed record keeping of each student in class for each set learning target. The expectation of modifying the curriculum for each student based on the outcome of the target-oriented assessment was too demanding given the teachers' workload. In a paper by Yeung Yiu Chung (1998), chairman of the Panel on Education of the Legislative Council, submitted to the council in 1998, it was reported that, in just two weeks, the signatures of more than 5,100 teachers from 250 schools were received in support of the motion to halt further implementation of the reform. TOC, the acronym for Target Oriented Curriculum, was used by some teachers as the abbreviation for "Totally Out of Control." TTRA, the acronym for Targets and Target Related Assessment, from which the TOC was derived, was nicknamed "Terrified Teachers Run Away" by the disillusioned teachers.

The challenges faced by teachers in the change process are well documented. For instance, Black and Wiliam (1998b) observed that, "Teachers clearly face difficult problems in reconciling their formative and summative roles, and confusion in teachers' minds between these roles can impede the improvement of practice" (p. 148). The challenges are, however, by no means confined to technical aspects. Many Asia-Pacific countries, including China, Taiwan, Japan, Korea, and Singapore, have long traditions of examinations, which also serve as a ladder for upward social mobility. These countries also share the culture of valuing hard work, competition, and "survival of the fittest," which might not be compatible with the assessment *for* learning philosophy (Shan, 2002). Conflict in cultural values between conventional and new approaches to assessment would imply different expectations from different stakeholders. For instance, parents might place stronger values on their children's excelling in examinations in academic subjects than in all-around development. Some principals might place priority on their schools' achieving top results academically. Such different expectations of the reform direction have made it difficult for teachers in their daily praxis.

Nevertheless, despite the challenges, the quality of teaching and learning is enhanced as a result of being better informed by the systematic gathering of accurate data on student learning, as evidenced by the research of Black and Wiliam (1998a). Teachers will be able to derive great satisfaction from students' enhanced learning. In a discussion on assessment for learning in the curriculum and assessment module, I asked my student teachers three questions: (1) What does assessment for learning mean to you? (2) Will assessment for learning ever work? (3) When will assessment for learning work? There were 20 student teachers in my group. All were experienced teachers in primary schools who had students with different levels of special needs (e.g., dyslexia, hyperactivity, etc.) and were being subsidized by the government for a one-year, full-time, in-service professional enrichment course leading to a teacher's certificate. All of them were cautiously optimistic toward the successful implementation of assessment for learning in their own classrooms when they returned to their schools the following year. One student teacher, Ms. Kam, expressed her views using her own learning in my module as an example. This is how she put it:

> Assessment for learning has worked. For example, for the assignment on literature review, we were free to select the articles and in the selection process, I came to better understand my learning needs, learning style, and interest. Then the format of this assignment helped me develop my writing skills and different genre of writing. In the process, I came to realize that it was just like preparing Chiu Chow tea. To brew high-quality Chiu Chow tea, we have to first warm up the teapot with hot water, put top-quality tea leaves in the teapot, then pour simmering hot water into the teapot, and pour-away the tea. This first round of tea is not for drink. Then we pour the second and third rounds of simmering hot water into the pot. The second round of tea so prepared is good quality tea but the third round is best. It has dawned on me that we

have to write our literature review in the same fashion—even with the finest articles at hand, we must be prepared to "pour away" our first and second drafts. The best comes last. I am learning throughout the whole process of this module through continuous reflection and self-assessment.

How to Implement Assessment for Learning in Your Own Classrooms

The Assessment Reform Group in the United Kingdom, which produced Black and Wiliam's (1998a, 1998b) report, identified 10 research-based principles (Assessment Reform Group, 2002) to guide classroom practice. The principles state that assessment for learning

- is part of effective planning of teaching and learning;
- focuses on how students learn, including both the "how" and the "what" of learning;
- is central to everyday classroom practice;
- is a key professional skill that needs to be nurtured through initial and continuing professional development;
- is sensitive and constructive in that comments focus on the work not on the person;
- fosters motivation by emphasizing progress and achievement rather than failure;
- promotes understanding of goals and criteria so that learners understand what they are trying to achieve;
- helps learners know how to improve through clear and informative guidance;
- develops the capacity for self-assessment so that learners can become more independent and reflective; and
- enables all learners to achieve their best and have their achievements recognized.

Based on these principles, teachers can translate assessment in learning into practice by

- clearly specifying for the students the learning goals and what is to be assessed;
- working out with students the standards they are aiming for;
- working in collaboration with peer teachers on assessment for learning strategies;

- encouraging and supporting students in developing the competence in assessing themselves by giving them sufficient experiences;
- developing the rubrics (descriptive rather than evaluative) for assessing the level of achievement;
- providing frequent feedback on the task and not on the learner;
- helping students to see where they are in relationship to their goals and supporting students in bridging the gap;
- fostering confidence in all students that everyone can learn;
- forming learning groups among students to foster peer support;
- adjusting your teaching based on feedback from students' learning;
- collectively reflecting with your peer teachers on the results of assessment and formulating new assessment for learning strategies or modifying existing strategies; and
- participating in professional development courses to develop capacity for self-assessment.

What Do You Think?

1. What mode of assessment would you like to implement in your own classroom? How will you decide which to use?

2. What are the relative pros and cons of assessment *of* learning and assessment *for* learning? Explain your answers.

3. What do you expect your students to say to you on your approach to assessment for them? Do you expect the parents to have the same views as the students?

4. What professional development programs on assessment would you consider to be beneficial to you? What are your goals in distinguishing between assessment *for* learning and assessment *of* learning from these programs?

5. What does assessment for learning mean to you? Will assessment for learning ever work? If so, when will assessment for learning work?

Suggestions for Further Reading

Black, P., et al. (2003). *Assessment for learning: Putting it into practice.* Berkshire, UK: Open University Press.

   This book describes a research project that examined the effectiveness of formative assessment in selected classrooms. The authors describe the benefits that teachers found in the project and provide suggestions for others who desire to improve formative assessment in their classrooms.

Brooks, J. G. (2002). *Schooling for life: Reclaiming the essence of learning.* Alexandria, VA: Association for Supervision and Curriculum Development.

Brooks urges educators to change their view on what educators should teach. Instead of looking at curriculum as separate from the lives of the students outside of school, the author challenges the read to consider combining the two. Her arguments are supported by examples from teachers, students, and parents.

Pellegrino, J. W., Chudowsky, N., & Glaser, R. (Eds.). (2001). *Knowing what students know: The science and design of educational assessment.* Washington, DC: National Academy Press.

This book provides insight into new ways of assessing students' performance in light of current research. The purpose is to provide readers with ideas for developing new forms of assessment, and examples are provided to illustrate these suggestions.

Smith, J. K., Smith, L. F., & De Lisi, R. (2001). *Natural classroom assessment: Designing seamless instruction and assessment.* Thousand Oaks, CA: Corwin Press.

The authors of this book argue that assessment should be a "natural extension" of instruction and should focus on students' strengths and help them surpass their weaknesses. The authors also discuss analyzing the results of these assessments as well as outside assessments.

References

Anderson, L. W., et al. (Eds.) (2001). *A taxonomy for learning, teaching, and assessing: A revision of Bloom's taxonomy of educational objectives.* New York: Longman.

Assessment Reform Group. (2002). *The 10 principles in assessment for learning.* Retrieved December 14, 2003, from http://www.qca.org.uk/ages3–14/afl/907.html

Biggs, J. (1995). Assessing for learning: Some dimensions underlying new approaches to educational assessment. *The Alberta Journal of Educational Research, 41*(1), 1–17.

Black, P., & William, D. (1998a). Assessment and classroom learning. *Assessment in Education, 5*(1), 7–74.

Black, P., & William, D. (1998b). Inside the black box: Raising standards through classroom assessment. *Phi Delta Kappan, 80*(2), 139–148.

Bloom, B. S. (Ed.). (1956). *Taxonomy of educational objectives: The classification of educational goals, by a committee of college and university examiners.* New York: Longman.

Boud, D. (1995). *Enhancing learning through self-assessment.* London: Taylor & Francis.

Bruner, J. (1966). *Toward a theory of instruction.* Cambridge, MA: Harvard University Press.

Butler, D. L., & Winne, P. H. (1995). Feedback and self-regulated learning: A theoretical synthesis. *Review of Educational Research, 65,* 245–281.

Gordon, C., & Debus, R. L. (2002). Developing deep learning approaches and personal teaching efficacy within a preservice teacher education context. *British Journal of Educational Psychology, 72,* 483–511.

Griffin, P. E. (2003). Unpublished lecture notes for the Master for Educational Management course, University of Melbourne.

Morris, P., et al. (1996). *Target oriented curriculum evaluation project: Interim report.* Hong Kong: The In-Service Teacher Education Programme (INSTEP), Faculty of Education, The University of Hong Kong.

Shan, W. J. (2002). *Quality assurance and assessment practices in elementary and secondary schools of Taiwan.* Unpublished manuscript.

12

A Seasoned Teacher's Experience with Technology

Pamela K. Miller

A s a result of state and national standards for teacher training, most teacher education programs contain a technology component as part of their curriculum. As Ms. Miller describes below, technology can range from basic tools that many people take for granted to more sophisticated equipment such as document cameras and two-way video technology. Despite what technology courses may teach preservice teachers to use, what is actually implemented will vary depending on what technology is available in each school. No individual chapter could begin to describe how every teacher uses technology, but Ms. Miller shares her personal experiences, which provide the reader with a picture of what might be available in a real classroom. The reader should keep in mind that some schools will have more technology readily available to students and faculty than what Ms. Miller describes, and yet some will have virtually no technology.

♦ ♦ ♦

One of the most exciting yet challenging educational tools for the classroom teacher is the use of technology. An incoming teacher will be exposed to various technological resources, and educators are expected to keep up with the advancement in technology. I am privileged to teach in a school district where I have access to various forms of technology. They consist of the basic resources such as a television and VCR, overhead projector, photocopying machines, and phone systems. More complex technology includes computers with printers, data projectors, scanners, the Internet, an e-mail system, and a variety of software programs. Regardless of the school district in which a new teacher begins a teaching career, technology will undoubtedly be used in one form or another, an indication that technology has become a permanent part of the educational process. An important reminder in the use of technology, however, is that it is not meant to replace the teacher or the curriculum. The classroom teacher is still the key to a safe and nurturing learning environment for every student. Technology's purpose is to enhance classroom instruction, further professional goals, and prepare our students for the technological world.

The more recent graduates of teacher education programs have an advantage compared to those of us who have been teaching for 15 or more years. In the beginning of our careers, having a television in the classroom to watch Channel One (an educational news program for schools) was the implementation of upgraded technology. Since that time, we have been required to receive training in the use of computers, software, e-mail, the Internet, and other technological tools. Because we did not grow up with these advantages, much of our technology education has come within the parameters of our working environments. Often, frustration has been a major obstacle to our acquiring technological skills because training was limited to in-service days or an occasional professional half-day. Support was rather limited in the beginning of our transition days to the use of technology in the classroom.

An important aspect of using technology within the classroom is learning to master an environment balanced between the integration of technology and the demands of a school district's expectations regarding curriculum and state standards. It is worth stating that technology is meant to be used as a supplemental learning tool and not as the total curriculum. The goal of this chapter is to share my experiences in the use of technology as part of the regular school day agenda as well as its implementation as a learning tool for students whose world is filled with technology. I cannot stress enough that the key word is *balance*. Attaining that balance may be challenging, but once it is achieved, wonderful results can materialize.

This chapter is divided into six subtopics presenting valuable information that may benefit any incoming teacher. My goal is for this information to help a preservice teacher understand some of the issues that educational technology raises in the mind of a seasoned teacher who did not grow up with technology; it is not intended to teach the reader how to use the technology discussed. I trust that by sharing my experiences and thoughts, the love for teaching and for students will be enhanced in the heart of anyone who chooses a career in education.

Basic Technology Within the School Building

As with any new job, there are many areas with which to become familiar in order to create a comfortable environment. At the beginning of the school year, becoming acquainted with the technology available in the school building will make teaching a little easier. Communication with other teachers, administrators, and staff may occur mostly through the use of technology. Acquiring knowledge in the use of photocopy and fax machines may become a necessary part of the school day. While these technologies may not necessarily directly relate to instruction, they have become a regular part of my job as a teacher.

The first important tool with which I have become acquainted is my school's e-mail system, which I use to contact others within my school and the entire school district. With laws to protect the privacy of students, it is crucial that a teacher use caution when sending information via e-mail, especially considering that we handle sensitive information about students on a daily basis. The importance of using caution when sending e-mails was never made clearer to me than as a result of my own mistakes as I learned how e-mail works. Perhaps one of the most important facts I learned is that e-mail is not a secure method for conveying private or sensitive information. For example, one could inadvertently send a message to several recipients at the same time if one is not careful. I made such an error in the first year my school implemented its e-mail system. Fortunately, I had replied to the sender concerning a relatively unimportant issue. I also have to use caution because students are often around my desk. If I were to leave an e-mail window open on my computer that contained private information, that information could be seen by wandering eyes. I have found that some e-mail systems may be quite simple to use, and others may have advanced features that require training to implement. Ultimately, I have learned to ask for help when I need it. I have countless times used the expertise of more experienced teachers or technology specialists in my school.

Another important form of technology that most teachers use is a VCR or DVD player, which may be used to show an instructional video that correlates with the curriculum. As I am not a very mechanically minded person, I soon discovered that to be confident in presenting the video as part of my instruction it was imperative that I know exactly where to push the play, pause, and rewind buttons without fumbling around in front of my students. Many students know more about these types of items than some of their teachers, which has been the case for me on occasion. One advantage to this type of situation is that it pleases a student greatly when he or she can demonstrate some form of knowledge that perhaps the teacher does not have. Despite this benefit to the student, I have found that it is still prudent for me to make sure I am prepared and know how to operate the equipment properly.

The last basic technological tool within the school building to consider is the photocopy machine. It can either be a user-friendly machine or one that causes much frustration. Depending on the budget of the school, photocopy machines can be anything from the latest model to an "oldie but goodie" model. Regardless of the machine, I have found it to be wise to ask for help if I am attempting to use an unfamiliar machine. When I was transferred to another building within my school district, the photocopy machine was completely different from the one with which I was familiar in my previous school. I was at a loss as to how to use the "new" one. No directions were posted in the copying room, which had always been my experience in the past. As with most other cases, I asked for help.

As a last point, working out the photocopy machine schedule according to the needs of everyone in the building can be challenging. I have always strived to plan ahead as much as possible for its use. Making my copies during my plan time has always proved to be a better time for me than trying to hurry to use the copier before classes start, which can be a frustrating experience. For example, I once realized that I would not have enough copies of a task that I would use for my next class. I dashed downstairs to the copying room in between classes hoping to make a few more. To my dismay, the machines were all occupied by other teachers who were using them on their plan times. I had no choice but to make other arrangements, a topic that I will address later. These experiences have taught me to plan ahead at all times.

Technology Tools for the Teacher

With technology becoming a vital part of the educational process, it is a wise teacher who takes advantage of the new skills and tools that appear on the scene. Depending on the technology funds of a school district, a regular classroom may have several forms of technology readily available for use. One of the most important forms of technology available to me has been my classroom computer. This is a wonderful asset to the teaching and learning environment that I strive to establish, and I feel that it aids me in completing all that I must accomplish each day. My experience in using the computer has been greatly enhanced as a result of the training that my school has provided my colleagues and me. As I have learned, those who are technologically oriented, whether they be other teachers or technology administrators, can offer valuable training in the use of those tools that are available to each individual teacher.

Once I reached a comfortable level in the use of my computer, I began exploring the various tools that I could use to assist my teaching and planning process. I set up my seating charts on my computer, which I can continually change as I determine the social makeup of my classes. I also create tests and quizzes or other resources for the curriculum. I am able to easily store on my computer documentation that needs to be saved throughout the year for administrators. I am able to communicate with my students' parents regarding their child's progress through the school's e-mail system; I also contact parents by creating personal letters and progress reports. As students are not often reliable in taking home written communication to their parents, e-mail has helped me to ensure that I keep better communication with my students' parents. These aspects of technology have helped me become a more efficient teacher, especially once the initial setup is complete.

With computers at an educator's disposal, it is inevitable that one will experience technical difficulties. In situations when I moved from one school to another, I learned early in the school year how to report problems and to whom. Depending on the situation, I must complete the proper forms to report a technological problem. In my school, I report these problems to a technology delegate. Sometimes, however, the problems are easily resolved by seeking help from a seasoned teacher. An important lesson I have learned in using technology is that a cooperative spirit is needed among all teachers whether it is over students or technological problems. For example, if my computer is not operating, another teacher is usually happy to allow me to use his or her computer for a brief moment. I am fortunate to have several colleagues who are generous in offering this type of support in such unusual circumstances.

An important lesson I have learned is that technology often breaks down at the very moment when I need it the most, either for teaching a lesson or for a last-minute test. For example, I was using a Web quest in the computer lab for the first time as part of enhancing a lesson. I had five classes using this particular Web quest, and we had bookmarked the Web site so we could go back to it every time we went into the computer lab. We successfully used it for two weeks, and we only had one day left for this unit. I took my first class into the lab, and to my frustration, no computer in the lab would open the Web quest site. We spent almost half of the class time trying to figure out the problem, but to no avail.

Needless to say, my students were in a state of confusion, and I did not really know what to do next. I had no other plans since we had been on this site several days prior to this incident. Fortunately, a student who was computer oriented began to hunt for a similar Web quest through a search engine and immediately found one that was comparable to the one I had planned in my unit. I had to improvise the rest of the lesson plan for that day, but remaining flexible allowed me to get through a tense moment. Once again, a student was able to come to the aid of his teacher in a time of frustration, but perhaps more important, I learned to always have an alternate plan ready in case the technology fails at the worst possible moment. In this case, it was only the particular Web site we had bookmarked that did not work. In some cases, the connection to the Internet may not be available, so I have alternate Web sites on hand, as well as tasks that do not require the use of computers. Having these backup plans available puts my mind at ease and prevents high levels of stress when the inevitable occurs.

In addition to the computer itself, one may add a list of peripherals such as digital cameras, scanners, DVD players, and data projectors. These items are of particular interest because there seem to be more and more opportunities to implement these technologies in order to further the curriculum in the classroom, to benefit the students, or to help the teacher in completing various duties throughout the school year. I finally learned to do a PowerPoint presentation for the first time with a lesson that I wanted to enhance for my students. It was exciting for me because my building had recently purchased the projector, so I had our building technology representative show me how to use it. My students were enthusiastic because it offered visual learning that was different from the traditional book and paper instruction. It was also something I had never used before, so they were intrigued with my new knowledge. Having experience with different technological tools will be a great asset to any new teacher's career. It is wonderful how technology can be incorporated into the everyday school agenda.

A final technology tool that one might take for granted, but that may benefit the students, is the overhead projector. Transparencies may be used to provide students with important information to be included in their notes, to engage students in activities related to the content of the lesson, and to provide visual supplements to the topic. I like using the overhead projector because it gives me the opportunity to face my students while writing or presenting information instead of always trying to write on the blackboard with my back turned to the students. It creates a more personal learning environment and provides an easier method for students to write down valuable information. The transparencies also allow me save the information for extended periods of time if the transparencies are stored properly (e.g., in a three-ring notebook). If I have students who are absent, they are able to get the transparencies from the notebook in order to copy needed information that was missed.

Technology and Student Safety

It is important to address pertinent information that every educator should know when dealing with the issue of students and their use of technology. In recent years, filtering systems have become much better at guarding students from sites that are inappropriate, but these systems are not foolproof. Every educator must be aware of laws and school policies regarding the use of technology for their own protection as well as that of their students. This information is not only for the use of the Internet but also for other technologies, such as taking pictures or videotaping in the classroom.

Many schools distribute an Internet agreement form to all parents at the beginning of the year. By filling out this particular form, the parents give permission to allow their child to use the Internet at school for the entire school year. By signing the form, parents also acknowledge that they are aware that their child is using the Internet at school. This form is extremely important, as the parent and the student agree that they will follow the appropriate guidelines for Internet use. Without the signed consent of the parent, students may not go online in any computer lab during the school day.

I have had students who did not return their signed Internet forms, so they were not able to go to the Internet in the computer lab. This has been frustrating at times because while the rest of the class is using the computers, that particular student must work on something else. If possible, I try to give the student something comparable to do without the Internet, but if this is not possible, the student can read a book or work on other assignments. It pays to follow up with parents on those students who do not bring back their permission/agreement forms, because it is difficult for students to complete certain assignments such as research papers when they do not have access to the Internet. I have also noted that online access is only available to some students at school, so following up with parents to get the signed forms is beneficial.

In my school district, teachers and staff are also required to sign an Internet use agreement form. School districts are usually particular about the Internet being used for educational purposes only, and my district requires us to agree that we will never visit any site that is inappropriate. What is more, the sites we visit can be traced. I have made a point to use the Internet for school and professional purposes only, and I save my personal Internet use for home. It is sad to say that there have been those who have made poor choices and have used the Internet at school beyond the educational parameters. Subsequently, they have paid the consequences. Teachers can lose their jobs, even with tenure, if they are found guilty of using the Internet inappropriately. The technology personnel in the school district can link any inappropriate use of a computer to its user.

The linking of Internet access to individual users leads to another important point: It is crucial that a teacher be aware of who has access to his or her classroom computer and restrict its use as much as possible. In my building, substitute teachers and assistants are not permitted to use a teacher's classroom computer. I have my own password for my computer, but I also pay close attention to ensure that my computer has been shut down at night and on the weekend.

With the security and protection of our students at the forefront of the minds of parents, teachers, and administrators, taking pictures and videotaping students in the classroom may require permission from parents. If I have projects planned that involve photographing or videotaping students, I always check with my principal to ensure that I am following the district's policy. For example, I wanted to videotape my teaching as part of a project I was doing for my master's degree. As I had suspected, I was required to obtain written permission from each student's parent. There were a couple of parents who did not want their student included in the videotape, so they sat in the back of the room out of the range of the camera.

On the other hand, I also had the experience of taking group pictures of my students to send to servicemen and servicewomen in Iraq as part of a class project. My district's policy for group pictures does not require parental permission as long as no names are attached. Whether consent is required or not, parents appreciate being informed about what the teacher is doing with video and photo images of their child. My experience has been that as long as names are not used with the photos, most parents will have no objections.

A Teacher's Support System

Having a strong support system has eased the frustrations that have cropped up with my use of technology. This support system includes other seasoned teachers, computer lab assistants, technology support personnel, students, valuable training, and last but not least, patience. It takes all these components, intertwined, to build a strong foundation of support that will last throughout the entire school year. The sooner I establish this support system, the sooner my frustrations are eased.

Becoming acquainted with the teachers in the building who are technology savvy can be the primary support for a teacher because they are easily accessible and can empathize with the frustrations that may occur. This is true because they have already experienced similar difficulties and have found solutions to these problems. There have been countless times that I have gone to other teachers or the technology representative in my building when I have had questions or problems with a given software program or other tasks involving some form of technology.

Computer lab assistants are also excellent resources. Because they deal with the computers in the labs, they often will have basic technical knowledge to help solve certain problems. The experience I mentioned earlier with the Web quest site not responding is a perfect example of the valuable assistance a computer lab assistant can give. They are also wonderful in helping find computer information for software programs and online information. The lab assistants in my school are also responsible for scheduling classes in the lab. Building a good relationship with them can be advantageous when incorporating technology into the curriculum.

Technology personnel in my school district are very busy people. Some districts have personnel who are responsible for meeting the demands of several schools within the district, while some districts are fortunate enough to have technology personnel for each individual school. Regardless of the situation, having to wait on the "techie" can be frustrating. In my school, we have one individual who is responsible for reporting all the technical problems for the entire building, and then we must wait for the district technology personnel to respond. Regardless of how technology people are distributed, it is inevitable that you will get to know them.

Students are another valuable resource within a support system. I am continually amazed by the knowledge that my students possess when it comes to technology. As I have previously described, there have been various times when a student has helped me solve a minor problem in the computer lab. Taking advantage of these moments has been a great opportunity to build teacher-student rapport as well as student self-esteem. Students love to help facilitate the learning process and little pleases them more than when they feel they have contributed their knowledge to benefit the teacher and their peers.

Acquiring the proper training for particular software programs and hardware tools can be challenging and is probably one area of technology where it is the most difficult to adequately satisfy the classroom teacher. Funding and time are usually the hindrances to meeting teachers' needs in this area, despite the fact that teachers would feel more comfortable in incorporating technology into the curriculum and using it in the classroom if appropriate training were available to them. With state standards requiring teachers to incorporate technology into instruction, I have actively sought out the training I felt I needed, which has included training provided by my school district and even additional course work provided by local universities. I am fortunate in that my school district also reimburses me for a large portion of the tuition fees that I pay for such courses.

My school district uses a program to keep track of students' grades. The school district provided training on the use of this program, which was extremely advantageous to me so that I could avoid making grievous errors in my students' records. This training also afforded me the opportunity to implement the different tools available within the grading program to keep better records of student learning progress as well as to establish communication with parents. A remedial software program was also instituted within my district to enhance our students' reading, mathematics, and English skills. As a result of my training in this software program, I was able to mentor the computer lab assistant when this program was networked into our building's computer lab.

Patience is last, but not least, on the list of the elements of a strong support system; indeed, it may be the most needed. Implementing technology is a valuable tool, but it may not always be reliable. This is probably a major drawback to its integration into the classroom. Difficulties may arise in the middle of its use. A computer lab schedule may change at the last minute because of the lab assistant's absence. A PowerPoint presentation may be flawed if the data projector does not work properly. A major challenge for me has been when I think an activity or a lesson on the computer will enhance my instruction, but then I discover that my students do not understand it or think it is boring. I have learned to become very familiar with the activity I want to use on the computer to offset any confusion or disillusionment that may arise. What I may think is wonderful may not always be the case for my students. I am continually learning as I strive to integrate technology into my instruction. I have learned that using technology does not guarantee a captivated audience.

A number of challenges may arise when incorporating technology into the lesson, but the main point to remember is not to panic. If plans do not go well, there is always a next time. Circumstances may develop that prevent me from using the technology that I have planned, so I have learned to have a backup plan. I keep other materials and ideas on hand for those last-minute changes. We do not live in a perfect world, and that is definitely the case with technology. Flexibility underlies patience, and I like to think that my patience and preparation make me a good role model for students on those days when Murphy's law seems to be in effect. I have had many of these days throughout my teaching career.

Available Software Programs

There are many wonderful software programs available to the classroom teacher, which are too numerous to include within the confines of this text. I will highlight a few that I have found valuable and instrumental for the enhancement of education. Many resources are available that may be adaptable to any teacher's classroom. The main programs mentioned here are those I believe to be pretty basic to the average school and classroom.

The World Wide Web is a tool that may be used to enhance the curriculum through the use of a Web browser. The Internet is a supplemental tool for students working on any kind of research project as well as other types of activities that may be part of the regular lesson. The textbook that I use for my curriculum also provides online access to a supplementary component to be used as an extended activity to the lesson; such activities are particularly beneficial to those students who are more hands-on learners or who have been absent for a while and need to catch up. Internet use is a wonderful asset for the teacher who is looking for ideas and lessons to complement the daily curriculum. Research modules and Web quests for projects are innovative tools to broaden students' horizons for a variety of skills and in-depth information about certain topics.

One of the requirements for our state standards is for students to complete a research paper. This tends to be a tedious task for most sixth graders, especially learning to develop a bibliography or works-cited page. The research process entails using the Internet as well as book resources. When we get to the point of using the Internet, I have my students use one search engine. From there, I show them how to use search terms in order to look for valid information. Before going to the Internet, in the classroom we have already broken the topics down into key words that the students will need to perform their search (e.g., land, climate, and history of a country). Specific guidelines are established in advance, which limit how many pages they are allowed to print. With the help of the librarian, students are shown how to cite Internet sources.

Many schools are implementing computer grading programs that allow the teacher to enter grades and track academic progress for each student. I personally endorse the use of this type of software, because I have learned to perform many useful tasks with it. Not only are grades tracked by the grading program, they can be calculated automatically once the program is set up to meet the teacher's needs. My school uses a program called Grade Pro. This software has been purchased by the school, and everyone in the building is expected to use it. It is the school's goal to use this program in the future to centralize the reporting of grades to the office in order to generate report cards. Right now, we must still enter the grades manually on a spreadsheet at the end of each grading period; however, everything else for the upkeep of grades is done by computer, which is much easier than keeping a traditional grade book. I also am able to have this program on my home computer so that if I don't have time to complete grades at school, I can work on them at home.

This program also allows me to print progress reports in order to determine which students have outstanding assignments. I am also able to keep track of my students' absences. Various charts and graphs can also be printed to compare a student's performance to the rest of the class. From these data, I am able to determine which students may need remedial or enhanced instruction.

Printouts, which show every assignment and the percentage/grade, are a wonderful supplement when talking to parents at parent-teacher conferences. When parents ask how their child is performing during any given time of the grading period, I can provide instant information with the overall grade and average, because the program automatically keeps track of this information on a daily basis.

The last software program I will mention is Microsoft Office. Many of today's teacher candidates are already familiar with this program, as they were probably required to use it in high school and college. Many school computers have this or another similar program installed, and they are wonderful tools. Excel, PowerPoint, Word, or any other version of these programs is complementary to any tasks a teacher may be required to perform. All of these tools can enhance instruction as well as personal use. I publish a newsletter each grading period, and I use Microsoft Word along with clip art to communicate with parents what we have been doing throughout the six weeks. I also have implemented the use of the scanner for scanning pictures of students to include in the newsletter.

Because I have used a PowerPoint presentation in my classroom for one of my lessons, my goal in the near future is to teach my students how to use it so they can create slides that will show their understanding of certain skills on which our standards are based. Enhancing instruction in this manner will give my students the opportunity to use their creativity, show any gained knowledge of the computer, and most important, demonstrate that they have learned the targeted skill. This would be a performance type of assessment that would be different from the traditional written test. This type of learning tool and assessment would also be beneficial to those students of diverse learning abilities. Students who need other methods of learning and assessment would be able to show their learning progress through this type of technology.

These examples are a very small part of what Microsoft tools afford the classroom teacher. Some programs may have more advanced functions, and one can also include additional items such as clip art or scanned images into documents. I have also been able to create word searches and crossword puzzles for lesson plans with much more to be utilized at a later date. Technology has brought many advantages to today's teacher, and this technology offers much support for the development of curriculum and the implementation of instruction.

Benefits of Using Technology

I purposely chose to save this subtopic for last, as it is my favorite one. Because I was introduced to technology after I became an educator, I can only whole-heartedly support its use as I have seen all of the positive effects it can have on both the student and the teacher. The valuable input technology has for the teacher has already been discussed so the conversation in this section will be centered on the positive benefits it provides to the students. With students living in a technological world, it is imperative that technology be used to enhance their education and to prepare them for the working world.

Integrating technology into classroom instruction gives students of all income levels, classes, and races an equal opportunity to gain experience and knowledge in its use, so long as schools that teach these students have such technology. It is true that many are concerned with the "digital divide" that has resulted in the great difference between the technology available to school districts in areas of lower income levels and that available in areas with higher income levels (see Kozol, 1992). I am fortunate in my own experience as a teacher in that my school district is able to train all of our students in the use of computers, whether or not they have computers at home. Even if school is the only place some students come in contact with technology, at least they will have experienced new knowledge much in the same manner as learning knowledge in any other academic subject. A potential drawback is that there will be students who have much more skill and expertise than others in technology as a result of the inequality among schools that have money and schools that do not.

It is even more important that schools ensure that all students have experience with technology because technology can have a positive effect in the learning growth of students labeled "low achievers," which may include behaviorally and academically at-risk or special-needs students. Having taught academically low-achieving students for 13 of my 15 years of teaching, I can endorse technology as a powerful tool for students who struggle to become successful learners. Offering a different avenue of learning builds self-confidence and self-esteem in these types of learners. What they cannot master under the traditional method of learning may often be mastered through the use of instruction on the computer. Additionally, I have seen behavior problems diminish as these students begin working more with their hands. Giving students a chance to prove to themselves that they can learn successfully is one of the most rewarding parts of being an educator. Not every student learns in the same way as another, and technology is a wonderful tool to use to cater to the needs of these individuals.

One of my five classes in my current position has been with students who are learning disabled. At the beginning of the year, they are always deficient not only in their English skills but also in their computer skills. As the year progresses, I take advantage of the computer lab as much as possible. I have seen this class grow the most compared to my other classes in their technological skills. Usually writing and spelling are difficult for this particular class of mine. By the end of the year, I have seen their English skills improve tremendously. I show them how to use spell check, and once in a while I have them actually type their rough draft on the computer instead of hand writing it. Their progress has amazed me throughout this year. Also introducing them to English activities on the Internet and using a Web quest project seems to enhance their ability to perform English skills at a higher level compared to the beginning of the year.

On the opposite end of the spectrum is applying technology for the learning enhancement of the gifted student. These students usually advance faster than their peers and need more challenges in their learning environment. A teacher may have a variety of learners in the classroom, so using technology is a wonderful tool for meeting the needs of those students who need a challenge. Allowing the gifted students to explore different activities online is an excellent way of enhancing their learning. Web quests as well as incorporating the creation of Web pages will challenge the gifted. These types of projects give the gifted students some room to use their creative abilities and advance at their own speed. Other types of computer work, such as using Microsoft Office, may also challenge them to explore their creativity while staying within the guidelines of the curriculum. I have allowed some of my higher-level students to incorporate their own ideas using technology into their research papers or group projects, especially when they are already highly comfortable with the use of the computer.

With no one student learning in the same manner as another, technology offers great benefits to the multiple intelligences a teacher will encounter among the students of a classroom. Howard Gardner (1999) promoted this theory of different intelligences, and I have seen this theory manifested in many different forms throughout my career. A student may function as a visual learner, a verbal learner, or a kinesthetic learner. In all, there are eight intelligences with the potential for a ninth. Using technology to meet the needs of all the different learners in the classroom is a wonderful way to provide variety in the learning environment (see McKenzie, 2004).

A teacher can decide what type of learning works best for certain students and plan to incorporate some form of technology in a successful lesson to reach these individuals. It requires work and planning to achieve this goal, but the rewards are great as a teacher becomes seasoned in education and learns how to meet the needs of individual students. PowerPoint presentations and supplemental lesson activities on the Internet will often meet the needs of some of the students. I have found that students who are poor writers with pen or pencil will often be able to get their thoughts down while using a word processor. Often, students show what they really know when the learning environment is geared for their personal learning success. Technology offers valuable resources to help create such success within the classroom.

Concluding Thoughts

The goal of this chapter has been to give the new teacher some insight into what one seasoned teacher uses in the form of technology on a regular basis. Technology is here to stay, and it has become an integral part of the educational process. As educators, we must offer our students the best education possible, and many wonderful opportunities are available with the use of technology in all its various forms. If an incoming teacher knows how to work with the resources available at the beginning of a school year, then perhaps one small part of becoming comfortable in the first year of teaching has been accomplished. Even though most new teachers have been exposed to much more technology than those of us who have been teaching for many years, there is still much to learn in the workings of any school. Each one of us has a different method for completing the finished product, which may involve technology.

While various forms of technology available to teachers have been discussed, the most important topic is the benefit that technology offers. The benefits for the students seem to outweigh all the arguments against the use of technology. Even though there are drawbacks such as not having available technological funding, teachers not comfortable with incorporating technology into the curriculum, the "digital divide" among student populations, and so forth, I believe the positives outweigh the negatives. We are living in a technology age, and it is vital for students to become educated with its use. It takes everyone within a school district working together to make the integration of technology successful, but it can be done if everyone involved becomes committed to its use. Technology is a learning tool that can only enhance student learning and the successful learning environment of the classroom.

Let me note here that the use of technology will never replace the classroom teacher. The teacher is the key to creating a positive learning environment that includes caring and nurturing. Machines and software programs cannot do that. They are still unreliable and will malfunction. The teacher is the one who puts the learning instruction together for students in the classroom. I may set up technology lessons or activities, but it still takes my planning and my time to work it into the curriculum. I have to know what the needs of my students are, and technology resources do not know that. I am the one who knows that one student may need extra reinforcement with writing skills or another needs to be challenged to enhance a project. Technology is a tool at the hands of the teacher who is the mastermind of the learning environment in the classroom. Using technology is to be balanced within the confines of meeting standards and the district curriculum.

We, as educators, are to not only impart knowledge to our students, but to also facilitate the learning process. Staying abreast of advanced educational issues includes technology. The more we are comfortable in incorporating it into our classroom instruction as well as our professional lives, the more benefits our students will reap. That is what education is all about: imparting knowledge and wisdom to the next generation. Educators have an awesome responsibility.

What Do You Think?

1. What technological skills do you believe students should have prior to graduating from high school? How should they obtain these skills? Whose responsibility is it to teach them these skills? When should they start learning how to use technology?

2. Describe how you have used technology to learn. Do you think you will expect your students to use technology to learn in the same ways or in different ways? How have you learned from these learning experiences? Explain your answers.

3. What are the benefits of incorporating technology into the curriculum? What are the dangers?

4. Describe your best classroom experience when a teacher used technology as part of the lesson? Why was this lesson the best? What would have made the lesson less effective and why? What might have made the lesson better?

5. Describe your worst experience when a teacher used technology as a part of the lesson? Why was this lesson the worst? What would have made it better?

6. How is technology affected by the inequalities in school funding? How do these inequalities affect students? Do you believe that this inequality matters?

Suggestions for Further Reading

Heinich, R., Molenda, M., Russell, J. D., & Smaldino, S. E. (2001). *Instructional Media and Technologies for Learning* (7th ed.). Upper Saddle River, NJ: Merrill Prentice Hall.
    This book offers the teacher a variety of ways to develop lessons using most of the technologies available for use in the classroom.

Mills, S. C., & Roblyer, M. D. (2003). *Technology tools for teachers: A Microsoft Office tutorial.* Upper Saddle River, NJ: Merrill Prentice Hall.
    As the title suggests, this book offers the preservice teacher a tutorial in using the various components of Microsoft Office. This book might be of particular interest to those who do not have a technology component in their teacher education program.

Roblyer, M. D. (2003). *Integrating educational technology into teaching* (3rd ed.). Columbus, OH: Merrill Prentice Hall.

The author maintains that integrating technology should always be based on theory and pedagogy. Technology should help meet teaching and learning needs. This book also provides specific ideas for using technology in specific subject areas.

Sandholtz, J. H., Ringstaff, C., & Dwyer, D. C. (1997). *Teaching with technology: Creating student-centered classrooms.* New York: Teachers College Press.

This book provides a collection of case studies and teachers' accounts of using technology in their teaching. It presents issues about the change in teaching and the role of the teacher and student as a result of current technology, as well as many other issues.

References

Gardner, H. (1999). *Intelligence reframed: Multiple intelligences for the 21st century.* New York: Basic Books.

Kozol, J. (1992). *Savage inequalities: Children in America's schools.* New York: Perennial.

McKenzie, W. (2004). *Standards-based lessons for tech-savvy students: A multiple intelligences approach.* Worthington, OH: Linworth.

Part V

Starting Your Career

13

An Employment Guide for Preservice Teachers

Joseph McSparran

I t is never too early to begin preparing for the job market. Preservice teachers should begin thinking about what kind of job they want and where they would like to work, and they should begin developing their portfolios and résumés. Field experiences prior to graduating from college are excellent opportunities to make the preservice teacher known and such experiences could result in a job offer upon graduation. Dr. McSparran presents the many issues that future teachers will face as they begin searching for a job. By thinking about these issues now, the reader will be ready and may be a stronger candidate for positions when that time comes. This chapter is not quite like the others in that it is more of a "how-to" chapter. It may provide more information than the beginning preservice teacher needs to know right away, but it is better to know early what is expected in order to be prepared for the future.

◆ ◆ ◆

Introduction

As a public school administrator for 25 years, I was very closely involved in the recruitment and selection of many candidates for teaching positions in my school district. As an assistant principal, high school principal, assistant superintendent, and superintendent, I took this yearly responsibility

223

very seriously as our team of recruiters selected the best possible candidates to join our ranks as educators in the school district. One of my former colleagues likened this process to a marriage, in that it had to be taken quite seriously if it was to survive as a lasting, long-term relationship. Given the seriousness of this recruitment and selection process, our administrative team approached this endeavor with a well-planned and very predictable format, to ensure that we were consistent in our approach to all teacher candidates and that we made the best possible use of the limited time available to select teacher candidates.

When I left public education and became an instructor in higher education, I was frequently asked by colleagues to speak to professional education classes about the employment process for teachers. I found that much of the experience I had had in this endeavor could be valuable for preservice teachers who were involved in locating professional positions. What follows is a compilation of practical ideas and strategies that I hope will prove to be of value in this process.

Locating Professional Vacancies

In recent years, school districts have found it to be relatively easy to advertise for professional vacancies. While professional listings in local newspapers and trade papers are still used in many districts, other sources are also available to ensure a wider distribution of announced openings. Current technology has made it extremely easy for school districts to announce openings and advertise for positions within their schools. With the increase in district Web sites, many schools use their district sites to advertise openings. Additionally, there are hundreds of related sites that post vacancies via the Internet.

College and university career services offices are always a valuable resource for up-to-date position listings. Many school districts send announcements regarding openings to career services offices and colleges of education for posting and/or distribution to preservice teachers.

Job fairs are an excellent source of information regarding available teaching positions. Teacher training colleges and universities frequently organize these fairs to provide their students with opportunities to learn about professional openings. While the format for these fairs can vary, most are organized so that teacher candidates can provide professional résumés for recruiters and also speak with school recruiters about possible openings within their districts. As a school administrator, I liked the job fair format because it provided an opportunity to conduct mini-interviews of several candidates in a relatively short period of time. I was able to learn a lot about a person in a 10-minute interview, so candidates should be prepared to do more at a job fair than provide recruiters with résumés and answer rudimentary questions about their candidacy.

In most instances, school districts will attempt to write or post vacancy notices that are as complete as possible. The announcements will highlight information such as the position opening, the grade level, and the specific school within the district. While concise, short announcements can minimize advertising costs, many districts have found that additional print information can save their office personnel unnecessary phone time when candidates call for ad clarifications or other related job information that was not included in the advertisement. However, if one needs additional information regarding an advertised position, the district office will be more than willing to provide these details. If a district simply states that it is seeking candidates for "all grade levels and positions," the candidate should place a call for more details. While the search for a professional position is extremely important, it is advisable not to waste one's time if the job is really of no interest. A simple phone call could save the job seeker a significant amount of time and effort.

Applications for Professional Positions

School district applications and styles of applications come in a variety of formats. While some school districts still use applications that they have personally designed, many districts have adopted a standard application, as designed and recommended by professional organizations. Standard applications have been incorporated in many districts to minimize the possibility of requesting information that could be construed as discriminatory. Some applications are available online and can be completed and submitted online, while others still require that the applicant complete forms by hand and use conventional mailing for submission.

Some school districts want to assess handwriting skills and will specifically ask that the application, or part of it, be completed by hand. If that is the case, the applicant should be certain to take the necessary time to be neat in completing the application and any supporting documents. If not otherwise specified, it is appropriate to type the responses to the application. Simply stated, a professional application must look professional to be well received. I can recall looking at several applications that were not completed neatly, which sometimes left me with a bad impression and led to the elimination of that applicant from the pool of potential candidates.

All questions or inquiries on professional applications need to be addressed or answered completely. Choosing to not answer questions, or leaving obvious gaps in responses, will undoubtedly raise questions (or possible doubt) on the part of the person who is reviewing the application. For example, if I reviewed an application that asked the candidate to develop a chronology of professional development, and a period of time was missing from that timeline, I would be certain to ask a direct question about that missing time period during the interview.

If the applicant is asked to submit professional documents with the application, it is important to send photocopies instead of the originals. A teaching certificate represents official licensure to teach and it is crucial that one not lose these documents. Instead, a candidate should keep these important papers in a safe place and bring them along at the time of the interview.

When one lists general references on applications, it is important to select people who can best address the applicant's strengths related to the position. General references can speak to the applicant's personal qualities and personality characteristics, but potential employers will want to know how well-prepared the candidate is to be a teacher. One should have a balance of references that are able to address all of one's qualities, both personal and professional.

It is important to contact the individuals in advance to obtain their permission before listing them as references. In addition to being certain that you can count on their endorsement, it is prudent to ensure that a current and valid phone number accompanies each reference. If reference checks are made during vacation periods, school phone numbers will be of little value. During my involvement with the recruiting process, I was frustrated when my attempts to contact an applicant's references could not be completed because the individual in question ". . . is on summer vacation and will not return for several weeks."

The Professional Résumé

The professional résumé should serve to present an accurate picture of the candidate for the professional position. It is imperative that the résumé present as much viable information as possible, but this does not imply that a multipage document will receive more attention than one that is more direct and concise. When I was involved in this process and encountered a résumé that was more than two pages in length, I would usually skim through the document in the interest of time. I appreciated résumés that were skillfully developed to direct my eyes to the pertinent information for the position. In that light, I recommend limiting the length of this document to two pages. It is important to avoid leaving out information that is critical to one's candidacy, as that might harm one's chances for additional consideration.

There is standard information that I look for when evaluating a résumé. The candidate should always include a current address, phone number, and e-mail address. There should also be a professional objective that is clearly stated in order to ensure that those who review the résumé will have a clear understanding of the candidate's professional goals and aspirations.

In addition to the basic information mentioned previously, I prefer to see an applicant's educational and professional preparation listed in descending order from the most recent date of completion. This should include complete names of colleges and universities, including credits and/or degrees received from each institution. In a similar fashion, one should include a listing of all professional experience, as well as a work history. Of particular importance is a listing of work experiences that relate specifically to professional preparation for the classroom.

I also look to see what affiliations related to the teaching field a candidate has. In addition, a candidate's interests and activities may be of interest to a potential employer. I am also interested in an applicant's honors and awards that are related to his or her area of professional interest.

On occasion, there might be additional information in reference to one's candidacy to include on one's résumé. For example, if the candidate is interested in coaching or assisting with clubs or school organizations, this is information that I might look for in this section. As an administrator who frequently struggled to find coaches and club sponsors, I was always encouraged to see that teacher candidates had an interest in various athletic and extracurricular programs, as well as a willingness to serve as a mentor, coach, or advisor for these activities.

Submitting Your Application/ Personal Contact and Follow-Up

While many school districts expect that candidates will mail application materials directly to the personnel office, technology has made it possible to submit these materials as e-mail attachments or fax transmissions. While technology has obviously resulted in easier approaches to the submission of these materials, candidates should consider the feasibility of relying on another less technical approach to the process, and a personal preference of mine—hand delivery. In consideration of this "slower" approach, the following are advantages and helpful hints that make a positive impression on me when I am conducting a teacher search.

Even though it is not likely that delivering an application packet will take much time, it is probable that delivering an application in person will mean being greeted by someone on whom one should make a good impression. One should dress appropriately and conduct oneself professionally even for such a brief visit. Hand delivery of application materials provides the candidate with the opportunity to personally meet someone in the district or school office, and it adds a face to otherwise very generic application materials. In such situations, it is a good idea to ask if it is possible to personally give the materials to an administrator or human resources officer. While it is presumptuous to expect to be interviewed on the spot, many administrators do encourage the practice of officially receiving application materials from candidates so that they can attach a face to an application when reviewing candidate files in the future. Throughout my career as a school administrator, I directed office personnel to inform me when candidates were delivering application materials so that I could meet them face to face. In many instances, this initial meeting provided an excellent opportunity to make a "first impression" assessment of potential candidates.

The employment process varies among schools and school districts. I always encourage applicants to ask about how the selection process works, because I believe that a candidate for a teaching position needs to know how and when the process will unfold in order to keep track of the proceedings. It is not a good idea to allow several weeks or months to pass without knowing about the status of the position for which an applicant has applied. If possible, it is a good idea to ask for the name of a specific contact person in the office who is responsible for collecting and cataloguing application materials. This can help to ensure that someone who is familiar with the candidacy addresses follow-up inquiries.

The Professional Interview

While success in being chosen for an interview will be due largely to strong academic preparation, an impressive application, and related credentials, there are some other basics that need to be remembered while waiting to hear from school districts regarding interviews.

Depending on the academic area and the popularity of the school district, there may be many applications for a single teaching position.

While it is generally customary to acknowledge receipt of a candidate's application materials, all school districts do not necessarily send out this notification. In such cases, an applicant should assume the initiative and contact the district to see if materials have been received. It is also important to remember that not all applicants will be granted an interview. During my tenure as a school administrator, I can recall some subject area files that contained in excess of 50 applications for a single teaching position—far too many to allow us to interview all candidates. For that reason, an applicant should call to check on the status of the application if he or she has not been contacted within a reasonable amount of time.

During the application process, it is crucial to ensure that a school district can contact the candidate to schedule an interview. When a candidate is not available during regular school hours, it is important to provide potential employers with a valid phone number or e-mail address where they can leave messages. It is frustrating if a school district interviewing six to eight candidates for each opening, is not able to contact an applicant to set up an interview date. As a former administrator, I can recall inviting other candidates in the recruitment process in lieu of a desirable candidate whom I was unable to contact. Candidates should also be certain that roommates, spouses, significant others, or parents are aware that school districts may be calling. Receiving a message from a roommate that "Some woman called about an interview, but I didn't get the number" could cost you a job and seriously damage a friendship.

When a candidate is contacted to set up an interview in a school district, it is a good idea to ask if the district has all the necessary application materials. Many districts will mention the fact that they need to see originals of certificates and clearance forms at the interview. Even if the district does not ask for this information, it is still prudent to have them at the time of the interview. A misplaced document could inhibit the interview process.

In addition to the previous documents, many candidates will bring portfolios with them to the interview. Specific artifacts that illustrate a candidate's strengths can prove to be valuable in an interview. Preservice teachers should begin collecting artifacts from the moment they enter their teacher education program. Items to include in a portfolio include papers that demonstrate growth in the profession, a statement of one's educational philosophy, special projects that highlight teaching abilities, lesson plans and other evidence of teaching experience, and special awards and honors that might help the candidate stand out among the other applicants.

When invited for an interview, a candidate should learn the exact time of the interview, as well as with whom and where the interview will take place. When not certain of the location and when it is practical to do so, taking the time to do a dry run will afford the applicant an opportunity to see how long it will take to get to the right location. It is a good idea to arrive a few minutes prior to the interview. While delaying the interview by arriving late is not good, waiting in a reception area for half an hour or more will do little to eliminate growing anxiety.

Because school districts approach the actual interview process in varying ways, it can be difficult to know what to expect when walking into a conference room or office for the interview. The number of individuals involved in the process also varies from district to district. Because of the importance associated with employing new teachers, my district interviews included a principal or assistant principal representing the school, along with a department supervisor or chairperson. Also, the central administration was usually represented by an assistant superintendent or the chief school administrator.

In some instances, the actual interview process is standardized and quite formal, while other settings are very relaxed. If the district is one that utilizes a prescreening tool, it will have already obtained valuable information about each applicant prior to the interview. One cannot assume, however, that all participants of the interview process have reviewed your credentials prior to the actual interview. Therefore, a candidate should be prepared to discuss experiences that may be described in the application packet.

While the interview should be the candidate's primary concern, the interview team is likely working on a tight time schedule, particularly if they are trying to complete several interviews in a short time span. Most interviews can be successfully conducted in 45 minutes to one hour, which really is not that long a period of time to determine if "the marriage of a teacher and a school district" is going to be successful. Consequently, as questions are asked during the interview, a candidate's response should be complete and concise. While practice does not necessarily make perfect, reviewing potential interview questions and formulating responses can prove to be quite helpful. A listing of several practice questions is given later in this chapter, as well as a section with questions a candidate may wish to ask during the interview.

Dressing for Professional Interviews

Assuming that the adage about first impressions is valid, personal appearance at a professional interview must be viewed as critical. While many school districts have abandoned more conservative dress codes for their staff, until entrenched as a member of the professional staff, one cannot assume that "smart casual" attire is appropriate, particularly for the interview. Conservative dress is always the best choice, and one for which an interviewee cannot be criticized. I have mentioned to many of my students who are preparing for interviews that the "casual Friday" philosophy is one that is interpreted by some school administrators as meaning that on one day of the week a teacher does not have to look professional, suggesting that looks beget performance.

While a neatly pressed sport jacket and slacks are acceptable, a conservative suit is still the best choice for men at the professional interview. A dress shirt and coordinating tie are a must, with special attention to everything being clean and neatly pressed. Dress shoes can finish off the overall appearance only if they are well polished. For women, it is important to remember this is a professional interview and not a cocktail party, so leave the party dress and stiletto heels in the closet. While conservative pant suits are acceptable for women in most professional work environments, a tailored business suit is considered most appropriate for a professional interview. Jewelry is quite appropriate to accent the outfit, but it should be conservative and not a distraction or a focal point for the interview team. Again, conservative and polished footwear should complete the ensemble for the interview.

On several occasions, students have asked me for an opinion regarding their appearance and whether or not certain personal preferences regarding their appearance could have a negative effect on their interview. Simply stated, if there is something about your appearance that you feel could be interpreted negatively, there is a good chance that you could be right. Unkempt hair, poorly trimmed beards, heavy makeup, garish jewelry, and unconventional piercings can draw attention away from the candidate's strengths as a professional. If one's commitment to one's physical persona is sincere and unfaltering, it is important to note that administrators may be looking for a more conservative role model for their classroom.

A Review List of Interview Questions

Developing a complete list of possible interview questions would be extremely difficult, if possible at all. The individual interviewer, the number of people comprising the interview committee, and the possible use of formal instruments will dictate the nature and design of questions posed to candidates. However, school districts that view the process as structured and formal will likely have a list of questions that they will ask all candidates being interviewed for a particular position. This was always very important to me as a school administrator when interviewing teacher candidates. Not only does this ensure that the committee will be using the same measuring device for all candidates, it also provides the ability on the part of the committee to compare and contrast candidates and their responses. Assuming that interview committees do prepare and review which questions they will ask, it is in the best interest of the candidate to consider the types of questions that could be asked and to practice possible responses to these questions. I have provided these questions to my students who are preparing for interviews and they have found them to be most helpful. If nothing else, the questions will provide an opportunity to formulate some general responses to a variety of inquiries.

The sampling of questions listed herein are standard fare, some are creative and thought provoking, and some are weak. This list is by no means exhaustive, but it does represent a cross section of possible questions. Please note that I have used all of these questions; a potential teacher candidate should review how to address each one while preparing for formal interviews.

1. Provide a brief narrative of highlights from your personal and professional background that you feel prepared you for this position.

2. Using only adjectives, how would you describe yourself? (*Note:* This is a favorite of many school district administrators. It is often asked to see if the candidate can follow simple directions.)

3. How would you describe a typical 10th-grade boy or girl? (*Note:* This can be adjusted to any grade or class, depending on the position that is open.)

4. Hypothetical situation: You have been hired for this position and during your third week in school you are visited by the principal. What would the principal see in your room? What would be taking place during a typical class?

5. Explain the elements included in your daily lesson plan. How is technology incorporated in your planning?

6. How would you plan for the diverse abilities of students in your classes?

7. What are the basic ingredients that make up your classroom management plan?

8. Why are you the best candidate for this position?

9. In what way(s) has your personal philosophy of education changed since the time you entered college?

10. What is your five-year career goal?

11. How would your instructional planning address the diverse learning styles of students?

12. What is your definition of a well-disciplined classroom?

13. What part does assessment have in your planning and what types of assessments would you use in your classes?

14. What do you consider to be your greatest academic strength, your strongest character trait, and an area of greatest personal interest?

15. What would you do to promote the integration of your subject with other disciplines?

Preparing Your Questions for the Interview

At some point in the interview process, the candidate will have an opportunity to ask questions. When I was involved in the interview and employment process, our committees used this as an opportunity to see how much thought a candidate had put into the process prior to the actual interview. It provides an opportunity for the candidate to ask questions that are of importance to him or her.

In preparation for this opportunity to ask questions, it is recommended that a candidate write out the questions on a note card or piece of paper. This provides a reminder of issues to be addressed. Of greater importance is that the committee knows that the candidate has taken the time to prepare questions for them.

One of the final questions that applicants should ask prior to leaving an interview concerns what the timeline will be for filling the vacancy, whether there will be a second interview, and how the candidates will be notified regarding their status with respect to the position. However, if there seems to be an inordinate amount of time beyond the stated time frame, the candidate may call the school district to ensure that his or her application has not been misplaced. A courtesy follow-up should be viewed by the district as sincere while also putting the candidate's mind at rest about the status of a particular position.

Some Considerations When
Offered a Professional Position

Receiving a phone call informing an applicant that he or she has been selected for a professional position results in a high level of excitement. While the candidate's immediate reaction may border on hysteria, remember that he or she is also interviewing the school district and may have issues or concerns that should be addressed prior to accepting the position. In preparation for an offer, it is necessary to ensure that all of your concerns and questions have been answered to your satisfaction and that this is *the* position you want. After signing a contract, it is too late to inquire about conditions of employment.

Understanding the process of employment from the time of accepting the recommendation for appointment is important. Typically, one is only recommended for hire by the administration, but officially hired by the school district's board of education. As a school superintendent, I always reminded candidates that the board of education and *only* the board of education does the hiring. While the superintendent or a personnel team may make recommendations for filling positions, only the board can make the final appointment at a regular meeting or advertised special board meeting. This means that as a candidate considering a number of positions or in the running for other positions, it is crucial one not notify other districts of one's withdrawal of one's candidacy until the board has acted officially on the recommendation of employment. Unfortunately, there are occasions when the board does not follow the recommendation of the administration. The lesson is: Do not sever potential employment opportunities with other districts until the board has confirmed employment.

While it is acceptable take "some time" to consider an offer of employment, most administrative teams work on tight time schedules. Often, an offer of employment is tied to a deadline for a decision. While a request for "some time" may really be the hope for an offer of employment from another district, administrators have faced this indecision in the past and know that they may be competing with other districts for a skilled teacher in the classroom. Therefore, a candidate offered a position should be prepared in situations such as this to make a definitive decision quickly.

Making the Most From Rejection Calls and Letters

Picking up the phone after the second ring, you are less than enthusiastic about the serious voice on the other end of the line informing you that another candidate has been selected for the position for which you applied and were interviewed. While many school districts inform unsuccessful candidates through the mail, those school districts that personally contact candidates can maintain respect and appreciation if they take the time to talk about the position and to offer some specific reasons for selecting a different candidate. As a school superintendent, I required administrators to personally contact all candidates that were interviewed, regardless of the outcome.

While a natural reaction might be to get angry with the caller, one should take advantage of these opportunities to inquire further about the interview and what one might do to improve one's interview skills in the future. If the rejection notification comes in the form of a letter, one could pick up the phone and call the person who chaired the committee to inquire about the interview, in an attempt to get specific reasons for not being considered for the position. For example, what did the successful candidate bring to the position that the other candidates did not possess?

School districts will be in a position in the future to interview for additional professional openings. If the candidate feels a particular district is an environment in which he or she would like to work, he or she may ask that the district keep the application active in the event that there is another opening in the future. Even if it is not a desirable school district, it is important to be professional at all times, even if it means swallowing one's pride. Dealing with damaged pride is far easier than dealing with the permanent damage that can be created when one starts burning bridges.

Substitute Teaching

While the current employment market appears to be improving for new graduates looking for teacher openings, a shortage of available positions continues to exist in many areas of the country. Graduates seeking positions in more attractive districts need to realize that they will face keen competition for scarce, permanent teaching positions; including those positions for which there are few certified teachers. Graduates interested in urban school settings or employment in areas of the country that are experiencing shortages will find employment somewhat easier. Early-retirement options and incentives have created some additional positions, but additional early-out incentive programs will be necessary to ease the current shortage of positions.

Substitute teaching receives mixed reviews by those entering the profession of teaching. Some younger teachers are committed to substitute teaching as a way to get started if a permanent position is not available to them, while others are not willing to agree to day-to-day short-term assignments. A number of considerations should be evaluated when looking at substitute teaching as a first position in the profession.

Some districts have a reputation for not employing teachers who serve their schools as regular substitutes; the reason being that good substitutes are difficult to find and they do not want to deplete what is usually a short list of available day-to-day substitutes. While some administrators will not readily admit to this practice, my experience has shown that it is the practice in some districts in an effort to ensure that good substitutes are on the list of the day-to-day possibilities. While one may have a difficult time getting a straight answer from some administrators regarding this practice, I would encourage candidates to inquire of other teachers and colleagues regarding the use of this employment approach.

If one is committed to teaching, the substitute route can be an excellent introduction to teaching. Substitute teaching can provide opportunities not only to practice the art of teaching, but also to showcase talents and abilities to supervisors and administrators. If one has had time to plan a substitute lesson and feels confident with the classes with which one is working, it would be appropriate to ask a supervisor or administrator to sit in on a class and observe. I always found this to be an ideal opportunity to evaluate potential candidates for permanent positions.

When entering the world of substitute teaching, one should limit the number of districts in which one will work in order to be available at their beck and call. Applying for substitute status in too many districts will limit one's availability on a regular basis, leading some districts to call teachers who are more readily available. In choosing districts in which to work, one should also consider the proximity to one's residence, especially since a substitute teacher may not receive a call until 6:00 a.m. that morning. A long commute might complicate the process.

When called to substitute, it is important to follow the lesson plans that are left by the regular classroom teacher. When regular teachers hear that the sub "did nothing," they may be reluctant to specifically ask for that substitute in the future. In the event that a teacher leaves no lesson plan, a substitute who makes an effort to provide something that is worthwhile for the students has a greater chance of recognition. Providing a written report that details what took place in each period will be appreciated. This attention to detail can result in specific requests for that particular substitute in the future and, ultimately, the possibility for longer-term employment.

A frequently heard comment from graduates regarding substitute teaching is as follows: "I'm not going to sub. I'll wait until the end of the semester or the end of the school year and then reapply. I have bills to pay, a loan to honor, and I really don't like the idea of not knowing when I'll be teaching." My response to this statement has always been the same: How will the semester or year off increase your value to a school? If you get another interview and are asked how you spent your semester or year, an administrator will likely be more impressed that you served as a regular substitute teacher rather than as a full-time employee in an area that has no relevance to your chosen profession. Entering the employment pool a year after graduation, with no additional work in the profession, at best places an applicant on equal ground with the current year's graduates. Regular substituting will serve to provide a candidate with an opportunity to practice the art of teaching and demonstrate one's commitment to the profession. If you want to teach, teach any way you can!

In Closing

As a guest presenter in professional semester classes at Kutztown University for the past several semesters, I have frequently started my presentation dealing with employment by asking some of the questions that are included in this guide. Without any formal introduction to the presentation, I select a student and ask the following: "In what way or ways has your philosophy of education changed since the time you entered college?" While I provide adequate wait time for a response, I do not hesitate, if the student is reticent to present an answer, to move to another student, posing another reasonable but thought-provoking question. In many instances, the students have commented that they feel a bit intimidated by the experience, due primarily to the fact that they are not given adequate time to think through their responses to the questions. My point in this exercise is that most students, if given the time to think about their responses to questions that could be raised in an interview, can do a good job of presenting responses. However, not preparing for possible questions in advance of the interview places the candidate at a distinct disadvantage—one that can be easily avoided.

It is *your* professional future, and you will do yourself a great disservice if you do not adequately prepare for all aspects of the employment process, particularly the professional interview. While professional preparation in an academic arena may be something for which candidates feel quite comfortable, preparation for the employment arena is frequently new and unfamiliar territory—territory that needs your complete attention if you are to be successful in your search for a professional position.

What Do You Think?

1. Provide a brief narrative of highlights from your personal and professional background that you feel will prepare you for teaching. What do you think your strengths are at this point? In what areas do you need more work and/or experience?

2. Describe what you believe to be the important elements that should be included in any daily lesson plan.

3. How are you going to plan for a diverse body of students in your classroom?

4. Write a short narrative describing your teaching philosophy. Then describe how your teaching philosophy has changed from the time that you entered college. What has caused your philosophy to change?

5. Describe your personality and then highlight what you believe are your greatest traits. How do these traits make you a good teacher?

6. How do you identify a "good" candidate and a "bad" candidate?

Suggestions for Further Reading

Feirsen, R., & Weitzman, S. (2004). *How to get the teaching job you want: The complete guide for college graduates, teachers changing schools, returning teachers and career changers* (2nd ed.). Sterling, VA: Stylus Publishing.

Feirsen and Weitzman discuss current issues that affect the job market for new teachers, including high-stakes tests, standards for certification, electronic portfolios, and online applications. They also offer unique suggestions for those who are experienced teachers but wish to work in another school district.

Moffatt, C. W., & Moffatt, T. L. (2000). *How to get a teaching job.* Boston: Allyn & Bacon.

The authors address where to look for a job, how to identify suitable positions and how to highlight your qualifications for the position. The authors' experiences and research offer the reader "behind-the-scene" information about how the search process works in schools.

Warner, J., Byran, C., & Warner, D. (2003). *Inside secrets of finding a teaching job: The most effective search methods for both new and experienced educators* (2nd ed.). Indianapolis, IN: JIST Works

This book offers advice from administrators and teachers on searching for teaching positions, developing a résumé, creating a portfolio, and producing a teaching video.

14

Tales From My
First Year of Teaching

Erin A. Mikulec

N o matter how many courses a person takes before starting his
or her teaching job, every teacher has concerns and issues to
address as they embark on a new career. Most of these issues can
only be answered by experience and the answers will vary from
teacher to teacher. This chapter presents a series of vignettes describing several of the experiences that a first-year teacher faced in her
new job. This chapter is not intended to prescribe ways to deal with
all students, but has a goal to convey the message that every new
teacher has concerns, and often the only way to resolve them is by
exploring one's options as a teacher and consulting with others.
Teaching is a process of trial and error. As Ms. Mikulec discusses, a
new teacher must not be afraid to be creative and try out various
methods, then evaluate and revise the methods for the future.

♦ ♦ ♦

It was my first day of school and the bell was about to ring. Soon I would
meet my first group of students and begin my new job as a high school
Spanish teacher. I had all of my handouts in neat stacks, counted out to
the precise number of students that were listed on my class roster. My
desk was perfectly arranged with books, lesson plans, paper trays, two
red pens, two green pens, and a few newly sharpened pencils. The anno-
tated instructor's edition of our textbook was lying open to the pages

we would begin with, marked by a perfectly pressed blue ribbon. The desks were all in neat rows and the chalkboards hadn't been written on yet. I was ready.

I decided to prop open my door before the bell rang. I took the extra wooden chair from beside my desk, opened the door, and put the chair in front of the door to hold it in place. It wasn't heavy enough and the door slowly closed itself. I looked at the clock. Only a few more minutes to go, I thought, as a strange feeling began to develop in the pit of my stomach. Better hurry things up a bit. I began pushing the chair across the floor back toward my desk when it hit a snag in the carpet. The chair stopped but I didn't. I went flying over it, slamming my shins into the side of it, completing a one-and-a-half somersault before landing flat on the floor. Glad no one was around to see *that,* I thought, looking down at my shins, which had begun to bleed, two red trails of blood running straight down toward my brand new school shoes. I ran to the bathroom, thinking I had about a minute before the bell. I cleaned up my shins, but couldn't hide the two big, purple welts that were growing on each leg. I started walking back to my room just as students were pouring out into the hallway. I was suddenly hit with an attack of nerves I hadn't felt before as I watched students going into my classroom. I hurried down to my room, my shins still aching and my heart racing. First thing, I said to myself, is to try to relax because they can smell fear. I took one last deep breath and headed into my classroom to meet my students.

You have just read the true and very embarrassing story of the beginning of my first day as a public school teacher. I chose to begin with this story for a few reasons. First of all, looking back, it is kind of funny. If there is one thing I learned in my first year, it is not to take yourself too seriously. I say this because something else I learned right away was that no matter how ready you think you are, there will always be surprises like this one.

The rest of this chapter is a collection of stories about things that happened to me during my first year of teaching. I chose to include these stories because, in each instance, I learned a lot from them. Of course, my experience will be completely different from someone else's, and not everyone would have handled these situations the same way I did. Nevertheless, the tales should give you an idea of what my first year was like.

Is There an Educator Discount?

I stared down at the pile of supplies in front of me. I had folders, both hanging and manila, pens, pencils, stickers, paper clips, sticky notes, a stapler with a box of 1,000 staples, colored paper, a tape dispenser with six extra rolls, and several boxes of pushpins.

"Cash or credit?" the clerk asked me, jolting me back to reality.

I handed him my credit card. It was August and school would be starting in a week. I had just found out which room would be mine, and I needed to get it organized as well as decorated. The department head had informed me that I would be receiving about $80 in funds to purchase supplies . . . in October. I couldn't wait that long. I needed these things now. I had already purchased a few things with which to decorate my room, which I had also paid for myself. I signed the receipt and left.

LESSON 1: BE PREPARED TO SPEND YOUR OWN MONEY.

As a first-year teacher, you won't have a wealth of things to put up on your walls nor will you have all the supplies you'll need. What about my $80, you ask? I ended up spending nearly all of it on more supplies in October. It went pretty fast. The good news is that some stores, especially office supply stores, do, in fact, offer an educator discount. Never feel shy about asking! I am sure to use mine whenever possible, especially when I'm spending my own money.

Paco, the Comfort Monkey

We were having our second chapter exam of the semester. The first one had gone pretty well, so I thought the second test would be a good time to include a speaking portion. When I had first announced this would be a component of the test, I saw every back stiffen in the classroom. I explained that the speaking portion of the test would be worth 10 points and would consist of speaking with me individually in Spanish for three minutes.

To get ready for the test, in class we practiced several speaking activities very similar to the ones that would appear on the test. The students had extra homework assignments to help them practice the vocabulary they would need. I had two whole days set aside so that each student would have his or her full three minutes. Finally, I made a transparency of the rubric I would be using to grade this portion of the test. I felt confident they were ready.

The first day of the speaking test arrived. I decided to go in alphabetical order in each class. In my first class, this happened to be one of my best students. She walked confidently up to my desk, sat down, and very casually completed her speaking test.

The next student to approach was a solid B student. In my mind, she had no reason to be concerned about this test. She sat down, face white and hands trembling. I tried to calm her nerves with words of encouragement. She smiled weakly. I asked her the first question and tears welled up in her eyes. I knew it wasn't a question of her ability or her knowledge of Spanish; she was nervous. I started to panic inside. If the rest of the class caught on to this, the test would be a disaster. I had to do something fast. I quickly glanced around by my desk for an idea. My eyes came to rest on a stuffed monkey that I had bought about a week earlier. He was the kind with long arms and legs that you could hang. At the time, I had no idea what I would do with it; I just thought he was cute.

I pulled down the monkey that was hanging from a peg on the bulletin board.

"Here, Jennifer, take the monkey. It'll help."

And strangely enough, it did. She breezed through the rest of her test.

I called up the third student. When I asked if he was ready, he looked at me and said, "Can I hold the monkey?"

He was not the last one. Nearly all of my students used this form of security in one way or another during their speaking test in order to not feel so nervous. Some kids held it like children hold a toy, others played with its Velcro hands, and a couple even fashioned it to sit on their shoulders. There were some students that didn't take it, and that is okay. They had their own ways of handling the situation.

The usefulness of the stuffed monkey did not end with that one test. It became a kind of class pet. Students would keep it at their desk if they were feeling anxious about a test grade or were having a bad day. I was astonished that in a room of 16- and 17-year-olds the desire to keep a stuffed toy at their desk did not raise ridicule. In fact, it also became a sign to the other students to give that student a little extra space or even that the student needed a little extra friendliness from his or her friends.

One day, a student came to class with red eyes. He confided in me that he had been fighting with his parents. I told him to take a "pass" day in class. "No," he said, "I'll be okay. But can I keep the monkey with me?" At the end of class, he brought it back to its hanging place and asked me if it had a name. I said no and asked if he could name it. "Paco," he said. "I like Paco."

LESSON 2: KIDS NEED COMFORT.

This might seem a bit simplistic, if not painfully obvious. Nonetheless, this experience helped me to realize a thing or two about staying in tune with the emotional needs of students. First of all, looking beyond the surface is crucial in being able to identify how students are feeling. For example, knowing that Jennifer was ready for this test helped me to look past her physical symptoms in order to pinpoint what it was she needed at the time. This led me to the even greater conclusion that the sense of comfort that the kids got from Paco had pretty much nothing to do with the toy itself. Instead, it came from their knowing that, no matter what, Paco was there in my room when they arrived in class everyday. If they needed Paco, he was there, and if they didn't, he would just hang around until they did.

She Is So Ugly

Everyday at the start of fifth period the school announcements come on television. The program is made to imitate an actual broadcast with student anchors. The students always look forward to watching them before class begins. One day as the announcements were beginning, I noticed that Jessica had come in a few minutes late to class. She had been crying. She looked up at the television and began crying again. I didn't ask why she was crying, but I sent her to the bathroom with a friend to get herself together. She came back a few minutes later ready for class.

The next day, Jessica was fine until the announcements began. Jessica looked up at the television and said, "She's so ugly!" and immediately burst into tears. She went to the bathroom by herself. I asked her same friend to go check on her. "Her boyfriend dumped her to go out with that girl," the friend told me quietly.

The next day, I headed Jessica off in the hallway before she got into the room. "Jessica," I said, "why don't you take the restroom pass until the announcements are over? As soon as they finish, come back to class."

She looked at me in disbelief. "Really?" she asked. I nodded. "Can Ashley come with me?"

I was hesitant to agree to it, but then decided that missing the announcements wouldn't be the end of the world for her friend, either. "Okay," I said.

Jessica and Ashley did this for the rest of the week. None of the other students seemed to notice, and they were always back on time ready to begin class. By the end of the second week, however, I was beginning to regret my decision. "Where do those girls go everyday?" one student asked. They were starting to take a little longer each day. I decided that the Friday of the second week I would tell them that they needed to stay in class, especially since Jessica seemed much happier than she had the week before. That Friday, everyone got ready for the announcements. I looked over at Jessica, whom I thought surely was getting ready to come get the pass and go to the restroom with Ashley. What I saw, however, was Jessica at her seat, chatting happily with another friend. She saw me looking at her and said, "I'm not going today. I'm over it."

LESSON 3: FOLLOW YOUR INSTINCTS.

In this case, my instincts told me that an ounce of prevention was worth a pound of cure. Allowing Jessica her time to "mourn" by leaving the room when her ex-boyfriend's new girlfriend came on air let her know that I understood about the things happening in her life outside of class. The second lesson I learned here, and probably the most important, is that when you treat your students like people, *real* people who can be given the kind of responsibility that I had given to Jessica, they will generally recognize those kinds of gestures as what they are meant to be. I had panicked when I thought she and Ashley were taking advantage of the situation, when, in reality, she had taken the time she needed and realized when she had reached the point of not needing that special privilege.

Stacy Was Here

I finished my school day at the middle school where I taught exploratory foreign language to seventh and eighth graders. I had them for the last two class periods of the day. For the most part, they were a good bunch of kids, although the eighth graders at times could be talkative and a small group of them disruptive.

One day as I was erasing the board, I noticed written in chalk in small curlycue letters "Stacy was here." I knew exactly who it was; there was only one Stacy in my class. She was a pretty bright student but had an attitude. She could be fairly passive-aggressive in the ways she might disrupt class, such as talking to her neighbor just enough for me to ask her to stop and then letting me know that she was just borrowing a pencil or returning an eraser. This seemed to be another way of doing the same thing.

The following day, I was erasing the board again. This time "Stacy was here" was written not once, but twice on the board. I erased them and went to my office to get my things before heading home. I was feeling a little frustrated because clearly she wasn't doing anything outwardly rude or disruptive, and perhaps that was why she continued to do it. When I got to my office, I saw the eighth-grade science teacher, and he asked me what was wrong.

"Well," I began, "I have a student that can't seem to resist leaving a little bit of graffiti for me. I know it might not seem like much, but I feel like she is doing it just to be defiant."

He asked who it was and I told him. "Stacy?" he asked in disbelief. "Really? I don't have any problems with her. I'm surprised that she would be acting that way."

We talked a bit about her behavior in my class. "I'll tell you what," he said. "I'm her volleyball coach. The next time you have any problem with her, send her to me. I'll have a talk with her, and we'll see if we can figure out what is going on with her."

The next day, I walked into class. I saw Stacy by the back chalkboard, leaving her signature curlycue letters for me.

"Stacy," I said. "Would you please erase that? We know you're here without seeing it written on the board."

She stared back at me, and I could see in her eyes she had no intention of erasing it. I repeated myself. "Stacy, would you please erase that? This is the last time I will ask you."

"I didn't do anything wrong," she said, sticking out her chin.

"No one said you did. I asked you to erase it and you haven't. Would you mind telling me why?" I was keeping my voice calm and steady, even though deep down inside I was feeling nervous about the possible situation that this could escalate to.

"I didn't do anything wrong," she said again. "What's the big deal?" Her voice was becoming more indignant. I kindly reminded her of what I had just said. She moved toward her seat. "*You* erase it then," she demanded as she pitched the chalk back into the tray.

I was having trouble not raising my voice. I felt as though she wanted me to shout at her. I took a breath. The bell was about to ring and I wanted this finished before it did.

"Stacy, would you please take a walk down to Mr. Burke's room? Just tell him I sent you. He'll understand what you are doing there."

Her face became bright red. The defiance was gone from her eyes and had been replaced by the faintest hint of worry. "Mr. Burke's room?"

"Yes. Go now before the bell rings. Tell him I sent you." She opened her mouth to protest just as everyone else began to settle down in their seats. I turned and walked toward the desk before she could react. I went about beginning class as she walked out the door.

She returned about five minutes later. She didn't look at me as she came in, but went right to her seat and didn't say a word. She left quietly and left me no messages.

I went to see Mr. Burke. He told me that he had asked Stacy why she was there and that she had said I had sent her for no reason. When he asked again, she explained what had happened. When he asked why she had decided not to erase the board, she had had no answer.

The following day, I went into class prepared for a similar show-down. She came up to me almost as soon as I got in the door. "Do you want me to pass out the books?"

I was a little taken aback. "Sure. That would help me out a lot." She smiled genuinely and began passing out the textbooks.

From that day on, Stacy was my right hand. If there was something to be passed out, she was the first to volunteer. If someone had missed the day before, she would ask if I wanted her to share her notes with that person. If she found something that belonged to a student not in our class, she would ask if I wanted her to take it to the office. I said yes every time.

LESSON 4: WORK WITH OTHER TEACHERS.

The first lesson from this story is that other teachers most likely have different relationships with students than you do. Maybe they see them at a different time of day or are involved with them as a faculty sponsor of some kind. They will be able to help you resolve the problem.

The second lesson here is that we have many students, and each one needs a different level of special relationship with you. Stacy was the kind of student that needed a special relationship with her teachers, even if it came in a negative way. I think that by involving another teacher, especially one with whom she got along well, Stacy realized that she wasn't just a "problem case" to me or to Mr. Burke, but rather that we both cared about her enough to try and understand why she was behaving the way she was.

Forget This

A mountain of papers waiting to be graded sat on my desk. There were two sets of homework assignments plus short essays. There was also the next chapter test to write, which would be given at the end of the week, and the quiz to prepare for tomorrow. Looking over at my paper trays, there was a small pile of memos and forms that I had retrieved from my mailbox earlier that day. Many things were dated and clearly needed my attention. I sighed heavily as I sat down and went to work.

I was exhausted. My brain just did not want to think about grading or writing exams. I especially did not feel capable of responding coherently to any memos or requests from the assistant principal's office or searching through the long list of names of students who would be gone on a field trip the following Monday to see which of mine were on it. My eyes were getting heavy and the heap of papers did not seem to be getting any smaller.

Caffeine was surely what I needed to buckle down and get this done tonight before going home. About 30 minutes later after my coffee, I was back to where I had started when a new thought crept into my head. Forget this, I thought. What good am I doing anyone right now? I am not paying very close attention to anything I am doing. I am going out.

I picked up my things and went to the movies, ignoring the creeping fear that this decision would result in an even more stressful situation tomorrow. My decision had, in fact, the opposite effect. It was great to turn off my teacher head for even a few hours and just relax and enjoy myself. The next morning I woke up about an hour early and went into school, feeling rejuvenated and able to tackle the pile of work that was on my desk.

LESSON 5: TAKE CARE OF YOURSELF!

It is easy to get bogged down in all the things you need to do to stay on top of everything. Making time for yourself will do you a world of good. It may sound silly to make a date with yourself to go to the gym, to see friends, or to sit home on a Friday night in your pajamas watching movies, but you will be thankful you did.

I Hate Spanish

Each student in my class has a small coin envelope in which to keep his or her participation points, which come in the form of paper tokens. Students receive these tokens for participating in activities, volunteering answers, or even as game prizes. Every four weeks, students should have at least 25 of these points to receive full credit for class participation. It was the end of the first four weeks, and I was collecting the envelopes for the first time.

I began emptying each envelope and counting the number of points inside for each student. I picked up Justin's envelope and flipped it over. He had written on the back in big black block letters "I HATE SPANISH." I was not sure what to think, so I counted his points and set his envelope aside.

The next day, I passed the empty envelopes back to their owners, but I kept Justin's. He approached me after class saying he had not gotten his. I pulled it out and pointed to what he had written. His face got red.

"I think you wanted me to see this, Justin," I began. "Is there something you want to talk about?"

"No, I just wanted to see if you would do anything."

I wasn't convinced as he took his envelope.

Justin was an extremely bright student. He had a high A in my class, and he seemed to get the grade with minimal effort. He really liked art. He would bring his ceramics pieces to class to show his friends, and he liked to draw. He had two other good friends in class with him, and they usually worked together in group activities. He was fairly quiet but participated regularly in class. He was not disruptive.

One day, I was walking around the room at the end of class helping students with an assignment they had for homework. It was tricky stuff, and I wanted to give them a start in class while I could still answer their questions. From the corner of my eye, I saw Justin at the front of the room blowing his nose. I went back to working with James, but noticed Justin's friend also at the front of the room blowing his nose as I moved on to help the next student. I had a strange feeling about it, but the bell rang and everyone left. A student lingered behind, as though she wanted to talk to me. When everyone had gone, she came to me and said, "I saw Justin and Tim go to your desk to blow their nose and then steal participation points from the box."

I thanked her for the information, telling her I was aware that they had been up there. I was mad! How dare they do something like that! I was going to pull them from their next class and settle this immediately. I walked over to some desks in the back of the room, fuming as I picked up a few scraps of paper on the floor. I noticed Justin's desk. Again, in big black block letters he had written "I HATE SPANISH." I tried to stay angry, even though I had a growing feeling that there was more to this than met the eye.

I decided to enlist the help of his counselor. I hadn't talked to her about Justin yet this semester, but I knew she would be a good source of information. I went to her office and asked her if she knew of anything going on with him lately. She told me that his mother has just called her a few days ago. She was worried that Justin was not behaving like himself. She asked the counselor to keep an ear out for any news.

I proceeded to explain what had just happened in class and about what he had written on the envelope earlier. I suggested that I thought there was more to this situation than appeared and that even though he had denied it earlier, he was trying to get my attention.

She agreed, and we called him down to her office. He froze in the doorway when he saw me, but then he sat down in the seat next to me. His counselor began.

"Justin, do you know why you're here?"

"Yeah, because of the points."

"Is that the only reason?"

"I think so."

"I found the message you left me," I said.

"What message?"

"What you left on your desk. We're concerned about you, Justin. What is going on?"

The next 10 minutes were intense. We talked about why he took the points, especially since he did not need them to boost his grade. At first, he said he did not know why, but then came around and told us that he had finished the homework I had given him and had gotten bored. "I do stupid things when I'm bored," he said looking down at the floor.

It did not surprise me he had finished ahead of everyone else. He was almost always the first one to finish. We asked if he felt like this in his other classes. He said he did in all of them except for art because he was always busy in art and could not get into trouble. His counselor asked me if I wanted to call his mom and tell her what had happened. I thought about it for a long time. "No," I finally decided. "I think we can handle this between the three of us."

"Do you want me to wash the desks?" Justin asked.

"That's a good idea," I replied and wrote him a pass.

I left the office, but he stayed to talk with his counselor. "I think there are some other things Justin and I need to talk about," she told me.

Justin came to my room during prep the next day. I had left out paper towels and a spray bottle with cleaner. He went about cleaning the desks while I worked at my own desk. Neither one of us said anything. About 15 minutes later, he announced he was finished. I opened my drawer to write him a pass back to class.

"Justin," I said, "I want you to do something for me."

"What?"

"When you get bored in class, I want you to draw."

"Is this a trick?" he asked skeptically.

I could not help but laugh. "No, it isn't a trick. I know you know what is going on in class and that you understand the material faster than anyone. So, when you start to feel bored, like you're going to do something you'll regret, I want you to draw."

He thought about it for a minute. "Okay," he said. "I can do that."

The following day, we began a new lesson. Everyone was taking notes, and I noticed that Justin finished very quickly. I peeked over to see that he had copied them all. He had, and he had taken out a new piece of paper and begun drawing. When everyone had finished, I asked some comprehension questions. When I asked for volunteers, Justin was the first to speak up, giving me the correct answer without so much as taking his eyes off his drawing.

Before I left that day, I went to check in with his counselor. She told me that after I had left, she and Justin had had a long talk about many things. They called his mother, who arranged for him to be tested for depression the following week.

LESSON 6: LISTEN TO WHAT KIDS ARE TRYING TO TELL YOU.

They may not always come out and let you know what is on their minds and half the time they may not even know themselves. Kids generally have a motive for acting out, which may not always be clear. The situation with Justin taught me to reflect on a student's behavior and not to react to it.

When Technology Attacks

The classes I teach at the middle school level are designed to be an introduction to foreign language with the hope that students will want to study a language in high school. Because of this, there is a strong focus on vocabulary as a means of introducing them to the language. I have a great Web site that I use to let the kids practice this vocabulary. It is easy for me to create fun activities for them, and they love nothing more than going to the computer lab to use it.

It was Friday. It had been a long week and I decided that it would be the perfect day to go to the lab since they had not been yet to practice with the new vocabulary we were learning. I checked to make sure no other class would be in the lab, and I signed us up for the seventh and eighth periods. The bell rang and I walked down to the classroom where I taught. I was halfway through the cafeteria when the PA came on. It was the principal.

"Please pardon this interruption. This is just to let you know that the network is down. Technical support should be here shortly. We'll let you know when it is back up."

I froze in my tracks. The network is down? The network is down! Class was about to start in less than a minute, and I had no plan! Since we were going to the lab, I hadn't planned any other activity. I walked into class, which was Spanish.

One of my students greeted me. "Hey," he said. "How come we never got Spanish names?"

"You're in luck," I said, wanting to hug him for giving me an idea. "That's what we are going to do today." I knew there was a section in our textbooks that did this very thing, and I began passing them out.

I quickly realized, however, that this activity wouldn't occupy the entire class time. I decided I would draw out the lesson as best I could. Just then, I heard the fire alarm. The kids jumped out of their seats and we made a beeline for the door and filed out into the parking lot.

The fire drill lasted only about five minutes. We got back into the room and finished our lesson on Spanish names. Before the dismissal bell rang, the principal was back on the PA. "Please pardon this interruption. The network is up and running again. You should now have access to your computers, e-mail, and the Internet." I was saved for eighth period.

LESSON 7: ALWAYS HAVE A BACKUP PLAN!

Since that day, I have compiled a folder of activities that can be done anywhere between five and forty minutes if need be. I have never been unprepared in this kind of situation again. And it has been my experience that technology isn't the only thing that can throw a wrench in your plans. Fire drills, assemblies, water main breaks, and two-hour delays are just some of the things that can change your lesson for you.

What You Do Today

It is January and the new semester begins in a week. At the high school, this means a new group of students since their schedules change between semesters. At the middle school, this means a new group of students for the next quarter since my classes are on a nine-week rotation.

I look at the handout that I passed out on the first day of school back in August. It is five pages long. I begin editing, taking out large portions of information that aren't relevant to the way I teach my class now. I revise my policies on makeup tests and homework assignments and create a new rubric for scoring class participation. It is a very different handout from the one I wrote six months ago. It is only two pages long.

The changes I made didn't come about overnight. When I began teaching in August, I had, or at least I thought I had, a pretty clear-cut idea of how my class would run. I had a great system for homework assignments and class participation, a solid plan for what tests and quizzes should be like, and a concise set of rules for expected classroom behavior. My system for organizing papers, taking attendance, and tracking makeup work seemed to work especially well in theory. But now, at the start of my second semester, I am making some pretty big changes as well as some small adjustments in how I approach all of these aspects of teaching. All of this has come through trial and error all semester, deciding what works and what does not, what needs to be tweaked and what needs to be trashed. I am confident that the changes will be positive ones for the coming semester, but I also know they will not be the last adjustments I make.

LESSON 8: WHAT YOU DO TODAY IS NOT WHAT YOU WILL DO TOMORROW.

The fact is there is good news and bad news about this job. The good news is that no two days are the same. The bad news is that no two days are the same. Everyday, you should evaluate how you do things and find ways to improve and fine-tune your teaching.

Tell Me Why

"That is it!" I thought to myself as I looked over at a group of four boys who had spent the past 30 minutes talking when I had asked them to stop. It was finals week and we were having study hall during class so people could study if they needed some extra time. This group of boys had asked me if they could play cards. "Can you play without talking?" I had asked. Yes, they had assured me.

Their silence had lasted about 10 minutes. When they began to chatter, I reminded them that this was study hall and to respect those who were studying. It died down for about 10 more minutes before starting up again.

"Gentlemen," I said sternly, "this is the last time I am going to ask you before you put away the cards."

Again, 10 minutes of silence before the chatter began, which brings us to the start of this tale. I pulled out four detention slips from my desk. I had not written any during the semester, and I really did not want to start during the last week, but I had had enough. I told them to put away the cards and to join me in the hallway.

As I got up to follow them, I realized that not having written any detentions, I did not have the faintest idea how to fill these things out! There were boxes to check, two different places for an account of the incident, a date to assign the detention, and it was in triplicate! Not wanting to show that I did not know how to fill out the form, I changed strategies quickly.

"Gentlemen," I began, "tell me why I should not fill out these four detention slips right now for your talking?"

This was met with a host of responses. Jimmy said he could not give me a reason, Thomas told me he just did not think it was a good idea, and Jeff told me I was going to do it no matter what they said. Brandon remained silent.

"Let's try again. Tell me why I shouldn't fill out these four detention slips for your talking?"

"We weren't doing it to make you mad," said Jeff. "We were just playing the game. It just got hard to play without talking."

"Why had I asked you not to talk in the first place?" I asked.

"Because other people are studying," said Thomas.

"And when you talk . . .?"

"It is disruptive," replied Jeff.

"And disrespectful to you and other people," said Jimmy.

"And so I should not fill these out because . . .?"

"Because this should be our warning," suggested Brandon.

"And it won't happen again this week because . . .?

"We know better," stated Thomas.

"And if it happens again this week I should . . .?

"Fill out the detention forms," Jimmy decided and the other three nodded.

I looked at them as I mulled it over in my head. "Fair enough."

LESSON 9: REMEMBER THE ULTIMATE GOAL OF DISCIPLINARY ACTIONS.

I stumbled upon this lesson because I did not know how to fill out a form, and I am glad because it helped me to realize this very important lesson. What had I wanted them to learn by giving them detention? I had wanted them to know that this week of study hall was important to many students, and that because of that when I said no talking, I meant no talking. It was not intended to be an edict given without reason, but rather I wanted them to understand why I was being especially firm about it this week in particular. I know that this message came across much better through the interaction that had taken place than if I had simply given them detention.

This is also a good example of something else that happens during your first year of teaching. There is so much to learn about policy and procedure! You hope much of it will be in your faculty handbook, but a lot of it is not. I looked in mine for instructions on filling out the detention forms and found nothing, so I ended up going to my mentor for more information. There are still many things like this I am not sure about, but I am learning as I go.

What Do You Think?

1. Think back to the first time you began your first field experience. How did you feel as you started on your first day? Were you nervous? If so, about what? What issues do you think you will have to face as you start your first year of teaching?

2. Think about your first day as a student. How did you feel? Imagine how your students will feel the very first day. What will you do to ease their fears?

3. You are obviously not ready to start teaching yet. What are some of the biggest concerns or issues that you feel you need to learn before you begin teaching?

4. Find an experienced teacher to interview about his or her first year of teaching. What did you learn from this interview? How does this teacher's first year differ from the experiences described in this chapter?

5. Which of the nine lessons presented in this chapter jumps out as being one of your biggest concerns about being a teacher? How so?

6. Select three of the nine lessons presented in this chapter and write about how you would handle these same situations if you were the teacher. Then compare your responses to the author's methods for dealing with these situations.

Suggestions for Further Reading

Kane, P. R. (1996). *My first year as a teacher*. New York: Signet.
    This is a collection of narratives written by twenty-five first-year teachers, describing both positive experiences and struggles they faced throughout the year.

Rominger, L. M., Laughrea, S. P., & Elkin, N. (2001). *Your first year as an elementary teacher: Making the transition from total novice to successful professional.* Roseville, CA: Prima Lifestyles.

The authors offer solutions to many of the common difficulties that new elementary teachers experience as well as suggestions for making the most of the first year and the years following.

Thompson, J. G. (2002). *First-year teacher's survival kit: Ready-to-use strategies, tools, and activities for meeting the challenges of each school day.* Indianapolis: Jossey-Bass.

This is a resource for preservice and first-year teachers who seek ideas for establishing a positive environment conducive to learning. It is rather comprehensive, addressing a variety of current issues facing today's educator.

Wong, H. K., & Wong, R. T. (2001). *The first days of school.* Mountain View, CA: Harry K. Wong Publications.

This book is especially good for the preservice teacher to read in order to begin thinking about educational issues prior to entering the profession. As the title implies, the authors suggest that many of the techniques be implemented at the beginning of the school year.

About the Editor

Paul Chamness Miller is Assistant Professor of Foreign Language Education in the Division of Teacher Education at the University of Cincinnati. He received a doctorate in foreign language education at Purdue University in 2003. Prior to pursuing his doctorate, he taught French in both rural and urban schools. He has taught French at the college level, as well as Foreign Language and TESOL (Teachers of English to Speakers of Other Languages) methods courses at the undergraduate and graduate levels. He has also taught courses in teacher education on exploring teaching as a career and on educational technology, in addition to supervising field experiences and student teaching. He has published articles in *Phi Delta Kappan, Multicultural Perspectives,* and the *Electronic Magazine of Multicultural Education,* and is a co-guest editor of a volume of *Research in Second Language Learning* on the topic of content-based instruction. He has also published book reviews in *TESL-EJ* and *Education Review.* He is a member of the board of reviewers for *CALICO* [Computer Assisted Language Instruction Consortium] *Journal* and *TESL-EJ* and is also an executive peer reviewer of *Educational Technology & Society.* His research interests include issues in second language acquisition, English language learners, and multicultural education. He also has a passion for recruiting students of color into teacher education.

About the Contributors

Wayne Au, a former high school English and history teacher, is currently pursuing his Ph.D. in curriculum and instruction from the University of Wisconsin, Madison. He is an editorial associate for the education journal *Rethinking Schools* and sits on the steering committee of the National Coalition of Education Activists. His work on critical classroom practice has been published in *Rethinking Schools, Rethinking Our Classrooms Vol. II, Beyond Heroes and Holidays,* and *Resistance in Paradise,* among others. In 2002, he received the Early Career Advocate for Justice Award from the American Association of Colleges for Teacher Education.

William Ayers is a school reform activist, Distinguished Professor of Education, and Senior University Scholar at the University of Illinois at Chicago (UIC), where he teaches courses in interpretive research, urban school change, and youth and the modern predicament. He is the founder of the Small Schools Workshop and the Center for Youth and Society at UIC. A graduate of the Bank Street College of Education and Teachers College, Columbia University, he has written extensively about social justice, democracy, and education. His interests focus on the political and cultural contexts of schooling as well as the meaning and ethical purposes of teachers, students, and families. His articles have appeared in many journals, including *Harvard Educational Review, Journal of Teacher Education, Teachers College Record, Rethinking Schools, The Nation,* and *The Cambridge Journal of Education.* His books include *A Kind and Just Parent: The Children of Juvenile Court* (1997), *The Good Preschool Teacher,* (1989), and *To Teach: The Journey of a Teacher* (1993), which was named Book of the Year in 1993 by Kappa Delta Pi and won the Witten Award for Distinguished Work in Biography and Autobiography in 1995. His latest books are *Fugitive Days: A Memoir* (2001) and *On the Side of the Child: Summerhill Revisited* (2003).

Christopher Blake is Vice President of Academic Affairs at Mount Saint Mary's University in Maryland. Previously, he was Professor of Education, Director of Teacher Education, and Chair of the Department of Education. His research interests include ethnography in teacher education and the role of teacher perspectives and voices in educational practices. He has also served as a university teacher and high school teacher of social studies in London, England.

Chris Carger is Associate Professor in the Department of Literacy Education at Northern Illinois University. Her research interests integrate the areas of bilingual education, English language learning, multicultural children's literature, and narrative inquiry. She stays in close contact with elementary education classrooms and is a bilingual program consultant. She also directs a service learning course each semester in which college students read aloud to Latino children and facilitate vocabulary and art experiences connected to multicultural children's literature. Her book, *Of Borders and Dreams: A Mexican-American Experience of Urban Education,* describes in detail her work with a bilingual student transitioning from elementary school to high school in Chicago.

Kin T. Chee has taught Japanese, Chinese, and English/language arts for 14 years in Grades 6 through 12 and is currently a teacher of Japanese in central New York. He has also taught in Singapore (Grade 6) and Japan (EFL). He is an active member of the Northeast Council of Teachers of Japanese and is a frequent presenter at workshops and conferences across the country, mostly on language pedagogy based on action research that he conducts in his own classroom. He was invited by the New York State Department of Education to serve on a committee to establish norming standards between New York State's Regents exams and SAT II test scores in Japanese and has served on a committee for the last five years to develop Japanese sample Regents exams. His article "Professional Needs of Non-Native Japanese Language Teachers" was published in the December 2003 issue of the *Canadian Association for Japanese Language Education Newsletter.* He received his master's degree in foreign language education from the University of Iowa.

Betty C. Eng is a Lecturer in the Department of Educational Psychology, Counseling, and Learning Needs at the Hong Kong Institute of Education (HKIEd), a major teacher education institute providing preservice and in-service training. Previously, she was a counselor with an international school in Hong Kong and at universities in the United States. A Chinese American, she was a faculty member in the Asian American Studies and

Women's Studies programs and in the School of Education at California State University, Sacramento, and a faculty member in the Department of Asian American Studies at the University of California, Davis, before making Hong Kong her home for 15 years. Her fields of interest are teacher knowledge, cross-cultural studies, gender, and counseling. She is currently an Ed.D. student at the Ontario Institute of Studies for Education at the University of Toronto. Her thesis is an exploration of teacher knowledge through personal narratives focusing on identity, culture, and sense of belonging.

Joseph McSparran is Associate Professor of Secondary Education at Kutztown University in Pennsylvania. He received his Ed.D. from the University of Pennsylvania. He teaches undergraduate courses on American education as well as graduate courses in school law. He also supervises student teachers. He has served as Director of the Allentown Alliance Project and as Director of the Urban Learning Center at Kutztown. He has also worked as superintendent, assistant superintendent, high school principal, and assistant principal in the public school system in Pennsylvania.

Erin A. Mikulec is completing her Ph.D. in Foreign Language Education at Purdue University. She received her master's degree from Middlebury College in Vermont. She is also currently a Spanish and French teacher at the middle school and high school levels. In addition to this teaching experience, she has taught Spanish for a number of years at the college level. She also served as instructor and field experience supervisor for preservice teacher education courses.

Pamela K. Miller is a sixth-grade English teacher in LaPorte, Indiana. She has been teaching for 15 years. The first 13 years of her teaching career involved working with students whom her school district determined to be "academically low achievers." Ten years of that time were spent teaching students through computer-assisted instruction. The next three years entailed piloting an academic program in which students were assisted in small groups for math, English, and reading. For the past two years, she has been teaching sixth-grade English to approximately 125 students. She is also involved in an after-school program with court-appointed students. This program services students in Grades 6 through 8. She is currently working on her master's of education through Indiana Wesleyan University.

Magdalena Mo Ching Mok is Principal Lecturer in the Department of Educational Psychology, Counseling and Learning Needs at the Hong Kong Institute of Education, where she teaches Curriculum and Assessment, Research Methods, and Education Project to preservice and in-service teachers. Before joining the Institute in 1999, she taught research methods to postgraduate students at Macquarie University in Australia for 10 years. She received her Ph.D. in education from the University of Hong Kong and her M.S. degree in statistics from Glasgow University. Her research interests are assessment, psychometrics, self-regulated learning, and school culture. She coauthored *Catholic Schools 2000* and published seven book chapters and over 30 international refereed journal articles.

Connie Monroe is Assistant Professor of Education at Mount Saint Mary's University in Maryland, where she serves as coordinator of secondary programs. Prior to entering the field of teacher education, she was a high school and middle school teacher of French and of English as a second language. Her research interests include the lives of teachers, teacher development, and the role of schools in society.

JoAnn Phillion is Associate Professor in the Department of Curriculum and Instruction at Purdue University. Prior to receiving her doctorate, she was an ESL teacher in Japan for six years and in Canada for three years. Her research interests are in narrative approaches to multiculturalism, teacher knowledge, and teacher education. She teaches graduate courses in curriculum theory and multicultural education and an undergraduate course in preservice teacher development with a focus on narrative. She is also involved in international teacher development in Hong Kong and Honduras. She was the recipient of the American Educational Research Association Division B Dissertation of the Year Award in 2000, the Purdue Faculty of Education Outstanding Teaching Award in 2002, and Purdue University Teaching for Tomorrow Award in 2003. She is the author of *Narrative Inquiry in a Multicultural Landscape: Multicultural Teaching and Learning* (2002). She has served on the editorial board of *Curriculum Inquiry* since 1999 and was appointed an editor in 2003.

Crystal Reimer is an adapted physical education (APE) teacher in Plano, Texas. She has taught public school (elementary, middle school, and high school) for eight years, including physical education and English. She has also coached several sports. She is currently teaching elementary physical education in Dallas, where her interest grew in programming for students with disabilities. She is currently completing her master's degree in APE at Texas Woman's University.

Teresa Rishel is Assistant Professor of Curriculum and Instruction and Middle Childhood Education at Kent State University. She taught and served as principal for a number of years at the elementary level prior to receiving her Ph.D. in Curriculum Studies from Purdue University, where she also received the Outstanding Dissertation Award from the

Department of Curriculum and Instruction in 2004. She published an article in Spring 2003, entitled "Letter to My Son: My Lived Experience with Suicide" in the *Journal of Critical Inquiry into Curriculum and Instruction.*

Jill Underly has been a history and sociology high school teacher in northwest Indiana for five years. She also coaches sports and sponsors several student organizations and is actively involved in the teachers' union in her school. She holds a master's degree in secondary education from Indiana University-Purdue University, Indianapolis.

Index